Becoming
Delinquent

With a new introduction by David Matza

Becoming Delinquent

Young Offenders and the Correctional Process

Edited by
Peter G. Garabedian &
Don C. Gibbons

ALDINETRANSACTION
A Division of Transaction Publishers
New Brunswick (U.S.A.) and London (U.K.)

Library of Congress Catalog Number: 2005048525
ISBN: 0-202-30795-6
Printed in the United States of America

Library of Congress Cataloging-in-Publication Data

Becoming delinquent : young offenders and the correctional process / Peter
 G. Garabedian and Don C. Gibbons, editors ; with a new introduction by
 David Matza.
     p. cm.
  Originally published: Chicago : Aldine Pub. Co., 1970.
  Includes bibliographical references and index.
  ISBN 0-202-30795-6 (pbk. : alk. paper)
   1. Juvenile delinquency—United States. 2. Juvenile justice, Admin-
 istration of—United States. I. Garabedian, Peter G. II. Gibbons, Don C.

HV9104.B416   2005
364.36'0973—dc22   2005048525

Introduction to the AdineTransaction Edition

Becoming Delinquent is a collection of research essays and articles edited by Peter Garabedian and Don Gibbons on the process by which juveniles are identi- fied or defined delinquent. Many, but not all, of the ideas and research projects were encouraged, funded, or supported by the various federal delinquency studies programs and curriculum development programs focusing on juvenile delinquency during the sixties and guided by precepts and persons associated with the Kennedy- Johnson War on Poverty.

The institutional model organized the various essays and studies published originally in 1970 and now reissued by AldineTransaction.

The collection serves as a valuable resource bringing together many of the best examples of the kinds of ideas and research shaping criminology, sociology, law, social work, psychiatry, and allied professions during the period.

The institutional model hypothesized, researched, refuted, modified, clarified, and explained throughout the book is best conveyed in the subtitle: Young Of- fenders and the Correctional System. During the period—say, the middle-sixties to middle seventies—avid discussions occurred among students, professors, researchers, and professionals about the effects of correction. Labeling, stigmatizing, selecting, defining, identifying, societal reaction, signifying, and framing were among the terms used to characterize this newly popular theory or idea regarding the causes of juvenile delinquency.

Nowadays the process pointed to would probably be called framing; the concept was already in use in the sixties, but framing was not as popular as labeling. Erving Goffman, followed by Ken Levi (in *Becoming a Hit Man*) and others referred to framing when considering how the character of young persons as well as adults was framed by reputations, stereotypes, and perceptions of self and others.

Correctional systems are among the finest examples of the institutional—as suggested in Erving Goffman's essay on total institutions in *Asylums*.

Most of the studies collected (including Lemert's) found mixed results and tended to modulate the strong formulations of labeling or framing in Howard Becker's *Outsiders* or Edwin Lemert's *Societal Reaction Theory*.

Institutional processing theory attained a certain degree of popularity during the sixties and the seventies despite the fact that gross characteristics of class and race did not appear to play a discernable role in selecting or apprehending juveniles in the studies collected. Many of the studies indicated that demeanor or uncooperative juvenile behavior played a role in whether authorities acted in a lenient or punitive manner, but that pure and simple discrimination or bias by race or class was hard to discern in the pattern of punishment or the attitudes expressed by correctional personnel.

Each chapter of this collection is an essay or research seeking to show the process by which identity is formed by an individual being processed, defined, or classified first by family and school and subsequently, if trouble is discovered, through police, juvenile court, probation, and prison. The correctional system interacting with a juvenile defines the delinquent. From the juvenile subjects' standpoint, a delinquent character is disclosed, made public.

The process model was critical and considered whether the correctional system was backfiring, doing more harm than good, resulting in blow-back, to use the current political science term (popularized by Chalmers Johnson) for a foreign policy or military alliances that backfire, the unanticipated consequences of social action (coined by Robert Merton many years ago).

Starting with family and school (Werthman's "The Function of Social Definitions in the Development of Delinquent Careers") and proceeding to (Short and Nye's "Extent of Unrecorded Juvenile Delinquency: Tentative Conclusions" and Murphy, Shirley, and Witmer's "The Incidence of Hidden Delinquency"), the reader of *Becoming Delinquent* is guided through the maze of an institutional system of correction encountering and identifying a juvenile behaving, sometimes, in a delinquent fashion.

Similar questions regarding the juveniles' basic character are assessed and defined through the correctional system: from the functioning of control agencies (Terry's "Discrimination in the Handling of Juvenile Offenders by Social Control

Agencies") to the police (Piliavin and Briar's "Police Encounters with Juveniles," Wilson's "The Police and the Delinquent in Two Cities"), and on to juvenile court (Lemert's "The Juvenile Court—Quest and Realities," Walther and McCune's "Juvenile Court Judges in the United States: Working Styles and Characteristics," Parker's "Juvenile Court Actions and Public Response"), then on to probation (Gross's "The Prehearing Juvenile Report: Probation Officers' Conceptions," Cohn's "Criteria for the Probation Officer's Recommendation to the Juvenile Court," Scarpitti and Stephenson's "A Study of Probation Effectiveness," McMillin and Garabedian's "Attitudes of Probation Officers Toward Due Process for Juvenile Offenders," and Garabedian's "Policy Questions in Delinquency Control: Perspectives of Police and Probation Officers"), and in the penal institution or training school for delinquents (Jesness's "The Fricot Ranch Study," and Eynon and Simpson's "The Boy's Perception of Himself in a State Training School For Delinquents").

The framing or labeling view had been posed against an older view, one that returned with a vengeance by the politically conservative eighties. Once the stronger statements of the labeling view had passed from the scene, the older view enjoyed a revival.

The older view—and once again the current view—since the eighties (though still challenged by critics) is that the correctional system deters (or corrects) by setting rational penalties that encourage people to avoid committing crimes for which their apprehension is increasingly likely after having been once apprehended. This utilitarian view that correction—if properly constructed and enforced—deters is represented by several of the contributors but the main focus of the collection is on considering and researching the possibility that the correctional system was hurting more than helping in dealing with juvenile delinquency.

Between the two contrasting and often conflicting views—that correction corrects and that correction stigmatizes—is the more prosaic view of the classic Cambridge-Somerville study that more or less concluded that correction does little or nothing.

The institutional view is scrutinized carefully in *Becoming Delinquent* and is considerably sharpened and modified by the various contributors. The first two sections set the stage for the complicated argument ensuing in the various chapters dealing with the police, probation, juvenile court, and penal institution.

The first essay is the insightful and perceptive description of the development of delinquent careers by Carl Werthman. Basing himself squarely in Erving Goffman's concept of the moral career of the mental patient in the total institution of asylums, Werthman usefully adapts the concept as the regular sequence of changes that career entails in the person's self and in his framework of imagery for judging himself and others (Goffman, *Asylums*, p.128).

Werthman states in his opening sentence a parallel usage with regard to the delinquent: "The moral career of the lower class juvenile gang boy often begins at age 6, 7, or 8, when he is defined by his teachers as 'predelinquent' for demonstrating to his friends that he is not a 'sissy,' and it ends between the ages of 16 and 25 when he either takes a job, goes to college, joins the Army, or becomes a criminal."

Carl Werthman's first chapter reflects a particularly creative version of lower-class juvenile gang theory that was well based in the general sociological standpoint of the sixties and seventies. In both the War on Poverty and in the substantive subcultural theories of Albert Cohen, Lloyd Ohlin, Richard Cloward, and Robert Merton and in the anthropological writings of Walter Miller, Oscar Lewis, and Charles Valentine, the idea of a lower-class-based subcultural juvenile gang delinquent was a basic premise of the social theory of young offenders.

But such allegations had been challenged and modified and the important contributions by James Short and Ivan Nye (1958) and Fred Murphy, Mary Shirley, and Helen Witmer (1946) still stand as critical reminders that the lower-class basis of juvenile delinquency is not quite as stark or noticeable if one tries to find out whether hidden delinquency or unrecorded juvenile delinquency is not also committed by middle-class, working-class, and upper-class youth.

Thus, a basic tension is injected into the discussion, and maintains whether police, court, probation, or training school (a.k.a. prison) practices and their effects on the delinquent career are considered.

How identify delinquents without framing subsequent development? Framing and deterrence theory are two potentialities of control. Control wishes to deter but sometimes its critics say control frames delinquent identity instead of deterring crime. There is no logical or empirical reason that both cannot be true. For many youth offenders, the relation between their behavior, their identity, and correctional agents remains a live one.

David Matza

Contents

Preface

The hallmark of urban society is bureaucratic organization. Today, individuals have relationships not only with other individuals but also with large-scale organizations. Over the years, our lives have become inextricably bound up with them so that it is now literally impossible to function adequately without some measure of contact with formal structures that have been established to serve human needs. Some of these organizations deal with physical products, as in the case of lumber mills that produce timbers, studs, and plywood. Others deal in ideas, such as colleges and universities, that are expected to generate new knowledge.

This book deals with the workings of "people-processing" organizations, an extremely important type of structure to which social control functions have been assigned in contemporary society. People-processing agencies work with human raw material and endeavor to convert it into another form, such as the rehabilitated alcoholic or mental patient. More directly, the organizations considered in this book process juvenile delinquents with the aim of changing them into law-abiding youths.

Not much sociological attention has been given to people-processing organizations until recently, and this is particularly true of correctional agencies. However, there is currently a pronounced move on the part of criminologists away from the study of "causation" and toward inquiry into social control agencies and their effects upon the persons they process. Part of this move has been stimulated by the growing tendency in American society to "criminalize" not only those behaviors that appear to involve considerable harm to persons and property but also those having to do with standards of proper conduct and morality. The latter activities, while distasteful to some, entail relatively little harm to persons and property. There is a growing feeling that "overcriminalization" works to the detriment of the justice and corrections system, exposing excessive numbers of persons to criminal sanctions at great cost to the general public.

Another reason for the move toward the study of control agencies is that many sociologists and criminologists have reached the conclusion that the causes of delinquency and crime are so varied and subtle that they cannot easily be discovered, if indeed they can be identified at all. This belief, coupled with the emergence of "labeling" theory in sociology, has led to the conclusion that the study of correctional agencies might be a more profitable line of inquiry. Then too, criminologists have turned to the analysis of correctional organizations out of the realization that this is the stuff of which sociological analysis is composed.

This book offers a sample of the literature on agencies that define youthful offenders as "delinquent," that process them on probation or in institutions, or that handle them in other ways that are intended to "rehabilitate" them. Our aims in assembling this collection are two-fold. We hope to provide a useful anthology which can inform the student of the social dynamics of the traditional types of correctional organizations which continue to process the great majority of juvenile offenders; recent innovations, such as community-centered treatment programs, are omitted from this book. In addition, we intend this reader to be a stimulus to further investigation, in part by identifying gaps and deficiencies in the evidence.

We wish to acknowledge the cooperation of a number of authors and the journals in which their essays appeared. We owe a special debt to Mr. James Clark, formerly of Aldine Publishing Company, for encouraging us to prepare this reader. As coauthors, we intend to divide the rewards for this work and to share equally in any blame for its defects.

PART ONE

Introduction

Delinquency and "Juvenile Delinquents"

Where do juvenile delinquents come from? The usual answer to this sort of question holds that social experiences of one kind or another produce juvenile delinquents who then become the subject of public concern. In turn, public attention takes the form of police apprehension of the deviant youth, court referral and court appearance, placement on probation, incarceration in an institution, and other experiences. This view of things implies that "delinquency will out," that is, those who conduct themselves in a lawbreaking fashion will inevitably reveal themselves and will get into the hands of the authorities. In the common view, the correctional machinery (police, probation, courts, etc.) exists in order to *react to* youthful misconduct after it has broken out.

But a moment's reflection will show that matters are not all that simple. To begin with, there is a large body of available research evidence which shows that much juvenile misconduct goes undetected, so that it does not become the subject of a correctional response. However, demonstration of this point does not require detailed empirical evidence, for most readers

2

can probably recall instances of youthful peccadilloes in their own backgrounds that did not receive a formal response from the correctional apparatus. Who among the readers of this book has an unblemished record of proper conduct?

The matter of being a "hidden" delinquent or an officially observed one is complex, influenced by many factors. However, the evidence generally indicates that:

1. Nearly all youngsters engage in acts of misconduct of varying degrees of seriousness sometime during the juvenile period of life.
2. About 3 per cent of all juvenile court–eligible children (youngsters between 7 and 18 years of age) actually get into the juvenile court each year, while double this number come to the attention of the police.
3. Those youngsters who get officially processed by the police or courts are most likely to be working-class children engaged in serious and repetitive acts of lawbreaking.
4. But some middle-class juvenile delinquents are found in the population of official offenders, while some youths engaged in relatively petty forms of misconduct are also found in that group.

It is also the case that law-enforcement and correctional agencies do much more than passively react to youthful offenders observed by them. The police stand as the major group of reactors-to-delinquency who sift and sort some juvenile deviants into the correctional machinery, where they flow by various paths into court appearance, probation, and the like. The police also sift other youngsters out of this correctional apparatus, so that they do not become "juvenile delinquents" (do not become adjudicated as such in a court). The processing of juvenile delinquents beyond the point of police contact is big business. Children referred to juvenile courts in the United States in 1967 (excluding traffic cases) numbered some 811,000 out of a total population of 31,000,000 children between 11 and 18 years of age. [1] During 1965, a daily average of 62,773 youths were incarcerated in juvenile institutions in the United States, while another 285,431 were under supervision in community programs (probation and parole). Institutionalized delinquents required 31,687 employees to process and supervise them, while another 9,633 individuals were employed as community correctional agents. [2]

The thrust of these remarks is that the law-enforcement and correctional system is a decision-making structure of heroic proportions. At a

1. Children's Bureau, *Juvenile Court Statistics,* 1967 (Washington, D.C.: U. S. Department of Health, Education, and Welfare, 1969), p. 10.
2. The President's Commission on Law Enforcement and Administration of Justice, *The Challenge of Crime in a Free Society* (Washington, D.C.: U. S. Government Printing office, 1967), p. 161.

number of points, someone must decide whether a lawbreaking youth is to be regarded as a "bad one" needing court attention or a "good kid" who only needs a mild tongue-lashing. Someone must decide whether a youth should be sent to a training school or placed on probation. Someone must judge whether a training-school inmate should be turned loose on parole this week, next month, or at some other time.

We might speak of the correctional process in metaphorical terms as a "people-processing machine." But in doing so, we ought to keep in mind the fact that this is not an automated operation which runs by itself. Instead, it is a system, or machine, staffed by human operatives who are engaged in making myriad decisions about what to do with the offender raw material that it processes. A graphic portrayal of the major elements of the correctional decision-making structure, identifying most of those points at which critical decisions must be made by someone, is provided in the diagram.

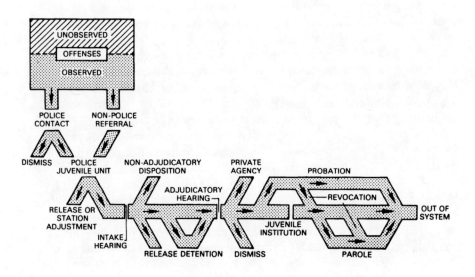

*The Juvenile Correctional Machinery**

* Don C. Gibbons, *Delinquent Behavior,* © 1970 Prentice-Hall, Inc. (Englewood Cliffs, N.J.). By permission of the publishers.

The Study of the Correctional Machinery

The varied parts of the juvenile correctional system in the United States add up to a vast bureaucratic structure given over to purposes of social control. This system warrants the same kind of sociological attention as the other large-scale organizations which play a prominent part in the social structure of modern societies. In short, one reason correctional organizations ought to be studied is that organizational analysis is the "stuff" of sociological inquiry.[3] The student of complex organizations has much to learn from an examination of the formal and informal rules of correctional organizations, role conflicts within them, and other organizational facets. Stated differently, it may be the case that prison guards, foremen, college administrators, and other bureaucratic functionaries, and the organizations within which they work all share many characteristics in common. The organizations within which they toil may show a number of common ingredients. If this be true, the study of correctional systems may inform us about organizational dynamics in other settings as well. This is a major *raison d'être* for the examination of correctional processes.

But there is another reason for the study of correctional processes. Perhaps these structures and the people who staff them have important effects upon the youths who are processed through them. Indeed, two different common-sense hypotheses have often been advanced regarding the repercussions of agency actions upon offenders. One of these holds that these experiences are harmful in effect, as illustrated, for example, in the view that training schools are "crime schools." In this conception, children who proceed through these institutions undergo deleterious experiences which drive them further into deviance by acquiring more hardened delinquent attitudes and more proficient crime skills. The other hypothesis is more sanguine, taking the form of an opinion that correctional agencies manage to succeed in deflecting offenders from delinquency by rehabilitating them.

In recent years, optimism concerning the curative effects of juvenile correctional processes has waned, and the pessimistic view that these experiences are negative career contingencies or experiences has become more common among sociologists. Those who hold this view tend to argue that correctional agencies unwittingly go about labeling youngsters as lawbreakers, or that they have other harmful effects which constrict the lawbreaker's chances to retreat from involvement in misconduct.

An early version of this position was advanced some years ago by Tannenbaum, who argued that official dealings with deviants constitute a process of "dramatization of evil." [4] He contended that official handling in

3. A useful collection of· readings illustrating this point is Amitai Etzioni, ed., *A Sociological Reader on Complex Organizations,* 2nd ed. (New York: Holt, Rinehart and Winston, 1969).

4. Frank Tannenbaum, *Crime and the Community* (New York: Ginn, 1938), pp. 19–21.

the courts, training schools, and related places often fails to divert the person from a deviant career; instead, such experiences alert citizens in the community to the presence of an "evil" person in their midst. Once a "bad" person becomes singled out, he is likely to be consistently thought of as "evil" in the future, quite apart from how he. actually behaves. Whether his deportment changes or remains the same, he continues to be seen as a "bad" person. In many instances, he develops sentiments of being unjustly dealt with, which operate as rationalizations for his misconduct. As a result, the end-product of correctional handling is the reinforcement of the very behavior the correctional agents are attempting to reduce.

There are a number of variables which ought to be considered in a full-blown exposition of the effects of correctional experiences upon offenders. First, these could conceivably have several different effects: *positive*, so that they propel persons out of deviance; *neutral* or *benign,* in which they have little or no impact upon offenders; and *negative*, in which they lead to the reinvolvement of the actor in additional lawbreaking. Quite probably some correctional encounters have more positive or negative repercussions upon deviant careers than do others. Thus, the first appearance of the lawbreaker in the juvenile court may have a markedly dramatic effect upon him, but later events, such as being placed in a forestry camp, may contribute little to his subsequent behavior. In short, to acknowledge that correctional agencies have deleterious effects does not mean that all such organizations are equally criminogenic in their workings.

Another consideration is that we ought not to lump all training schools, all probation agencies, or all other correctional structures together when we look at the question of their impact upon delinquent careers. For example, those wards who are processed through a state training school in a progressive correctional system may be influenced by institutionalization in quite different ways than are wards in a punitive, harsh training school. Then too, offenders ought not to be lumped together as though correctional organizations have the same impact upon all of them. Instead, we ought to entertain the possibility that incarceration in a training school might have very different meanings for first offenders as opposed to urban, gang delinquents who are wise in the ways of institutions.

Dimensions for Study

There are at least five dimensions or aspects of correctional organizations about which we should like to have detailed information. To begin with, there is *the nature of the organization* and the behavioral processes that go on within it. Here, attention is focused upon questions of the sort: What are the functions of the organization? Are some of these formal or stated, while others are informal and unstated? What are the rules, formal and informal, governing organizational processes? What is the nature of the organizational hierarchy, status system, and role definitions? Are there role conflicts within the organization, centering about discordant tasks being carried out by the personnel in the system? In short, there is a series of questions about organizational structure that engage our attention when we study complex organizations of any type.

A second concern in the analysis of correctional organizations has to do with the *perspectives of the "consumers"* of the service, that is, the general public in whose name these agencies operate. To what extent are citizens' views of correctional goals congruent with the actual operation of agencies? A third dimension is closely related to this one, namely, the *perspectives of the employees* or agents within correctional systems. Among other things, we want to know whether their views are in tune with those of citizens. Also, what of organizational consensus? Do agents within a particular correctional operation share a body of understandings about tactics and strategies for dealing with offenders? We may find that, in some organizations, the workers are in violent disagreement about the nature of the work task. A fourth dimension, related to these above, is the *persepctives of the offenders.* To what extent do offenders agree with the image of them held by the workers or citizens? Do they see themselves as "bad" persons in need of punishment or rehabilitation? Do they regard the conditions of probation or the rules of the institution as fair and just? How do they perceive the organization and its functionaries as it operates upon them?

The final dimension of correctional organization analysis, the *impact of the agency upon offenders,* is the most difficult one to study. As we have already noted, these structures may have positive, negative, or benign effects upon the human material they process. But how do we measure this impact? Suppose we find that training-school wards generally become more docile and cooperative during their stay in the institution. Is this an indication of basic change on their part that will carry over into their life after release from the institution? Perhaps, but it may simply be a manifestation of "playing it cool," in which wards are engaged in a transitory adjustment to the school. Their cooperative behavior may be short-lived once they are released from the institution. Clearly, the measurement of agency impact must take place some time after the offender has moved through the organizational experience. All of this is made even more difficult by the problem of separating out agency effects from other experiences which play upon offenders and influence their behavior. Thus successful adjustment upon release from custody might be the product of the correctional experience, but it might also be due to other contingencies, such as the availability of a post-release job, school placement, or some other factor. Given the complexity of the task of assessing correctional outcomes, it is little wonder that relatively little research has been conducted on this question.

Prologue

This book is about the correctional decision-process, correctional organizations, and the dimensions of analysis identified above. It begins with the delinquent population and endeavors to identify the major characteristics of juvenile lawbreaking. In particular, it attempts to identify the sorts of youths who most often remain as "hidden" delinquents and the kinds that get observed in their lawbreaking acts. The text then moves through the major parts of the correctional machinery in much the same way that offenders are processed through it, starting with police contact, moving to the juvenile court, then on to probation, and finally through incarceration in an institution.

In all of the sections of this book, we shall marshal what information we can on the five dimensions of correctional agencies enumerated above. But let us recognize at the outset that there are important gaps in the available evidence. One of the main tasks in the connective discussions at the beginning of each part will be to identify some of these soft spots in the evidence. The book can be viewed as somewhat programmatic in that it identifies problems for empirical investigation.

Before moving to the study of specific correctional processes, let us examine a general essay by Werthman concerning the impact of social definitions upon delinquent careers. In his lucid and insightful paper, he shows some of the ways in which the opinions, views, and definitions of persons with whom the offender interacts condition his self-perceptions and his opportunities for conforming and deviant conduct. Although Werthman's essay deals in part with interactions between delinquents and correctional organizations, it also speaks to the broader question of social intercourse between deviants and those who react to them. The essay serves to remind us that the offender is not some kind of alien from another social world, but instead he is, in various ways, the product of social influences in which we are all implicated.

1. The Function of Social Definitions in the Development of Delinquent Careers

CARL WERTHMAN

THE MORAL career of the lower class juvenile gang boy often begins at age 6, 7, or 8 when he is defined by his teachers as "predelinquent" for demonstrating to his friends that he is not a "sissy," and it ends between the ages of 16 and 25 when he either takes a job, goes to college, joins the Army, or becomes a criminal.[1] Although much of his behavior during this period can be seen and is seen by him as a voluntary set of claims on one of the temporary social identities available to him as a lower class "youth," his final choice of an "adult" identity will depend in large measure on the way his moral character has been assessed, categorized, and acted upon by his parents, teachers, and officials of the law as well as on the attitudes and actions he has chosen in response. How the boys embrace

Reprinted from the President's Commission on Law Enforcement and Administration of Justice, *Task Force Report: Juvenile Delinquency and Youth Crime* (Washington, D.C.: U. S. Government Printing Office, 1967), pp. 155–170.

1. The concept of a moral career has been defined by Erving Goffman as "the regular sequence of changes that career entails in the person's self and in his framework if imagery for judging himself and others." See Erving Goffman, "The Moral Career of the Mental Patient," in *Asylums* (New York: Doubleday, 1961), p. 128.

these identities, how adults tend to define and treat them for doing so, and how the boys respond to these definitions and treatments is thus the subject of this paper.[2]

The Identity Materials of the Delinquent

Although the special conditions of youth as a status do not dictate, provoke, or account for "delinquent" behavior, these conditions constitute the structural possibilities that allow it to exist; and, as suggested by the fact that most gang boys leave the streets as soon as they are forced to make a living, one of these conditions concerns the way young people are related to the economy.[3] Since they are required by law to attend school until the age of 16 or thereabouts, they are virtually forced to remain financially dependent on their parents during these years, and this state of dependence diminishes the magnitude of their responsibilities considerably. They do not have to support themselves or a family, and the schools are equipped to run quite well, if not better, without them. Unlike adults, they are thus left relatively free to organize their lives around noneconomic pursuits. Looked at another way, however, they are also deprived of occupational categories and activities as ways to differentiate themselves from one another.

In the adult world, occupations are the major source of social identity. The jobs themselves are used to classify and rank, while the norms governing performance are the principal criteria by which competence and character are judged. In the world inhabited by youth, however, identities must be constructed from other materials; and on the whole, these materials are limited to the activities that take place in schools and those engaged in and around them.[4] The school provides a number of instrumental training roles for those who wish to pursue them, but if a student is neither academically nor politically inclined, these roles are likely not to have much meaning. Particularly in elementary and junior high schools, it is not so

2. The data on which this study is based consists of taped interviews with 56 "core" members of 11 "delinquent" gangs or "jacket clubs" plus observations and more informal conversations involving over 100 members of these 11 gangs. The boys were drawn from the clientele of a delinquency-prevention program in San Francisco called Youth for Service, and the research was conducted largely out of their offices for a 2-year period. Of the 56 boys interviewed on tape, 37 were Negro, 11 were Mexican, and 8 were Caucasian. This report is thus based primarily on a sample of Negro gang boys.

3. To the extent that these conditions rule out the possibilities of deviance, they can be referred to as elements of "structural conduciveness." See Neil J. Smelser, *Theory of Collective Behavior* (New York: Free Press, 1963), p. 15.

4. Although the family can be seen as an important source of emotional support for the various contests that go on outside it, there is little important contribution it can make to the genesis of public identities since most young people do not spend time together in the same home.

much what you *do* that counts but rather what you *are,* since everyone tends to be doing about the same things.

In the absence of occupational titles, a rich vocabulary of identity categories tends to emerge, a vocabulary that often includes referents to physical or anatomical features, clothing styles, places, possessions, special membership groups, and a general relationship to the administration of schools.[5] In addition, each of these categories tends to be associated with certain skills and attributes of character as well as with the activities in which these skills and character traits are generally displayed.

As Erving Goffman has elegantly made clear, however, there are certain skills and attributes of character, particularly those most prized by gang boys, that can only be claimed by aspirants to them in social situations where something of consequence is risked; and since the school facilities available for nonacademic character construction are generally limited to games, it is not surprising that boys who wish to play for higher stakes tend to use each other, the law, and sometimes even school officials in order to demonstrate their claims.[6]

It is impossible to prove that one is cool, courageous, or "smart," for example, without a situation in which there is something to be cool, courageous, or "smart" about, just as it is difficult to gain a reputation for being "tough" unless the skills involved are occasionally put to a test. In situations where it is possible to claim possession of these attributes, the reward won or utility gained, in addition to whatever material goods may be at stake, is an increment in status or reputation, a commodity that

5. Just prior to the completion of this study, for example, the high school population of San Francisco had divided itself into four major groups. The lower and working class Negroes, Spanish-speaking minorities and whites were referred to as "bloods," "barts," and "white shoes," respectively, while the fourth group, the "Ivy Leaguers," contained the middle and lower middle class segments of all three races. The relationship to schools implicit in this vocabulary is obvious, and all four groups were easily identifiable by uniform. The "bloods," "barts," and "white shoes" were further broken down into gangs by districts and each gang had its own jacket. Moreover, the district and gang distinctions took precedence over race in racially integrated districts so that the lower class Negroes and whites living in predominantly Spanish-speaking areas wore the "bart" uniform and were referred to by members of their own race as such.

In the city of Albany on the other side of San Francisco Bay, the vocabulary adopted by the students in the all-white high school is devoid of ethnic references but certainly no less to the point: the students who congregate during recess on plots of land in the middle of the school have been entitled the "quadrangles"; the students who meet in the parking lot outside the school are called just that, "parking lots"; and the remainder of the student body is referred to as "uncommitted," presumably because they occupy the territory between the parking lot and the quadrangle that surrounds the school on four sides.

6. I am indebted to a recent unpublished paper by Goffman for much of the analysis of gang activity that follows. See Erving Goffman, "Where the Action Is: Or, Hemingway Revisited" Center For the Study of Law and Society, University of California at Berkeley, 1965.

youth, like adults, spend a sizable amount of time attempting to obtain and protect. Conversely, the risks include the possibility of damaging the body or the pocketbook as well as the chance of being shown to lack whatever skills or attributes of character the situation calls for. In addition, when the law is being used to prove possession of moral character, there is also the probability of being observed or discovered and thus sanctioned by the State. Goffman further suggests that risky situations should be entered voluntarily if a person wishes others to grant him possession of the desired attributes without any contingent doubts: and when this happens, he says, there is "action" to be found.[7]

Claiming title to these character traits can be more difficult than it may first appear, however, since risky situations do not arise very often in the course of an average day. In fact, as Goffman points out, most people manage to arrange their lives so that matters of consequence such as physical safety and a money supply are protected from unnecessary risk, although as a result these people encounter few situations in which the most heroic of social virtues can actually be claimed rather than assumed.

Yet if someone with an adult status actually decides he desires "action," there is always Las Vegas or a risky job, while a lower class gang boy is more or less forced to create his own. If he wishes to prove that he is autonomous, courageous, loyal, or has "heart," not only must he take a chance, he must also construct the situation in which to take it; and for most gang boys this means that risky situations must be made from whatever materials happen to be available on the streets and at schools.[8]

On the streets, the various activities defined by law as "thefts" provide perhaps the best examples of the way gang boys use laws to construct and claim identities. In order to become usable as identity materials, however, the situations in which laws against theft are broken must be carefully selected to insure that sufficient risk is present. Unlike the professional thief who takes pride in knowing how to minimize the occupational risks of his trade, most younger gang boys create risks where none need be involved.[9] Joyriding, for example, is ideally suited for this purpose since "cool" is required to get a stolen car started quickly; and once started, the situation contains the generous though not overwhelming risk of detection. Moreover, given the wide range of risky activities that can be en-

7. As Goffman puts it, "action" can be located "wherever the individual knowingly takes chances that are defined as voluntary, and whose conduct is perceived as a reflection on character." (*ibid.*, p. 48).

8. It was largely on the basis of an argument such as this that Norman Mailer suggested "medieval jousting tournaments in Central Park" and "horse races through the streets of Little Italy" as delinquency prevention programs for the City of New York. See Norman Mailer, *The Presidential Papers* (New York: Bantam Books, 1964), p. 22.

9. See Edwin H. Sutherland, *The Professional Thief* (Chicago: University of Chicago Press, 1937).

gaged in once the cars are stolen, joyriding is viewed as an abundant source of the anxiety, excitement, and tension that accompanies the taking of risks for its own sake, a complex of emotions often referred to as "kicks."

> (Did you guys do much joyriding? Yeah. When I was about 13, I didn't do nothing but steal cars. The guy that I always stole with, both of us liked to drive so we'd steal a car. And then he'd go steal another car and we'd chase each other. Like there would be two in our car, two in the other car, and we'd drive by and stick out our hands, and if you touch them then they have to chase you. Or we'd steal an old car, you know, that have the running boards on it. We'd stand on that and kick the car going past. Kind of fun, but, uh, it's real dangerous. We used to have a ball when we'd do that other game with the hands though.

In addition to joyriding which was almost always done at night, the younger gang boys I studied also located two risky daytime situations in which to engage in theft. On Saturday afternoons, they would delight in trying to steal hubcaps from a parking lot next to a local supermarket, and on special occasions, they enjoyed breaking into gum and candy machines located in a crowded amusement park. In the parking lot, the challenge consisted of making away with the hubcaps without being seen, while in the equally crowded amusement park, the risk consisted of darting through the customers and away from the police after making sure that the theft itself had been observed.

> (What else did you guys used to do when you were in Junior High School?) Well, we would sometimes, three or four of us, maybe go to Playland and rob the machines. That would be a ball cause, see, what we'd do is maybe have two guys start fighting or maybe jump on a sailor or something like that. In the meantime, the other two guys would go back in there while the police was, you know, chasing the others, while we was back there breaking the machines open, you know. There was about five or six of them machines. So then the cops would always see us cause somebody would yell for them. So they would stop chasing the other guys and start chasing us. We had a lot of fun up there.

Even among the younger boys, however, thievery was sometimes undertaken for motives other than "kicks" or "fun." Shoplifting, for example, was viewed as a more instrumental activity, as was the practice of stealing coin changers from temporarily evacuated buses parked in a nearby public depot. In the case of shoplifting, most of the boys both wanted and wore the various items of clothing they stole; and when buses were robbed, either the money was divided among the boys or it was used to buy supplies for a party being given by the club.

> Like we'd give a party on a Friday night. Well, we know the bread man come Thursday. And we know what time he gets there and what

time he leaves, so we know what time to be there to get the bread. And
then we know where to get the tuna fish and the Kool Aid. That's simple.
Just walk into any store and steal that. I used to call everybody so they
get up. Let's say two gonna go get the bread. The other two gonna go
out to the streetcars cause early in the morning they just leave their
money on the bus cause there ain't nobody around. Get some coffee at
the Fire Department. So they go on and hit the streetcar and get the
money, something like that.

Yet these thefts were not perceived as exclusively instrumental. Practically as soon as the gang was formed in elementary school, its identity
system differentiated into "thieves" and "fighters," and both types of boys
were perceived as performing some function for the group. Thus, even
when the purpose of theft was defined as instrumental, the act itself was
quickly communicated to the other gang members since it was a source
of identification as well as party supplies.

Our club was organized. We had a mutual understanding between us.
Everybody in the club had something good about them or something
bad. Everybody had some kind of profession. Like Ray, he was the
fighter, always throwing his weight around when we had a fight or something. Little Johnnie and Ronnie, they were what we called the thieves.
They was the best! I mean those two could steal anything. Then, like
Arnold couldn't spell his name. He couldn't spell Arnold. I mean, boy
he needed help.

As the members of a gang get older, their perception and use of theft
become increasingly instrumental; and if they are still in the gang after
graduating or getting expelled from high school, theft turns into a particular version of the "hustle." These hustles still involve risks, but the
risks are no longer incurred exclusively for what can be demonstrated
about the self by taking them. The possible sanctions faced are much
more serious than they were in junior high school. Moreover, the boys
now need the money. Without it they would find themselves hard pressed
to sustain a daily round of socializing with ease. Thus, their relationship
to the risky situation changes as both positive and negative outcomes
become more consequential; and as this shift takes place, the actual thefts
themselves are talked about less and less. Where a boy happens to be
getting his money becomes his own private business, a policy that gradually evolves as attempts are made to cut down the probability of detection.
Yet the boys still do not see themselves as professional thieves, even
after they have graduated from high school. As long as they can rely on
their parents for room and board, the hustle is viewed as a transitory,
impermanent, and part-time way of simply getting by. It is not conceived
of as an "adult" training role, even though it is an instrumental relationship

to the economic world. On the other hand, if the boys remain on the streets after 18, they are no longer stealing for "kicks."

The laws against theft are not the only materials used by gang boys to demonstrate moral character. On the streets, they also tend to use each other for this purpose, activities that Goffman has called "character games."

> I assume that when two persons are in one another's presence it will be inevitable that many of the obligations of one will be the expectations of the other (and vice versa), in matters both substantive and ceremonial. Each participant will have a personal vested interest in seeing to it that in this particular case the rules the other ought to obey are in fact obeyed by him. Mutual dependence on the other's proper conduct occurs. Each individual necessarily thus becomes a field in which the other necessarily practices good or bad conduct. In the ordinary course of affairs, compliance, forbearance and the mechanisms of apology and excuse insure that showdowns don't occur. None the less, contests over whose treatment of the other is to prevail are always a possibility, and can almost always be made to occur. The participants will then find themselves committed to producing evidence that will cause a re-assessment of self at the expense of the assessment that will come to be made of the other. A "character game" results.[10]

Goffman further suggests that a claim to possess "honor" is what initiates most character games, honor defined as "the property of character which causes the individual to engage in a character contest when his rights have been violated and when the likely cost of the contest is high." [11]

Like other forms of "action," then, character games are played at some risk but also presumably for some reward.

As Short and Strodtbeck have pointed out, fighting is perhaps the classic example of a gang activity that is best understood with this model.[12] After observing gang boys in Chicago for a number if years, these authors concluded that most fights take place either when a "rep" for toughness is suddenly challenged by a situation that the gang boy cannot avoid confronting or when a challenge to within-group rank appears, either from inside or outside the gang. In the first instance, the gang boy is handed a chance to appear "honorable," perhaps even a chance he did not want; while in the second instance, the boy will provoke a character contest to reaffirm or reclaim his status in the gang after it is challenged by a streetworker or another boy, sometimes during an absence in jail.

Although it is quite true that most older gang boys will only fight

10. Goffman, "Action," p. 60.
11. *Ibid.*, p. 63.
12. James F. Short, Jr., and Fred L. Strodtbeck, *Group Process and Gang Delinquency* (Chicago: University of Chicago Press, 1965), pp. 248–264; also J. Short and F. Strodtbeck, "Why Gangs Fight," *Trans-Action*, I (1964).

when their reputations or ranks are threatened, the younger boys can sometimes be found initiating fights even though they have not been provoked. These fights are consciously sought out or searched for in an attempt to build a reputation where none existed before, and the boys are referred to as "looking for trouble" because they are "coming up." In these situations, an attempt is often made to select the target carefully. Not any rival gang will serve as a suitable object on which to build a rep, and thus, as in the following case, a gang invading "rival territory" may decide to go home if the members cannot find boys who are big or important enough to prove a case.

> Remember when them guys from Hunters Point came over looking for us? Man, it got real bad there. Cause when we made the papers, you know, everybody thought we was something. So then they all come lookin' for you. Gonna knock off the big boys. So a whole bunch of these little kids from Hunters Point came lookin' for us one night. They was coming up, and they figured they could beat us or something. (Did you fight?) No. We wasn't in the neighborhood that night. They found a bunch of guys their age but they wasn't interested in that. They just went home.

Particularly among younger boys, a great deal of bullying is apparently also inspired by attempts to build rather than protect reputations. For example, a schoolteacher in Washington, D.C., recently told me that her fourth grade class already contained a boy who had earned the nickname "tough cat," a nickname that was apparently achieved by beating up younger, older, bigger, and smaller boys virtually at random.[13] After the nickname was given to a single boy, it then became a free-floating identity aspired to by others in the class and could be claimed for the same activity. Once the boys get to high school, however, this sort of fighting tends to be perceived as "unfair."

> When I was in Junior High some kids called me king of the school, and there was about seven of us. You know, we ran that school. Those girls, they kinda looked up to us. We didn't let nobody go with nothing. It ain't nothing now, but we all would get in front of the line—Get out the way, let us through—you know. There wasn't about seven of us. Want some money, just ask for it and they glad to give it to you cause they scared. It was just that we was seven bullies I guess. Cause we'd snap our fingers and they'd do what we tell them. See, that was when we was younger. The girls, they went for all that cause they didn't know no better than you. They liked to see somebody being bad then. Big show-offs. Somebody who's a lot of fun. See, they like that then. But now that you get older, they don't go for it so much no more.

13. I am indebted to Ethel Rosenthal for this observation.

There may be a parallel here between the apparently "senseless violence" engaged in by very young boys and the more serious instances of "random violence" some times found among gang boys at the very end of their "delinquent" careers. In the oldest gang I worked with, all of whose members were between 20 and 25, a few of the boys would occasionally stab strangers miscellaneously, ostensibly for having received a "dirty look." Most of these stabbings seemed to occur when the boys were in the process of bragging about their past exploits and their virtually non-existent "reps."

It is possible that for very young boys, the task of building a "rep" can involve creating an audience for this behavior where none previously existed, and this task may involve selecting targets miscellaneously in order to establish the rules. In the case of older boys, however, the instances of random violence seem to occur just after most of the real audience for this behavior abandons this source of identity for an occupation, at which point the boys who still wish to retain an identity by engaging in acts of violence may choose to imagine that this audience still exists. Although the consequences of these audience creation problems are clearly more serious among older boys than among younger ones, both tend to be defined as "disturbed" by their immediate audience of peers.

Regardless of whether fights are entered into voluntarily or involuntarily and regardless of whether they take place in situations that are imagined or real, the basic principle involved in this mode of identity construction seems to be clear: the fight is defined as a situation in which reputation or rank can be won or lost. Whether a particular fight will be entered into depends on the expected values of the various outcomes, and these values can vary considerably from boy to boy. It is no accident, for example, that situations involving violence are often perceived as "turning points" by ex-gang members when contemplating their past careers. Particularly among older boys, it is easy to see how reputations can get large enough so as not to be worth the risk of defending.[14] Similarly, in areas where it is tacitly understood that certain affronts can only be revenged by attempting to kill the offender, the person offended may simply decide to leave town rather than run the risk of being sent to jail or killed in defense of his honor.[15]

In addition to fighting, there are also other activities in which gang boys use each other to claim and construct identities. The behavior described by Miller as "verbal aggression," also known variously as "ranking,"

14. I encountered two boys who dropped out of gang activity for this reason. In one case, the boy decided it was time to leave after he was shot at twice in one week from passing automobiles driven by members of different rival gangs.
15. Claude Brown, *Manchild in the Promised Land* (New York: Macmillan, 1965), p. 171.

"capping," or "sounding," seems to involve some of the same principles found in fights.[16] As Matza has pointed out, this activity amounts essentially to a process of testing status by insult, and thus honor is the quality of moral character at stake.[17] Goffman has called these encounters "contest contests," situations in which someone forces someone else "into a contest over whether or not there will be a contest." [18] Like fighting, it involves risk and can thus have a bearing on status. Unlike fighting, however, it is not engaged in to demonstrate toughness or courage but rather to display a type of verbal agility that gang boys call "smart."

Short and Strodtbeck have also suggested that the "utility-risk paradigm" might shed some light on the high percentage of illegitimate pregnancies that gang boys produce while engaged in another type of "interpersonal action" discussed by Goffman, namely "making out."[19] Sexual activity sometimes begins very early among gang boys, and there is typically a great deal of it throughout a career. Most of the Negro boys claimed to have lost their virginity around the age of 8 or 9, and some were having intercourse regularly in junior high school. During most of the years spent in a gang, girls are seen primarily as objects for sexual play, and it is not until the age of 16 or older that they are sometimes treated with anything resembling respect. Ultimately, however, it is marriage that takes most boys out of the gang, thus providing one of the few available legitimate excuses for leaving the streets.[20]

Although Short and Strodtbeck suggest that two separate risks are involved in illegitimacy, the first being the probability of engaging in sexual intercourse with a given frequency and the second being the probability that these actions will eventuate in parenthood, only one of these risks is used as a source of identity. Success or failure at "making it" with a girl is socially risky since the outcome affects status in the gang, while it is doubtful that the risks involved in gambling without contraception are considered a source of pleasure independent of the act itself.

The gang boy thus aspires to an identity that puts him in a special relationship to risk. When he is around his friends, he often creates the situations in which he chooses to exist, an act of creation that involves selecting out certain features of the social environment and then transforming them into the conditions that allow him to define a self. In part, these risks are taken for their own sake since a reputation can be built on this capacity alone and the emotional reward is a "kick." In part, there

16. W. B. Miller, H. Geertz, and S. G. Cutter, "Aggression in a Boy's Street-Corner Group," *Psychiatry*, November 1961, pp. 283–298.
17. David Matza, *Delinquency and Drift* (New York: Wiley, 1964), pp. 42–44.
18. Goffman, "Action," p. 68.
19. Short and Strodtbeck, *Group Process*, pp. 44–45, 249–250.
20. Walter B. Miller, "The Corner Gang Boys Get Married," *Trans-Action*, I (November 1963), 10–12.

are also honor, courage, and loyalty involved, special attributes of moral character that can only be demonstrated in situations of risk. Taken together, however, these risks seem to represent a set of special claims to the status of "men," a status they are culturally and structurally forbidden to occupy until the "delinquent career" comes to an end. Why gang boys rather than others decide to take these risks is a difficult if not impossible question to answer. Yet it is possible to look at how the gang boy deals with the mechanisms that ordinarily prevent these risks from being taken.

The Genesis of Autonomy

Although the absence of adult economic responsibilities can be seen as conducive to the development of unconventional identity formations among youth, young people are also politically dependent on adults. A person under age 18 is always in the legal custody of someone; and if he proves to be beyond control by parents, he can always be adopted by the State. In effect, this means that young people can be ordered to obey the rules established for them by their parents since the law can be appealed to if these commands are not obeyed.

In most instances, however, this parental power develops into authority. As a rule, young people simply assume that parents are a legitimate if sometimes difficult source of rules and thus obey them voluntarily.[21] Perhaps more important, it is precisely this authority relationship that allows at least the preadolescent to define himself as "a child." He implicitly surrenders all autonomy and thus does not exercise whatever capacity he might have to make his own decisions. In return, he can afford to feel "protected."

In addition to establishing their own authority, parents also have a vested interest in endowing school teachers with a temporary "title to rule." This legitimacy is sometimes conferred in subtle ways but most techniques are easy to observe. Parents caution their offspring to behave and get good grades, then teachers are visited to determine whether these prescriptions are being obeyed. In instances where there is a dispute between teacher and child, parents rarely voice criticism to a son or daughter—however much the teacher may be castigated for ruining the future of the family in the privacy of a bedroom.

To further insure that the authority of school personnel is legitimated, boys and girls are made aware that these officials can and do inform parents of their misadventures. Parents, teachers, and other adult officials thus see to it that children are not allowed to segregate roles. Since parents typically have the ultimate power, they become the center of a communi-

21. Max Weber, *The Theory of Social and Economic Organization,* trans. A. M. Henderson and Talcott Parsons (Glencoe: Free Press, 1947).

cations network for other adult authorities. Whether the child is at school or on the streets, he is made to feel that none of his behavior can be hidden from his parents.[22]

The youngsters who define themselves as dependent do not mind being the subjects of this friendly conspiracy and most would feel very insecure without it. They often cannot tolerate a segregation of roles, even when the communications network is broken by accident and thus they often feel the need to confess their sins in order to relieve themselves of the responsibility for hiding information. These "confessionals" are considered rewarding moments for parents who take pride in constructing leakproof systems of surveillance over their offspring. They are looked upon as indicators of "trust."

Precisely how this network of authority is cultivated and maintained remains something of a psychosocial mystery. Yet the fact remains that as long as parents can manage to have their ideals about the behavior of their offspring either aspired to or even vaguely achieved, there is precious little chance, as we will see, that policemen and probation officers will end up defining them as "delinquents," provided, of course, that the number of crimes committed is kept to some reasonable limit. Although I encountered a great many parents who had come to look upon the trip to jail as "routine" by the time their sons were 16, I found none who said that at an earlier point in life they had not hoped for something better. In practically every case, it was possible to locate a set of expectations that was perceived by parents either to have broken down or never to have developed, despite the fact that many had also come to view the news of "trouble" as a more or less "normal" event.

The situation that these parents find themselves in can perhaps best be described with a vocabulary developed by Harold Garfinkel for the analysis of how stable social activity systems are "constituted," become "disorganized," and are "reconstituted." [23] Garfinkel suggests that routine social activities are defined in the most fundamental sense of that word by a set of "constitutive" or "basic" rules, i.e., rules that are used to make behavior recognizable as an act or event in some known order of events. Unlike institutionalized norms (or "preferred rules" as Garfinkel calls them), the "basic" rules do not specify how a person is to act in an activity but only the range of possible acts he could perform as well as the social category of person he is if he takes part in them. As examples of "basic rules," Garfinkel cites those that "constitute" the game of tictactoe: "Play

22. It is largely for this reason that vehicles for public transportation such as buses become scenes of mass confusion when children ride them unsupervised to and from school. The bus drivers do not have access to parents and the children know it.

23. Harold Garfinkel, "Some Conceptions of and Experiments with 'Trust' as a Condition of Stable Concerted Actions," ms.

is conducted on a three by three matrix by two players who move alternatively. The first player makes a mark in one of the unoccupied cells. The second player, in his turn, places his mark in one of the remaining unoccupied cells. And so on. The term 'tictactoe player' refers to a person who seeks to act in compliance with these possible events as constitutively expected ones." [24]

Garfinkel further suggests that in order for an activity system to be "stable," the people involved in the activity must "trust" each other, "trust" defined as a condition in which the participants expect one another to act in compliance with the basic or constitutive rules. If these rules are violated, the activity is in danger of becoming "confused" or "disorganized" since people will find themselves without a context in which to interpret the meaning of the act committed by the violator and thus will not know how to respond to him. In addition, there is often a feeling that the condition of "trust" has been broken and the people who believe themselves to be participants in the activity are likely to get anxious, frustrated, or angry.

In groups such as families, friendships, and businesses where participants are quite committed to one another for personal, economic, and legal reasons, some attempt is usually made to "normalize" the situation. This can mean that there is a renewal of belief in the other person's commitment to the previous rules or that the rules will change, in which case an act or event that was not previously understood will come to be perceived as "normal" or "routine." If a "basic" rule is added or subtracted, however, the result is a new activity.

Following this conceptual scheme, we can see that where the participants in an activity include an "authority" as well as others who are seen as "subordinates," the set of basic rules establishing the activity will always include a rule which constitutes this relationship. From the point of view of a subordinate, moreover, this rule will be one that says: I choose to obey all the preferred rules or norms that are established for me in this activity by the category of person who is designated the authority, say a parent, a teacher, or perhaps even all adults.

In addition, we can predict that where an authority has a part in some activity, it will be important to him that his subordinates act in compliance with the basic rule establishing the source of preferred rules, or, put another way, that his subordinates "trust" him. From the point of view of the authority, moreover, the important issue about all acts becomes not whether they are being performed in accordance with a particular rule but whether they are being performed in accordance with the rule establishing who it is that properly establishes the rules themselves.

24. *Ibid.*, p. 6.

This problem is frequently and simply illustrated among the parents of preadolescent and "predelinquent" boys, many of whom are described as simply "out of control." In these cases, what the parents seem to be describing are situations in which no stable pattern of mutual expectations has developed at all. Whatever preferred rules they attempt to establish as a way of ordering the activities of the family are more or less randomly ignored by their offspring. In the neighborhood where this study was done, for example, there were always a certain number of boys on the streets who, from the point of view of their parents, had "suddenly disappeared." They were usually classified as "runaways" after failing to appear for 1, 2, or 3 consecutive nights, but since they only rarely proved to be more than 10 blocks away from their houses at any time and during an absence might even faithfully attend school, this classification was sometimes not adopted until a week of absence had elapsed. In some cases, the inability to predict an appearance was almost total. These parents could rarely count on their sons either to be at school, at home for meals, or sometimes even in bed. For example:

> (How do you handle Melvin when he gets into trouble?) Well, we figure that weekends are the main times he looks forward to—parties and going out. So we'd say, "You can't go out tonight." You know, we'd try to keep him from something he really wanted to do. But he usually goes out anyway. Like one night we was watching TV, and Melvin said he was tired and went to bed. So then I get a phone call from a lady who wants to know if Melvin is here because her son is with him. I said, "No, he has gone to bed already." She says, "Are you sure?" I said, "I'm pretty sure." So I went downstairs and I peeked in and saw a lump in the bed but I didn't see his head. So I took a look and he was gone. He came home about 12:30, and we talked for a while. (What did you do?) Well, I told him he was wrong going against his parents like that, but he keeps sneaking out anyway. (What does your husband do about it?) Well, he don't do much. I'm the one who gets upset. My husband, he'll say something to Mel and then he'll just relax and forget about it. (Husband and wife laugh together.) There's little we can do, you know. It's hard to talk to him cause he just go ahead and do what he wants anyway.[25]

25. The family being described here is perhaps a classic example of a "disorganized" activity system since the son himself could rarely count on the appearance of his parents. Both worked, the father as a free-lance garage mechanic and the mother as an Avon saleslady, and both enjoyed taking spur-of-the-moment trips to Las Vegas. This meant that when the boy disappeared, he often returned to find his parents gone and vice-versa. Moreover, given the fact that random disappearances tend to stop around age 12, these family situations are often as unpredictable to sociologists as they are to the family members involved. The boy being discussed, for example, had an older brother on the honor roll at a local San Francisco high school during the same period that he asked his streetworker whether he could be admitted "voluntarily" to Juvenile Hall when he felt that his family situation was unmanageable at home, a desire that is not uncommon although rarely acted upon by the younger boys.

The initial response of most parents to this behavior is anger, a sense of betrayal, and a feeling that the family situation has become "disorganized." After a while, however, this lack of predictability becomes virtually "routine." Passing one of these mothers on the street, she might report that "Charles is gone again." Only wistfully would she ask me whether I had seen him or happened to know where he was. She already knew that by and large Charles made up his own mind when to come and go. Since she did not know where, however, she was curious.

Although it is often hard to judge how the absence of parental trust is perceived by the boys involved, in most cases it seems to be taken as a simple matter of fact. When the very young boys are asked why they "ran away," they often do not seem to know; and when they are asked on the streets why they do not return home, their answer is usually, "because when I do I'll get a beating."

These children, most between the ages of 6 and 10, were the most puzzling people I met on this study. Their behavior always seemed to make perfect sense to them, but it also seemed to make so much sense that they could not produce accounts for it. Although they sometimes exhibited a touch of bravado, they were only rarely defensive, and most managed to carry themselves with what can only be described as miniature adult poise. When they were not in motion or suddenly running away, they assumed the posture of "little men," often shouldering their autonomy with great dignity but rarely with perfect ease.

These children are a testimony to the fact that basic rules about authority are not accepted automatically, even among the young. The assumption of dependence must be cultivated before it can be used as a basis for control, and this becomes quite clear when for some reason their assumption is never made. In these cases, the children often demonstrate a remarkable capacity to take care of themselves. In fact, one could argue that the preadolescent who does not conceive of himself as dependent on his parents also does not really conceive of himself as "a child," particularly when he loses his virginity at 8 and supports himself on lunch money taken from classmates. Once the authority rule is rejected, the family as an activity system becomes an entirely new game. Politically the child is not an adult, but sociologically it is hard to argue that he is still a child.[26]

When the gang boy gets on in years, there is often a violent showdown with a father; and regardless of whether these fights are won or lost, most

26. Herb Gans notes the tendency among working class Italians in Boston to treat their children as "little adults." It could well be that the posture of the boys described in this paper is simply an exaggerated version of lower class socialization generally. See Herbert J. Gans, *The Urban Villagers* (New York: Free Press, 1962), p. 59.

parents simply resign themselves to viewing "trouble" as "normal" or "routine."

> My father don't get smart with me no more. He used to whup me, throw me downstairs, until I got big enough to beat him. The last time he touch me, he was coming downstairs talking some noise about something. I don't know what. He had a drink, and he always make something up when he start drinking. He was trying to get smart with me, so he swung at me and missed. I just got tired of it. I snatched him and threw him up against the wall, and then we started fighting. My sister grabbed him around the neck and started choking him. So I started hitting him in the nose and everything, and around the mouth. Then he pushed my mother and I hit him again. Then he quit, and I carried him back upstairs. Next morning he jump up saying, "What happened last night? My leg hurts." And all that old bullshit. He made like he don't know what had happened. And ever since then, you know, he don't say nothing to me.

Similarly, mothers also seemed to resign themselves quite quickly to the possibilities of future "trouble." Where there was no father in the house, they often placed the blame for their son's behavior on his absence. But even in situations where the father was present, they continued to offer what advice and support they could, once it became clear that punishment was no deterrent. On a day-by-day basis, whatever efforts at direction were exerted tended to be directed at keeping the boys in the house on weekday evenings, at least until they did their homework, and trying to get them home at a reasonable hour on Friday and Saturday nights. In most instances, however, even these attempts at control gradually broke down, particularly among the older boys and those who were either suspended or permanently out of school. As time wears on, a long unexplained absence from home as well as phone calls from the police become socially expected parts of the family activity system itself.

> Well, like last week, you know. Last Saturday I came home about 4 o'clock and they got kind of excited. And they didn't say nothing that night. But the next morning they kept talking "where you been" and all this. And I told them where I had been and they said okay. They told me to stay in this weekend but they didn't say nothing about it this weekend so I went out last night and tonight. (When she tells you not to do something, do you go along with her or what?) Like you mean stay or something? Oh, if she say stay in, I talk to her about it for an hour or two and then she get mad and say, "Oh, get out of the house. Leave." That's what I been waiting for.

Not only is the assumption of autonomy the important issue at home, it also has important implications for the way gang boys are defined and treated by school officials as well as for the ways they often fight back.

Most young people adopt a posture of deference in the presence of adult authorities because this posture is a taken-for-granted assumption about the self. To gang boys, however, this posture becomes a matter of choice. They can defer or not defer, depending on their mood, their audience, and their feelings about a teacher; and for many teachers, the very existence of the assumption that submissiveness is a matter of choice becomes sufficient grounds for the withdrawal of "trust."

Autonomy and the Schools

The posture of premature autonomy is carried directly into the schools and the result is the "predelinquent." As early as the first and second grade, his teachers find him wild, distracted, and utterly oblivious to their presumed authority. He gets out of chairs when he feels like it; begins fighting when he feels like it; and all of this is done as if the teacher were not present. Even the best teachers find him virtually unmanageable in groups, even though the best teachers also seem to like these boys.

Once the boys begin proving they are "tough," there seems to be little the school can do to stop them. If they are suspended, they come to school anyway; and if they are transferred from one class to another, they return to the first class or to whatever teacher they happen to like. The social system of the third grader is an arena of social life that very much needs to be explored. It is certainly the beginning of the "delinquent career," and in some respects it seems to be its wildest phase. The boys seem immune to sanctions, and thus bullying, theft, and truancy are often blatantly displayed. It is not really until the fifth or sixth grade that organized gangs begin to form, and, in a certain sense, it is not until this age that the boys can be brought under systematic group control. Most of my work was done with older boys, however, and thus this discussion must be confined to them.

Recent sociology on gang boys has been very hard on the schools. Cloward and Ohlin suggest that lower class delinquents suffer from unequal "*access* to educational facilities"; [27] Cohen points to their "*failures* in the classroom"; [28] and Miller and Kvaraceus argue that a "*conflict* of culture" between school administrators and lower class students is precipitating delinquent behavior. [29] Although there are many differences between contemporary sociological portraits of the lower class juve-

27. Richard A. Cloward and Lloyd E. Ohlin, *Delinquency and Opportunity* (Glencoe: Free Press, 1960), p. 102.

28. Albert K. Cohen, *Delinquent Boys* (New York: Free Press, 1965), p. 116.

29. Walter B. Miller and William C. Kvaraceus, *Delinquent Behavior: Culture and the Individual* (National Education Association of the United States, 1959), p. 44. See also Walter Miller, "Lower Class Culture as a Generating Milieu of Gang Delinquency," *Journal of Social Issues*, XIV (1958).

nile delinquent, the same model of his educational problem is used by all authors. Regardless of whether the delinquent is ambitious and capable,[30] ambitious and incapable,[31] or unambitious and incapable,[32] the school is sketched as a monolith of middle class personnel against which he fares badly.

Yet data collected by observation and interview over a 2-year period on the educational performances and classroom experiences of lower class gang members suggests that pitting middle class schools against variations in the motivation and capacity of some lower class boys is at best too simple and at worst incorrect as a model of the problems faced by the delinquents.

First, some of the "trouble" that gang boys get into takes place on school grounds but outside the classroom. There is some evidence, for example, that gang boys tend to view the rules against fighting, smoking, and gambling the same way they view the laws against theft, as opportunities to demonstrate courage in situations that entail some risk. As suggested in the following quote, the boys sometimes sound thankful for these rules.

> (What do you guys do when you cut school?) Well, like everybody, you know, everybody get together and say, "Everybody cut Friday and we'll go to Luigi's house." So, you know, a lot of boys and girls go up there and we have a party. Drinking. Having a good time. Otherwise if we have a day off from school, you know, during the weekend, and we gave that, it probably wouldn't be too much fun cause it'd be almost legal. You know, when I first went to Gompers, we used to be able to smoke in the halls cause the ends of the halls was all concrete. We used to be able to smoke there. I didn't hardly ever smoke there though. We used to go smoke in the bathroom. It seemed like, you know, smoking was better to me since I had to hide to do it. It seem like everything at that school, you have to do it backwards to make it seem more better to you.

Second, during middle adolescence when the law requires gang members to attend school, there seems to be no relationship between academic performance and "trouble." Gangs contain bright boys who do well, bright boys who do less well, dull boys who pass, dull boys who fail, and illiterates.

Finally, the school difficulties of these boys occur only in some classes and not others. Good and bad students alike are consistently able to get through half or more of their classes without friction. It is only in particular classes with particular teachers that incidents leading to suspension flare up. We thus need to see how the same gang boy may become a

30. Cloward and Ohlin, *op. cit.*
31. Cohen, *op. cit.*
32. Miller, *op. cit.*

"troublemaker" in one classroom and an "ordinary student" in another. To do this, it is again worth using Garfinkel's scheme to look at the classroom as a place where a range of possible activities or "constitutive orders of events" can take place, including the most common and mutually related set known as "teaching and learning." This is not the only activity that can take place in classrooms, however, as suggested by the fact that many young people, including gang boys, tend also to see the classroom as a place to see friends, converse by written notes, read comic books, eat, sleep, or stare out the window. For example:

> If I'm bored then I have to do something to make it exciting. First, second, and third ain't too bad because I get me two comic books and they last me three periods. (You read comic books for the first three periods?) Yeah. See in my first three periods I got typing, English, and some kind of thing— Social Studies I think. In them three periods I read comic books, and the next three periods I got Shop and I got Gym and then I got Math. Them last three periods I don't read comic books because I only bring two, and they only last three periods.
>
> Friday we had a substitute in class named Mr. Fox, and I had a headache so I went to sleep. (Why were you sleeping? Were you out late the night before?) No, I wasn't. I just had a headache. And I went to sleep cause my head was hurting. They wasn't doing nothing but talking. About this and that, Sally and John, and I just went to sleep. The class wasn't doing nothing but fussing, fooling around, talking, so I went to sleep.

When it becomes clear to a teacher that he is in the presence of people engaged in activities other than "teaching and learning," there are a number of ways he can choose to respond to this observation. One thing he can do, for example, is decide to overlook whatever other activities besides "learning" are taking place and decide to "teach" with those people who show signs of wanting to learn. In these classrooms there is rarely "trouble."

> (Have you ever had any good teachers, Ray?) Yeah, Mr. F. and Mr. T. in junior high school. (What made them good?) They just help you, you know. They didn't want you always working all the time. As long as you keep your voices down, you know, and don't be talking out loud and hollering, you could go on and talk in groups and have a good time. (They let you have a good time. Did they flunk you?) Yeah, they flunked me. But I mean it was my fault too cause they gave me all the breaks, you know. Anything I asked for, they gonna give me a break. But, you know, I just never do right anyway.

One possible danger of ignoring people who engage in activities other than "learning" is that these people will always be overlooked, even when they decide to enter the "learning" activity. When this happens, there is the possibility that the person overlooked will resent not being allowed to enter the activity.

> Like this one stud, man, he don't try to help us at all. He just goes on rapping (talking) to the poop-butts (squares), and when we ask a question he don't even pay no attention. I don't think that's fair. We there trying to learn just like anybody else! (All the time?) Well, sometimes.

The teacher may also, if he wishes, agree to participate in the activities preferred by the other people in the classroom, in which case either a different order of events or some mixture of this order and "teaching" gets constituted. Activities such as "talking to friends," "having fun," and "horsing around" then becomes "normal" events that can go on at different times in the same room. In these classrooms also there is rarely "trouble."

> Like my Civics teacher, he understands all the students. He know we like to play. Like, you know, he joke with us for about the first 15 minutes and then, you know, everybody gets settled down and then they want to do some work. He got a good sense of humor and he understand.

When confronted with activities other than "learning," however, there are also teachers who tend to feel not only that their rights to teach are being violated but also that the basic rule establishing their authority is being broken. In addition to perceiving that their honor has been challenged, these teachers are also likely to conclude that "trust" is no longer warranted; and when these feelings are communicated to gang boys, the result is almost always defined as "getting smart." In some cases, the teacher will insult them in return; but in most cases he will resort to the imperative and begin to issue "commands." This is a sure sign to gang members that the teacher no longer trusts them to comply with the basic rule establishing his authority. Conversely, however, the boys tend to view these commands as abridgments of their own rights to autonomy, and thus the prospect of a "character contest" arises.

> The teachers that get into trouble, they just keep pounding. You *do* this! You know, they ain't gonna ask you nice. You just do this or else, you know, I'm gonna kick you out of school. All that old foul action. Like in Math class, this teacher always hollers. He always raises his voice and hollers, "Do this work!" All that old shit. Everybody just looks at him. Don't say shit, and just sit down, talk, wait around, you know.

This breakdown of trust on the part of teachers does not always occur as one event in a developmental sequence as suggested by the examples quoted above. There are also teachers whose previous experience has led them to define their students as "untrustworthy" right from the start, and they will thus communicate this lack of trust on the first day of class.

Similarly, by the time the boys have been through junior high school, they have experienced enough teachers to know that this category of person also cannot always be trusted to honor their claims to a choice about the activities they wish to engage in. Most gang boys will therefore test the limits of the classroom situation before making up their minds whether a teacher can be trusted. This is done by purposely violating a rule preferred by the teacher in such a way as to suggest that their participation in the classroom is a voluntary act and should be acknowledged as such with the proper amount of respect. If the teacher responds to this move by becoming either angry or afraid, the boys know they are dealing with someone who is either "tough," "smart," or "lame." On the other hand, if the teacher responds by acknowledging the right while insisting that the rules still be obeyed, he is considered "straight."

In addition to the issue of who decides what activities take place in classrooms, there are also other disputes that sometimes arise. For example, although the students may be willing to comply with the rule establishing the teacher as the source of preferred rules, they may also feel that there are limits to the kinds of things a teacher can legitimately make rules about. These issues are most likely to arise when teachers feel it is within their jurisdiction to make rules about the dress and physical appearance of the people engaged in the activity of "learning." To the extent, moreover, that a gang boy feels that his moral character has been reconstituted by the teacher because of the clothes he wears, he is likely to experience a grave sense of injustice.[33]

> The teachers would start on the hair and go on down to the dress. Cause I was getting this scene a lot of times. Telling me to get a haircut.
> "No, I'm sorry. I don't need one."
> "Why don't you get a haircut?"
> "Well, this is my hair, and I feel if you were to get it cut, you'd have to pay for my clothes also."
> "Well, ain't nobody saying anything about your clothes. I mean, you're a nice dresser."
> I said, "Well, then I wear my hair the way I want."

Other problems of a similar nature arise in classrooms, particularly those having to do with the grounds used by teachers to evaluate the student in his capacity as a "learner." [34] In all these cases, the basic sequence of events is the same. First, the boys behave in a variety of ways for a variety of reasons. If they are tired, they sleep; if they are bored, they

33. For a general discussion of the problems created by contingent or purposive infraction of irrelevant rules, see Erving Goffman, *Encounters* (Indianapolis: Bobbs-Merrill, 1961), pp. 17–85.
34. These issues are discussed in the author's M.A. thesis, "Delinquency and Authority" (Department of Sociology, University of California at Berkeley, 1964).

read comic books; if they are energetic, they may feel like "having fun"; and if they do not yet trust the teacher, they may test him.

Second, this behavior is defined by the teacher. If he does not see it as part of the "teaching and learning" situation, he may tolerate or ignore it. If it is transformed into an "event" in the "teaching and learning" activity, the teacher either interprets it as a violation of a preferred rule or as a challenge to his authority. In both cases the moral character of the gang boy is likely to be reconstituted; but if the act is only considered a violation of a preferred rule, the teacher may ask a boy politely to stop. If it is viewed as a challenge to authority, however, the response will be sharper since the teacher will feel that his honor is at stake.

Finally, the boys themselves must decide how to act. If the request to stop is made politely, their own sense of honor is not offended and they are likely to cease whatever it is they are doing. If the teacher's retort is derogatory, however, the boys are likely to view the teacher's defense of his rights to authority as a violation of their own rights to autonomy and thus the character contest is on. If the boys do not concede the contest, they challenge the authority of the teacher directly, and this challenge tends to take one of three forms: it can be done subtly with a demeanor suggesting insolence; it can be done directly with words; or it can be done forcefully with violence. All three methods are used in the encounter described below:

> The first day I came to school I was late to class so this teacher got smart with me. He didn't know me by name. See a lot of people have to go by the office and see what class they in or something. Like there was a lot of new people there. So you know I was fooling around cause I know nothing gonna happen to you if you late. Cause all you tell them, you got the program mixed or something.
>
> When I came into the class you know I heard a lot of hollering and stuff. Mr. H. was in the class too. He's a teacher, see. I guess he had a student teacher or something, you know, because he was getting his papers and stuff. So Mr. H. went out. Well this new teacher probably wonder if he gonna be able to get along with me or something. Cause the class was kinda loud. When I walked in the class got quiet all of a sudden. Like they thought the Principal was coming in or something.
>
> So I walk into class and everybody look up. That's natural, you know, when somebody walk into class. People gonna look up at you. They gonna see who it is coming in or something. So I stopped. You know, like this. Looked around. See if there was any new faces. Then a girl named Diane, she say, "Hey Ray!" You know, when I walk into class they start calling me and stuff. They start hollering at me.
>
> I just smile and walk on. You know. I had my hands in my pockets or something cause I didn't have no books and I just walk into class with my hands in my pockets a lot of times. I mean I have to walk

where I can relax. I'm not going to walk with my back straight. I mean you know I relax. (What were you wearing?) About what I got on now. I had a pair of black slacks and a shirt on. My hair was long and I had taps on my shoes. I had kinda boots on but they weren't real high boots. They came up to about here.

Then I looked over at the teacher. I see we had a new teacher. He was standing in front of the desks working on some papers and doing something. He looked at me. I mean you enter by the front of the classroom so when you walk into the classroom he's standing right there. You gotta walk in front of him to get to the seats. So then I went to sit down. Soon as I passed his desk he say, "Just go sit down." Just like that.

So I stop. I turn around and look at him, then I went and sat down. (What kind of look did you give him?) You might say I gave him a hard look. I thought you know he might say something else. Cause that same day he came he got to hollering at people and stuff. I don't like people to holler at me. He was short, you know, about medium build. He might be able to do a little bit. So I say to myself, "I better sit down and meditate a little bit."

So I went and sat down. I sat in the last row in the last seat. Then he say, "Come sit up closer." So I scoot up another chair or two. Then he tell me to come sit up in the front. So I sat up there.

Then you know a lot of people was talking. A lot of people begin telling me that he be getting smart all day. You know Stubby? He is a big square but he pretty nice. He told me how the teacher was. And Angela start telling me about how he try to get smart with her. He say, "This is where you don't pick out no boy friend. You come and get your education." I mean just cause you talk to a boy, that don't mean you be scheming on them or nothing. It just that you want to be friends with people.

Then he say something like, "You two shut up or I'll throw you out on your ear!" So he told me he'd throw me out.

So I say, "The best thing you can do is ask me to leave and don't tell me. You'll get your damn ass kicked off if you keep messing!"

Then he told me to move over on the other side. See I was talking to everybody so he told me to move away from everybody. And so I moved to the other side. He told me to move three times! I had to move three times!

And then he got to arguing at somebody else. I think at somebody else that came in the class. You know, a new person. So while he was talking to them, I left out. I snuck out of class.

So I walked out the class. Went out in the yard and started playing basketball. We were supposed to turn in the basketball out there so I took the ball through the hall on the way back in. I was gonna go back out there and play some more. See I had the ball and I passed by his class and I looked in. I seen him with his back turned and I didn't like him. That's when I hit him. I hit him with the ball. Got him! I didn't miss. Threw it hard too. Real hard!

Faced with behavior like this, a school administrator has a number of sanctions at his command. He can suspend the boys, alter their grades, and some are not above violence.[35] Yet most of these sanctions have little meaning to the boys, particularly during elementary and junior high school. When the boys are young, they simply assume they will graduate from high school, even if they flunk every course. In part, they know they will be passed on automatically every other semester since the school considers them a menace to the younger boys if they are left behind; and in part, they are simply too young to care much about time. For example:

> (Did you ever flunk a grade?) No. I just never passed. Every other term I passed. Ha. Ha. Cause you see they had to pass me in the low seven. So in the high seven I flunk. So they pass me to low eight. Low eight I flunk. They pass me to the high eight. The high eight I flunk. And so on like that. (You can't flunk twice in the same grade. Is that it?) They see that you ain't gonna do it anyway so shit, they just go on and put you up in the next one. In high eight they transferred me. That's when I moved. I went to Benjamin Franklin, and Mr. B., whatever you call him, he was Principal there. He said he was gonna try me out in high nine. So I went there and I flunked. And there was another Principal who came and took over. He took over cause Mr. B. got transferred some place else. He say after summer if I bring my birth certificate to prove I was 16, he was gonna transfer me to high school. So I brought it to him after the summer, and Mr. P., the Principal at the high school, he said he was gonna try me out and put me in my right place. (What's your right place?) High junior. (So you went from high nine to high junior?) Yeah. (How are you making out in high junior?) Well, I'm still trying to make it. Knocking me out some Z's and getting me some A's and B's.

It is only when the boys get to high school that the sanctions meted out by the school begin to matter, and by then it is sometimes too late. Before the high school years most boys simply assume that the future will take care of itself; but in the sophomore and junior years of high school, the future becomes the present. Graduating, finding a decent job, and marrying the right kind of girl all become problematic, and the boys thus develop some stake in passing courses. Yet here again, any increase in the subjective importance of sanctions also depends on the objective

35. Although a Principal may not feel that his school is demeaned by violence, he sometimes feels that he and his teachers are. This attitude often leads to the hiring of lower status specialists such as gym teachers and janitors to administer the beatings. Apparently these people are felt to be of sufficiently low status not to be offended by violence.

facts of a boy's situation, and these situations tend to vary directly with mental capacity. Many of the boys who are bright enough to graduate from high school make some attempt to do so, but the boys who are illiterate or consistently F students invariably fail. Consider this conversation between three boys who have all been in the same neighborhood gang since fifth grade. The gang began breaking up in the junior year of high school when some of the boys made a serious attempt to graduate. The first boy speaking is the vice president and the second boy speaking is the president. Notice the difference in the way they perceive their fates.

WERTHMAN. Do you guys think it is important to graduate from high school?

VICE PRESIDENT. Hell yeah! That's the most important thing in your life right now. If you ain't got no high school diploma, you ain't got shit! You oughta least have 1 or 2 years of college so you can say "I've been to college." I tell you, like if I was gonna get married like after I got out of school and my wife had a little more education than me, I'd rather feel embarrassed than marry her. Cause in the old days, all a man was supposed to be for was work and fighting wars. His woman was at home washing clothes and taking care of babies. OK. Then it was fine. Cause then she could go to school and get some education and help her husband. But now it's more the man's responsibility cause the ladies done lost respect like they done had back there. I mean they don't do as much for a man as they did back then. Now they depend on the man no matter what. They look for the man to do. And if the man can't do, well naturally she gonna get her ass out. She gonna get hip quick. Get her somebody that can. You know.

WERTHMAN. What about you, Charles, are you going to graduate from high school?

PRESIDENT. No comment. (What do you mean, "no comment?") I'm not saying nothing. (Why not?) Well, I mean if it wasn't too late I'd try and change it. But the way I see it now there's no need to even try to catch up cause I know I can't do it within these next 3 months. So I'm not even going to try. I plan on being a bum anyway. See, my uncle's a bum and he's making it.

WERTHMAN. How about you, Billy?

MEMBER. Me myself, I don't care if I don't get no job, if I'm a tramp or something. I can stay in the house and steal hub caps and sell them and get some food and pay the electricity and stuff. And that'd be all right because you don't have to pay no rent. (But what if you want to get married?) Well if you want to get married, man, you steal some hub caps and you get some food money and you can pay the electricity and stuff. You ain't got to worry about paying the rent. (Do you think you will graduate from high school?) Hell no. They gonna kick me out any day now. If I go back tomorrow, I think I gonna get kicked out for good.

A gang boy's career as a "delinquent" in the schools is thus a somewhat problematic affair. It begins in earnest around the fourth or fifth grade when he comes to the attention of his teachers for paying no attention to them, beating up other students, and forcing his colleagues to surrender their lunch money. During junior high school the fights are better organized and the posture adopted towards teachers turns from unconcern to insolence. And in the last years of high school, the boys either graduate or depart, usually at the school's request. For most of these years, the school regards him as hopeless, and they suspend him regularly for his activities in the presence of other boys as well as for his attitude towards the authority of the school itself. Most of this behavior, however, is designed to claim an identity that the school itself cannot stamp out. What the boys do on the streets with one another is beyond the scope of their control although they punish it severely when it happens to take place on school grounds.

Whether the boys are given the chance to engage in character contests with teachers, however, is directly affected by the school itself since what is made of an act depends almost entirely on how it is defined and evaluated by the teacher, including the issue of whether or not the act is a violation of the basic authority rule. The boy is using the teacher to define himself as autonomous; and, like his behavior on the streets, he often creates or provokes the situation in which he then defends his honor. Yet if a teacher is willing to concede the fact that school is meaningless to some boys and therefore that other activities besides "teaching and learning" will necessarily go on in class, and if he is willing to limit the scope of his jurisdiction to the activity of "teaching and learning" itself, then his authority is likely to remain intact, regardless of how much it may be "tested." Whether or not he wishes to persuade the boys to join the learning process is another matter, but it is precisely at this point that we see the merits of defining authority, after Bertrand de Juvenel, as "the faculty of gaining another man's assent." [36]

The Delinquent and the Police

As Aaron Cicourel has recently attempted to demonstrate, the transformation of gang boys into official "delinquents" by policemen, probation officers, and juvenile court judges is perhaps best looked at as an organizational rather than a legal process since the criteria used to contact, categorize, and dispose of the boys often has little to do with break-

36. Bertrand de Jouvenel, *Sovereignty: An Inquiry into the Political Good,* trans. J. F. Huntington (Chicago: University of Chicago Press, 1957), p. 29.

ing the law itself.[37] In part, this discretion can be traced to the rather diffuse conception of justice that has arisen in juvenile courts, and in part it can be traced to the situation of the police. Regardless of how this discretion is explained, however, it remains a fact, and one that is not lost on the juveniles themselves.

In studies of how boys are contacted by the police, the distinction between policemen and juvenile officers is often made, largely because these two groups often tend to organize their work in different ways. As Harvey Sacks has suggested, the task of the patrolman can perhaps best be defined as "inferring the probability of criminality from the appearances persons present in public places"; [38] and as David Matza has pointed out, this task "is similar in almost every respect to that faced by the sociologist." Both must "classify individuals" into a set of social or legal categories since "true indicators rarely exist." [39] The indicators mentioned most frequently by both policemen and gang boys are the juxtaposition of race and neighborhood plus an odd asortment of clothing, hair, and walking styles. [40] Stated generally, however, the patrolman tends to contact people who "look suspicious," and then, by using various techniques of interrogation, he tries to link the person he is interrogating to the universe of possible and reported crimes.

Although it is difficult to imagine how this process of detection by patrolmen could be organized in any other way, it is the source of considerable outrage among gang boys. Practically as soon as a patrolman makes contact with a boy, the structure of the situation becomes visible and reveals the patrolman's mistrust. If the boy did not happen to be a Negro walking through a white neighborhood and if he did not happen to be sporting boots and long hair, his moral character would not have been called into question and he could walk the streets without insult, risk, or fear. As one boy put it, "Them cops is supposed to be out catching criminals. They ain't paid to be looking after my hair!"

In many cases, the gang boy responds to patrolmen the same way he responds to schoolteachers who subtly or not so subtly cast aspersions on his moral character. By acquitting himself with a straightforward nonchalance or indifference and refusing to proffer the expected signs of

37. This discussion of the police relies heavily on an unpublished manuscript of Cicourel's. See Aaron V. Cicourel, "The Social Organization of Juvenile Justice," ms. See also John I. Kitsuse and Aaron V. Cicourel, "A Note on the Uses of Official Statistics," *Social Problems*, II (Fall 1963), 139–152.
38. Harvey Sacks, "Methods in Use for the Production of a Social Order: A Method for Warrantably Inferring Moral Character," ms., p. 4.
39. David Matza, "The Selection of Deviants," ms., p. 32.
40. These indicators are discussed at length in Carl Werthman and Irving Piliavin, "Gang Members and the Police," in David J. Bordua, ed., *The Police* (New York: Wiley, 1967).

deference that typically denote respect, he challenges the authority of the policeman who then must either arrest the boy, use his "billy club," or withdraw from the encounter by saving face as best he can. Once again, the gang boy takes a risk in a social situation, only this time the situation is one he did not construct. When he chooses to challenge the authority of the patrolmen, he is defending his pride, his honor, and his social self respect. He does this at a risk, however, since his "rap sheet" includes field interrogation reports and thus continues to grow.

Members of juvenile bureaus tend to make contact with gang boys on other grounds. Their job is usually to investigate specific complaints, often filed by neighbors, parents, and the schools. Unlike patrolmen, they are trying to trace a single crime to its source in a universe of suspects rather than proceeding from the suspect to the universe of possible crimes. Their task is thus a great deal more specific, and they have a great deal more information to go on. Once suspects are contacted, however, the process of detection proceeds more or less the same way. A variety of interrogation techniques are used, including false accusations and lies about the amount of information possessed. The success of these techniques is reflected by the fact that over 90 percent of juvenile convictions in the United States are gotten because the boys "confess."

Yet these confessions do not mean much, since the "delinquent" is defined by the police as a boy with a questionable moral character rather than as a boy who has merely committed a crime. Depending on a host of criteria, the juvenile officer may decide that he is dealing with a boy who is "guilty but essentially good," in which case he is likely to let him go. The *magnitude of the offense* involved becomes a factor in dispositions because a murder, rape, or robbery casts more of a shadow on moral character than a stolen bicycle or a broken window; and the number of *previous contacts* that the boy has had with the police is used the same way. These contacts are typically recorded on an easily accessible "rap sheet" or file; and, as Cicourel points out, these files often contain contacts made on the flimsiest of contingent grounds. Yet once they are placed on a rap sheet and described in five words of official code, they tend to become pregnant with meaning and take on a life of their own.

Perhaps more important than these two offense-related criteria are the judgments made by juvenile officers about the type and quality of *parental control*. One of the main concerns of the juvenile officer is the likelihood of future offense, and this assessment is made largely in terms of the "kind of parents" a boy happens to possess. Thus, the moral character of the parents also passes under review; and if a house appears messy, a parent is missing, or a mother is on welfare as well as defensive and annoyed, the probability of arrest appears to increase significantly. As

Cicourel points out, moreover, these judgments about family life are particularly subject to bias by factors related to class.[41]

The *age* of the offender is a factor in dispositions, and it is also related to parental control. The extent to which young people, as opposed to their parents, are held responsible for their behavior does not remain uniform as they are growing up. An offense that the police might treat lightly when committed by a 12-year-old may pose the prospect of arrest if committed 4 or 5 years later, and thus most gang boys become more selective about the risky situations they enter and what they do for "kicks."

Although the age of the offender, his family situation, his prior arrest record, and the nature of his offense all enter into the dispositions made by juvenile officers, recent students of the police suggest that perhaps the most important factors affecting dispositions are related to *demeanor*. Cicourel found that the decisions made by juvenile officers were strongly influenced by the style and speed with which the offender confessed.[42] If a boy confesses to his misdeeds immediately, or at least immediately after being offered lenient treatment by the officer for doing so, this act is taken as a sign that the boy "trusts" adults, in which case it is further assumed that his attachment to the basic authority rule is both sound and intact. On the other hand, if the boy proves to be a "tough nut to crack," he is viewed with suspicion. It is said that he is "hardened," does not "trust" authority, and is therefore probably "out of control." Piliavin and Briar also report that boys who appear frightened, humble, penitent, and ashamed are also more likely to go free.[43] Like the test for "trust," these indicators are used to measure respect for the authority of the law. Similarly, in a study of the differential selection of juvenile offenders for court appearances, Nathan Goldman reports that "defiance on the part of a boy will lead to juvenile court quicker than anything else." [44]

The juvenile officer, like the probation officer, thus seems to make arrest decisions on the basis of a more or less complete gestalt. A series of minor brushes with the law, when added to a negative school report, a "bad" family situation, and suspicious associates, often does the same damage to imputed moral character as the insolent behavior that gets a "bright boy" from a "good family" defined by the juvenile officer as a "punk."

As far as the boys themselves are concerned, these indicators of moral character determine the basic facts of their situation in the eyes of the

41. Aaron Cicourel, "Social Class, Family Structure and the Administration of Juvenile Justice," ms.
42. Cicourel, "The Social Organization of Juvenile Justice," *op. cit.*
43. Irving Piliavin and Scott Briar,' "Police Encounters with Juveniles," *American Journal of Sociology* LXXX (1964), 206–214, reprinted below in this volume.
44. Nathan Goldman, *The Differential Selection of Juvenile Offenders for Court Appearances* (National Council on Crime and Delinquency, 1963), p. 106.

law. As the boys get older and their arrest records longer, the consequences of taking risks increases accordingly, as does the magnitude of courage they can demonstrate by taking them. Perhaps the most important fact about a gang boy's situation, however, is his relationship to the system of sanctions used to enforce the law. This system consists of a gradual decrease in the civilian freedoms granted a boy by the terms of his probation, and a series of detention facilities that are graduated by age and seriousness of offense.

Like the facts of his situation as determined by the police, his relationship to this sanction system affects the fatefulness of his acts. A boy who knows that the California Youth Authority awaits him if he is caught for theft or joyriding one more time can demonstrate possession of more courage for the same act than the boy who has never been caught. To the extent that boys do not drop out of gangs as they move through this sanction system, the fatefulness of their acts increases, and they tend to constitute an increasingly select elite. In the identity system of the gang world, reputation increases with the fatefulness of the situation in which a boy is willing to take a risk, and thus the boys who have been sent to the more important prisons can flaunt this fact as evidence that they have paid and were willing to pay a more significant price for maintaining an identity on the streets.

> They think they is bad because they have gone to jail. Most of them, that is. They come out with a big build or something like that and they think they is bigger than somebody else, you know, they done learn some slang in jail and may have won a few fights up there or something and think they can whup everybody when they come out. They think they is halfway bad. They done beat up somebody that was supposed to be the baddest up there in jail where they was. Being in jail doesn't make them badder, but it makes them think different than before they left. The stud who's been in jail expects you to respect him when he comes back. You know, before he goes in you respect him and he respects you, but when he comes back he expects you to respect him more. Like the kid in the Marathons who went in weighing 75 pounds and came out weighing 100, looking for me [laughter].

The identity system of the gang world actually tends to be somewhat more sophisticated than this. In practice, every boy and every gang tends to view their own particular relationship to these institutions as the one of most value. When comparing themselves to the gang described above, for example, a somewhat younger group of boys tended to pride themselves on having more boys in school and having been sent to jail less often, all of which seemed to prove to them that they were "smarter."

> The Marathons, they much bigger than us, but half of them crazy. They equip their heads with something else. Like they don't have no

imagination, you know, no fear. When they go do something they do it. They act like if they ever got started you have to kill them to stop them. But we got the smartest guys. Half of them (the Marathons) ain't going to school. They all go to jail. If we had to plan something we'd get them. They don't have any sense. Only one they got in there that's smart is Johnny, and he's crazy himself. We just think quicker than they do. You know, when it comes down to going to jail or getting into trouble, we just think quicker. And we been through more than they been through. You know, like where to hit 'em to hurt 'em most. They ain't learned that yet. There's only one club in this district and that's the Conquerors [laughter].

On the other hand, when these same boys compare themselves to non-delinquent neighborhood cliques, they denigrate school and pride themselves on taking more risks.

No. School ain't going to make you whup them, and it ain't necessarily going to make you smarter neither. It don't teach you nothing about how to get along with the bitches [girls] or all them other dudes [boys]. What are these cafeteria-eaters going to do when they get married or when they go to a dance? Some stud hits on [makes a play for] the bitch they is with, and what they going to do? They gonna talk some more shit in the cafeteria. And those guys never been to jail. They just don't know what's happening. Them books don't teach you nothing about the streets, and that's where them cats is going to spend the rest of their lives.

The second effect of the sanction system concerns the use of the rules themselves. If a boy is ordered by the court not to associate any more with his friends, the court has in effect created a rule that allows the boy to demonstrate greater loyalty to them. He has the opportunity to prove himself an even better comrade than he could ever have proved before, and thus again the sanction system can function in two quite different ways.

Third, there is the fact that the courts sometimes create their own special rules to judge the "improvement" of a boy, but when these rules are violated, there is a sense in which they have artificially created the very rules by which the boy is then condemned. Consider, for example, the following conversation between this researcher and a 12-year-old boy who had just run away from his foster home. He had been living with "Uncle Eddie," his mother's brother, essentially because his older brothers were in jail, his father deserted the family some years ago, and, as a result of these actions by other members of the family, his mother was declared "unfit" and Danny was forced to leave home.

(Why did you stay away from school yesterday?) I felt like comin' to San Francisco to see my mother. (Didn't you go back last night?)

Yeh, but my cousin Darlene said they was lookin' for me, you know, my probation officer. He came to visit me in school and couldn't find me. I got scared so I came back up here. (Where did you stay last night?) I slept in a friend of mine's car. I figured I better not go home. I don't want to get my mother in dutch. They'll call her and if she says I'm home that'll get her in trouble. (What do you think your probation officer will do when he finds you?) He told me he was going to send me to C.Y.A. like Billy if I got into any trouble down there, you know, at my Uncle Eddie's. I don't want to go to C.Y.A.

(Well what do you plan to do now?) I don't know. I figure I could keep running. I could stay with my brother up in Tahoe, but it's tough bein' on the run. What do you think I should do? (I don't know either. Let's discuss it. You're the one that has to make the decision. How do you like living down at your Uncle Eddie's?) I don't like it. They talk about me behind my back, and they say bad things about my mother. And Eddie's no good. He won't even buy me gym clothes. They told me at school I can't go to gym class unless I got the clothes, and he won't get them. He said he already bought me some and I lost 'em but he's lyin'. He never bought me no gym clothes. (Would you rather live somewhere else?) Yeah, but they won't let me come home. They say I got too many friends up there and the school won't let me back. But all my friends have left, and I could go to a different school. I know I could make it. But they won't let me. I know they're going to send me to C.Y.A.

(Well, it looks to me like you have two choices. You could either keep running and take your chances on getting caught, or go back and take your chances on getting sent to C.Y.A.) [After a long silence.] Well maybe C.Y.A. wouldn't be so bad after all. [He tries hard to fight back tears and succeeds.]

This is a good example of what can happen with probation restrictions. A boy is sent to a foster home because he comes from a broken one and then plays hookey in order to come back. The truancy is produced by the desire to see his mother, and the terms of his probation make this act an offense unless it is properly approved. The boy is thus in danger of being sent to the California Youth Authority for committing an offense that was actually created by the courts themselves.

Yet the fact remains that boys who *do* remain on the streets to face increasingly serious sanctions *do* take more serious risks than other boys; and in terms of the logic underlying the identity system itself, they at least can see themselves as more committed than others to this round of life. The most serious change in their situation occurs, however, when the police finally decide to "crack down." The boys are warned to "stay off the streets or else." After this injunction has been issued, the character of the streets is fundamentally transformed. The neighborhood, the territory, and the hangout cease being places where it is merely dangerous to be found. If the boys continue to stay in the streets, there is a near perfect probability that they will spend at least some part of their remaining years of youth in jail.

This sudden escalation of the risks involved in remaining on the streets as well as the fact that these risks are present in a large area of space can have a decisive and damaging effect on a gang boy's identity as a "delinquent." During most of the years he spends in a gang, he uses a great many objects to demonstrate his courage and autonomy in situations of risk. As suggested above, there are laws, school rules, teachers, girls, and rival gangs as well as the police. When the police make this final move, however, they effectively surround or encompass him with one source of identity material. Practically everywhere he goes, he is in a situation of risk that is defined by the police; and if this goes on for a long enough time, this identity begins to leave a permanent impact on a boy's conception of himself. His only choice is either to leave the streets or define himself exclusively in relation to the police. Although most boys still leave the streets rather than surrender to this identity as a permanent or "adult" way of life, there are some who begin losing the capacity to imagine themselves as anything else; and when this happens, there is a chance that the boy will graduate into adulthood as a self-defined criminal.

Contingencies, Risks, and Opportunities

There is some evidence to suggest that most gang boys have a conception of how and when their careers as "delinquents" will end. As Short and Strodtbeck have recently reported, most look forward to becoming stable and dependable husbands in well-run households, despite their reluctance to voice these expectations around one another and despite the fact that some become fathers out of wedlock along the way.[45] Similarly, although about half the boys interviewed by Short and Strodtbeck anticipate problems in securing "good paying honest jobs," their images of family life make it clear that the great majority expect to be holding down some kind of conventional occupation when they become "adults."[46] During most of the years spent in gangs, however, these occupational concerns are neither salient nor relevant. The boys understand that as long as they are defined and define themselves as "youth," they are not the people they will someday become; and for this reason

45. Short and Strodtbeck, *Group Process*, pp. 25–46.
46. See James F. Short, Jr., Ramon Rivera, and Ray A. Tennyson, "Opportunities, Gang Membership, and Delinquency," *American Sociological Review*, February 1965, p. 60; see also Delbert S. Elliott, "Delinquency and Perceived Opportunity," *Sociological Inquiry*, Spring 1962, pp. 216–228.

they have little difficulty identifying with two apparently conflicting sets of attitudes, values, and behavior patterns.

As we have seen, the issue of whether a particular career will come to the expected conventional end is often resolved in large measure by how a boy deals with a host of contingencies that arise before the end of the career arrives, particularly those associated with the way he is defined and acted upon by parents, teachers, policemen, probation officers, and judges of the juvenile court. At the early stages of the career, it is often difficult for the boys to make objective assessments of the risks they run in defining themselves since the implications of these acts for the way moral character is defined, evaluated, and acted upon are only known "after" the acts themselves have taken place. This is particularly true in the case of the police where many more rules are invoked to pass judgment on the offender than were actually involved in the offense, particularly since these judgments are often made on the basis of how he behaves in four different institutions at once. As Howard Becker has suggested, "deviance is not a quality of the act a person commits, but rather a consequence of the application by others of rules and sanctions to an 'offender' "; [47] and there are many instances in which the criteria used to reconstitute moral character are simply seen by gang boys as arbitrary, unfair, or outright illegitimate.

Yet regardless of how a boy feels about the rules that have been used to judge him, these judgments often alter the objective facts of his situation, and this requires him to make new decisions. He must decide, for example, whether to use his probation restrictions as an excuse to leave the gang or as a new and riskier source of identity material, just as he must decide how he feels about the fact that his parents may no longer trust him. By viewing the "delinquent career" as a more or less stable sequence of acts taken in risky social situations in order to claim an identity or define a self, often followed by changes in the rules and judgments that make up these situations, and followed again by new choices of the self in response to these changes, it is possible to see how a gang boy could arrive at the age of 18 or 21 to find that his situation makes it costly, painful, or difficult for him to take the conventional job that he always expected to take, particularly if the boy has come to view the conventional world as a place full of the kinds of people who have labeled him a "delinquent." [48]

This process can be seen quite clearly in the schools where the initial payoff in female acclaim for fights and risky character contests slowly

47. Howard S. Becker, *Outsiders* (New York: Free Press, 1963), p. 9.
48. This process has been described in somewhat different terms by Lemert as a transformation from "primary" to "secondary" deviance. See Edwin M. Lemert, *Social Pathology* (New York: McGraw-Hill, 1951), p. 75.

vanishes during high school. The "big men" in 7th grade often become school rejects in the 10th or 11th, and thus they do pay a price for their early notoriety, only this price cannot always be foreseen.

Once a gang boy gets beyond the age of 18, moreover, his situation changes rather dramatically. Whether he likes it or not, he now has a choice to make about what identity system to enter. He could get married, get a job, and assume the status of a full-fledged "adult"; he could decide to postpone this decision in legitimate ways such as joining the Army and going to school at night; or he could decide to remain for a few more years as an elder statesman on the streets, in which case he will continue to make use of the identity materials available to youth.

The decision he makes at this point in his career will depend in part on his situation. If he managed to graduate from high school, he may well decide to go on to college; but if he was expelled from high school, he may feel either bitter or reluctant about going back to night school to get the high school degree. He knows that he has been administratively reborn in the eyes of the law, and thus the risks he takes by staying in the streets increase considerably since he now may be processed by the courts as an adult. On the other hand, if his status in the gang world is still high, he may not want to trade it right away for a low-paying blue-collar job; and he knows he will be rejected by the Army if he has a jail record of any kind.

In short, it is at this point in his career that the "opportunities" available to him will affect his behavior, his attitudes, and the decisions he makes about his life.[49] If there are no legitimate options open to him, options that at best would not make him suffer a sudden decrease in status and at worst would allow him not to face his ultimately dismal status-fate as an adult, then he may well decide to stay on the streets, despite the greater consequences involved in taking risks. He may adopt a "hustle," and he may also adopt a full-blown ideology along with it. Since he now views the conventional world as a place he is expected to enter, he tends to develop a "position" on it. Jobs become "slaves"; going to school becomes "serving time"; and in some cases the assumptions about marriage and getting a conventional job are replaced by fantasies about the quick and big "score." These are no longer the "delinquent boys" described by Cohen.[50] They are the self-styled aristocrats described by Finestone and Sykes and Matza.[51] They have an answer to everything, and they always "know the score."

49. This view suggests that the various processes discussed by Cloward and Ohlin tend to affect outcomes of the transition between youth and adult status at the end of the delinquent career. See Cloward and Ohlin, *op. cit.*
50. Cohen, *op. cit.*
51. Harold Finestone, "Cats, Kicks, and Colors," *Social Problems*, V (July 1957), 3–13; G. M. Sykes and David Matza, "Techniques of Neutralization: A Theory of Delinquency," *American Sociological Review*, XXII (December 1957), 664–670.

After a few years of this existence, these boys are really at the end of their "delinquent" careers. Some get jobs, some go to jail, some get killed, and some simply fade into an older underground of pool rooms and petty thefts. Most cannot avoid ending up with conventional jobs, however, largely because the "illegitimate opportunities" available simply are not that good.

NOTE: The research on which this paper is based was initiated by the Survey Research Center at the University of California in Berkeley on a grant from the Ford Foundation and was later moved to the Center for the Study of Law and Society on the Berkeley campus, where funds were made available under a generous grant from the Office of Juvenile Delinquency and Youth Development, Welfare Administration, U.S. Department of Health, Education, and Welfare, in cooperation with the President's Committee on Juvenile Delinquency and Youth Crime.

PART TWO

Delinquency: Hidden and Observed

ANY SENSIBLE discussion of the extent of juvenile delinquency must start off with the question "What is delinquency?" It is not, as many people suppose, simply or solely crime carried on by juveniles. The delinquency statutes throughout the United States are extremely broad in definition, so that they allow the juvenile authorities to assume control over all kinds of youths engaged in all sorts of misbehavior. Indeed, the laws empower the juvenile court to take charge of youngsters who exhibit vague *conditions*, such as "immorality," as well as those who are implicated in specific acts of misconduct.

The provisions of the Welfare and Institutions Code of the state of California illustrate the wide range of the delinquency laws in this country. That statute declares that California juvenile courts have control over dependent children—youths who are in need of parental care, who are destitute, or who are physically dangerous. Courts are also given control over persons under 18 years of age who violate city, county, or state laws. In addition, court control is extended to youths who disobey their parents, habitual truants, and youngsters who are "in danger of leading an idle, dissolute, lewd, or immoral life." [1]

1. State of California, *Welfare and Institutions Code, 1965* (Sacramento: Department of General Services, 1965), p. 35.

Given omnibus laws of this kind, it is apparent that nearly all juveniles could be said to be juvenile delinquents at some time during the period of childhood. But what sorts of acts occur most frequently? Are officially designated delinquents involved in serious acts which would be crimes if carried on by adults, or are they principally engaged in petty acts? What of those youths who remain "hidden" or undetected? Are their delinquencies fairly petty ones, or are they implicated in serious acts?

These questions are fundamental ones. It is argued by many that one of the major factors influencing the prospect that an offender will become officially tagged as delinquent is the seriousness of his conduct. In this view, hidden offenders often remain undetected in part because their acts are relatively inconsequential ones which do not warrant official concern. The opposing view assumes that undetected offenders are as involved in misconduct as are officially processed ones, but owing to favorable social and economic circumstances their acts are overlooked by the police and the courts.

Our view on these matters appeared in the introductory section, where we observed that, although nearly all juveniles engage in acts which could be subsumed under the existing statutes, youths who get into the hands of the police or the courts are a minority of all juveniles. Those youngsters who get officially processed tend to be ones engaged in serious and repetitive acts of lawbreaking. However, youths who have been involved in relatively petty offenses are sometimes found among officially tagged offenders at the same time that some perpetrators of serious acts of lawbreaking manage to escape the attention of the authorities.[2] This view lays major stress upon offenses as determinants of official action against juvenile deviants, but it also holds open the possibility that the social characteristics of lawbreakers also play a part in the response to their activities.

The character and extent of delinquency in American society are noted in the Figure. That diagram suggests that official delinquents are frequently youths who have engaged in serious acts while hidden offenders are more commonly involved in relatively innocuous acts.

The next two selections are designed to flesh out this picture of the extent of youthful deviance. The study by Short and Nye is one of the major ones dealing with hidden offenders, for a large number of subjects were quizzed as to their involvement in a large variety of acts of misconduct. The study also allows us to compare the deviant careers of undetected offenders with those of officially processed ones, because samples were drawn from training schools as well as from high-school groups. The reader will note that much petty misconduct is reported by hidden delinquents. The training-school wards admit that they have done

2. The evidence on the extent of delinquency is discussed in detail in Don C. Gibbons, *Delinquent Behavior* (Englewood Cliffs, N.J.: Prentice-Hall, 1970).

these things too, but they also confess to serious forms of youthful law-breaking and they also report themselves as engaging in these endeavors more than once or twice. Thus, training-school subjects cannot be said to be closely similar to hidden delinquents in high schools.

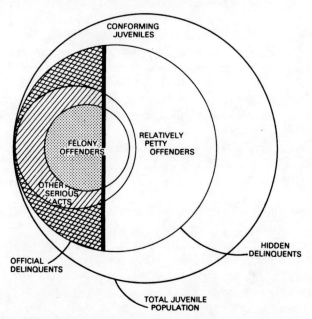

Delinquency and Nondelinquency in American Society*

* Don C. Gibbons, *Delinquent Behavior,* © 1970, Prentice-Hall, Inc. (Englewood Cliffs, N.J.). By permission of the publishers.

The second essay in this section by Murphy, Shirley, and Witmer is one which puts the results of studies such as those by Short and Nye in perspective. The latter indicates that many youths who have escaped the delinquency tag are nonetheless involved in misconduct, albeit fairly petty in form. But the investigation by Murphy, Shirley, and Witmer suggests that lawbreaking among working-class groups is vastly more common than indicated by official statistics. These two studies taken together suggest that total delinquency is much more widespread than indicated by delinquency rates based on official cases. However, these rates seem to be quite good indicators of the total volume of youthful misconduct. Areas in which delinquency rates are low do show less total delinquency than do areas where official rates are high.

2. Extent of Unrecorded Juvenile Delinquency: Tentative Conclusions

JAMES F. SHORT, JR. and F. IVAN NYE

THE FREQUENCY and nature of delinquent behavior committed by adolescents never arrested or committed to institutions has been regarded by criminologists as an important but unknown dimension of delinquent behavior. The informed layman also is aware that only a portion of delinquent behavior is followed by arrest and conviction; further, that conviction and committal to a "training school" is much more likely to follow delinquent behavior if the adolescent is from the "wrong side of the tracks." The picture of delinquent behavior obtained from official records only, and particularly the punitive action of the courts, is known to be incomplete and seriously biased.

That concern with unrecorded delinquency is high is indicated by the great interest shown in the pioneer studies of Robison, [1] Schwartz, [2]

Reprinted by special permission from *The Journal of Criminal Law and Criminology,* Copyright © 1958 by Northwestern University School of Law, Volume 49, Number 4.

1. Sophia Robison, *Can Delinquency Be Measured?* (New York: Columbia University Press, 1936).
2. Edward E. Schwartz, "A Community Experiment in the Measurement of Juvenile Delinquency," reprinted from *National Probation Association Yearbook,* 1945 (Washington, D.C., U.S. Government Printing Office, 1947).

Porterfield,[3] and the Cambridge-Somerville Youth Study,[4] in texts and in recent papers by the writers.[5] Cohen has called for an extension of such studies,[6] and a number of other investigators are pursuing research projects dealing with unrecorded delinquency.[7]

The methodology of the investigations which form the basis for this paper have been described elsewhere and will not be repeated here.[8] The present paper deals with (1) types and frequency of delinquent behavior as indicated by 23 specific delinquent acts ranging from driving without a license to grand larceny and drug use, and by the use of delinquency scales derived from these items; (2) comparison of delinquent behavior in western and mid-western high school students; and (3) comparison of unrecorded delinquency with official records of delinquency.

The data were gathered by anonymous questionnaire in the classroom under the supervision of the writers. A 75 percent sample was taken from the three western high schools (cities of 10,000 to 30,000 population) and a 100 percent sample in three smaller mid-western communities. Approximately 99 percent of the questionnaires were usable.[9] In addition to being considered generally suitable for present research purposes, these particular communities possessed the positive advantage that active and informed lay people were ready to sponsor the project and interpret it to the community.

The measures of delinquent behavior used in this paper are based upon a list of behavior items commonly referred to in the laws relating to delinquent and criminal behavior. Delinquency has been defined in descriptive terms rather than in terms of legalistic categories. For example,

3. Austin L. Porterfield, *Youth in Trouble* (Fort Worth: Leo Potisham Foundation, 1946), chap. 2.

4. Fred J. Murphy, Mary M. Shirley, and Helen L. Witmer, "The Incidence of Hidden Delinquency," *American Journal of Orthopsychiatry*, XVI (October 1946), 686–696.

5. Albert K. Cohen, *Delinquent Boys: The Culture of the Gang* (Glencoe: Free Press, 1955), pp. 37–41. For the authors' statement as to the importance of such data, see James F. Short, Jr. and F. Ivan Nye, "Reported Behavior as a Criterion of Deviant Behavior," *Social Problems*, Winter 1957–58.

6. Albert K. Cohen, "Sociological Research in Juvenile Delinquency," paper read before American Orthopsychiatric Association, March 1956.

7. The authors are aware of studies under way in Chicago, Kansas City, Indiana, Tennessee, Columbus, Ohio, New York City, and in the state of Washington.

8. F. Ivan Nye and James F. Short, Jr., "Scaling Delinquent Behavior," *American Sociological Review*, XXII (June 1957); F. Ivan Nye, *Family Relationships and Delinquent Behavior* (New York: Wiley, 1958), chap. 1; James F. Short, Jr., "The Study of Juvenile Delinquency by Reported Behavior—An Experiment in Method and Preliminary Findings," paper read at the annual meetings of the American Sociological Society, Washington, D.C., 1955.

9. Questionnaires were administered by one or both writers, assisted by other staff members or graduate students of the Department of Sociology of the State College of Washington. For further methodological details, see the references cited in note 8 above.

we refer to stealing things of a certain value, rather than to descriptions of property offenses, e.g., robbery, burglary, larceny, etc.

High School Populations

Because they seem likely to be more representative of the general population than are college or training school populations, we have concentrated our research on high school populations. Table 2.1 presents the percentage of boys in our two high school samples, western and midwestern, and in the western training school group, who report committing each of 21 delinquency items, and the percentage who admit committing these offenses more than once or twice. Table 2.2 presents these data for the high school and training school girls.

From these tables it is apparent that the types of delinquent behavior studied are extensive and variable in the populations studied. We have compared students in the western and mid-western samples in order to secure an estimate of the stability of responses in two non-institutionalized populations. Populations in these two regional samples differ in such respects as city size and population mobility. The mid-western sample is comprised of three small communities: a suburb of a large city, a rural town, and a consolidated rural school district. The western sample comprises three small contiguous cities. The population of the mid-western communities has been fairly stable since 1940, in contrast to the rapid population growth experienced by the western cities. These samples are alike in important respects, however. Ethnic composition is similar, both populations being overwhelmingly native caucasian, and age and sex are controlled. Perhaps of greater importance, both populations are non-institutionalized.

Few statistically significant differences between our two non-institutionalized groups are found in Tables 2.1 and 2.2.[10] This may be taken

10. Samples from both finite and hypothetical universes are treated. The western state samples represent 25 per cent regular-interval samples of the high school population. Mid-western and training school samples represent 100 per cent samples of the individuals in those selected grades in the mid-western high schools and 100 per cent samples of the training schools.

Nine of 21 possible comparisons of the percentage of western and mid-western boys who admit committing these offenses are significant at least at the .05 level. Eight of these 9 offenses are committed by a higher percentage of mid-western boys. When percentage of boys admitting commission of these offenses more than once or twice is compared, only 6 significant differences (at the .05 level) are found, 5 of these being higher for the mid-western boys. When mid-western and western girls are compared as to commission of these offenses, 5 significant differences are found, all being committed by a higher percentage of mid-western girls. Only 1 significant difference between these groups of non-institutionalized girls is found when percentages admitting commission of the 21 offenses more than once or twice is compared.

Table 2.1. Reported delinquent behavior among boys in three samples

Type of offense	Percent admitting commission of offense			Percent admitting commission of offense more than once or twice		
	M.W.	*West*	*Tr.S.*	*M.W.*	*West*	*Tr.S.*
Driven a car without a driver's license or permit	81.1	75.3	91.1	61.2	49.0	73.4
Skipped School	54.4	53.0	95.3	24.4	23.8	85.9
Had fist fight with one person	86.7	80.7	95.3	32.6	31.9	75.0
"Run away" from home	12.9	13.0	68.1	2.8	2.4	37.7
School probation or expulsion	15.3	11.3	67.8	2.1	2.9	31.3
Defied parents' authority	22.2	33.1	52.4	1.4	6.3	23.6
Driven too fast or recklessly	49.7	46.0	76.3	22.7	19.1	51.6
Taken little things (worth less than $2) that did not belong to you	62.7	60.6	91.8	18.5	12.9	65.1
Taken things of medium value ($2–$50)	17.1	15.8	91.0	3.8	3.8	61.4
Taken things of large value ($50)	3.5	5.0	90.8	1.1	2.1	47.7
Used force (strong-arm methods) to get money from another person	6.3	–	67.7	2.4	–	35.5
Taken part in "gang fights"	24.3	22.5	67.4	6.7	5.2	47.4
Taken a car for a ride without the owner's knowledge	11.2	14.8	75.2	4.5	4.0	53.4
Bought or drank beer, wine, or liquor (including drinking at home)	67.7	57.2	89.7	35.8	29.5	79.4
Bought or drank beer, wine, or liquor (outside your home)	43.0	–	87.0	21.1	–	75.0
Drank beer, wine, or liquor in your own home	57.0	–	62.8	24.1	–	31.9
Deliberate property damage	60.7	44.8	84.3	17.5	8.2	49.7
Used or sold narcotic drugs	1.4	2.2	23.1	0.7	1.6	12.6
Had sex relations with another person of the same sex (not masturbation)	12.0	8.8	10.9	3.9	2.9	3.1
Had sex relations with a person of the opposite sex	38.8	40.4	87.5	20.3	19.9	73.4
Gone hunting or fishing without a license (or violated other game laws)	74.0	62.7	66.7	39.6	23.5	44.8
Taken things you didn't want	15.7	22.5	56.8	1.4	3.1	26.8
"Beat up" on kids who hadn't done anything to you	15.7	13.9	48.7	3.1	2.8	26.2
Hurt someone to see them squirm	22.7	15.8	33.4	2.8	3.2	17.5

Table 2.2. Reported delinquent behavior among girls in three samples

Type of offense	Percent admitting commission of offense			Percent admitting commission of offense more than once or twice		
	M.W.	West	Tr.S.	M.W.	West	Tr.S.
Driven a car without a driver's license or permit	60.1	58.2	68.3	33.6	29.9	54.4
Skipped School	40.3	41.0	94.0	10.1	12.2	66.3
Had fist fight with one person	32.7	28.2	72.3	7.4	5.7	44.6
"Run away" from home	9.8	11.3	85.5	1.0	1.0	51.8
School probation or expulsion	2.7	3.7	63.4	0.3	0.2	29.3
Defied parents' authority	33.0	30.6	68.3	3.7	5.0	39.0
Driven too fast or recklessly	20.9	16.3	47.5	5.7	5.4	35.0
Taken little things (worth less than $2) that did not belong to you	36.0	30.0	77.8	5.7	3.5	48.1
Taken things of medium value ($2–$50)	3.4	3.9	58.0	1.0	0.6	29.6
Taken things of large value ($50)	2.0	1.3	30.4	1.7	0.9	10.1
Used force (strong-arm methods) to get money from another person	1.3	—	36.7	0.3	—	21.5
Taken part in "gang fights"	9.7	6.5	59.0	1.7	1.1	27.7
Taken a car for a ride without the owner's knowledge	5.4	4.5	36.6	1.0	0.6	20.7
Bought or drank beer, wine, or liquor (including drinking at home)	62.7	44.5	90.2	23.1	17.6	80.5
Bought or drank beer, wine, or liquor (outside your home)	28.7	—	83.9	10.8	—	75.3
Drank beer, wine, or liquor in your own home	54.2	—	71.1	16.4	—	42.2
Deliberate property damage	21.7	13.6	65.4	5.7	1.6	32.1
Used or sold narcotic drugs	1.3	0.5	36.9	0.3	0.3	23.8
Had sex relations with another person of the same sex (not masturbation)	5.4	3.6	25.0	1.7	0.5	12.5
Had sex relations with a person of the opposite sex	12.5	14.1	95.1	4.1	4.8	81.5
Gone hunting or fishing without a license (or violated other game laws)	20.6	20.3	27.5	5.7	3.9	21.3
Taken things you didn't want	6.4	3.6	43.0	0.7	0.6	13.9
"Beat up" on kids who hadn't done anything to you	5.7	3.1	37.8	1.0	0.9	18.3
Hurt someone to see them squirm	10.4	9.3	35.4	1.0	1.1	20.7

as an indication of stability and reliability of the responses obtained from the two samples. Comparison of 16 and 17 year old high school boys on a seven-item delinquency scale, based upon these same data, indicates agreement between the two groups of boys in 90.7 percent of the scale responses.[11] We note that such differences as are found in Tables 2.1 and 2.2 indicate that delinquent behavior is somewhat more widespread in the smaller, older, more structured mid-western sample than in the larger, newer, growing western communities.

The most common offenses reported "more than once or twice" by high school boys and girls in Tables 2.1 and 2.2 are traffic offenses, truancy, and drinking. Boys also report considerable fighting, stealing (of small things), heterosexual relations, and game violations.

Comparisons of western instutionalized and non-institutionalized boys and girls on the delinquency items in Tables 2.1 and 2.2 indicates that significantly higher proportions of the "official" delinquents commit virtually all of the offenses, and commit them more often, than do the high school students.[12] Exceptions to this pattern are found only in the case of homosexual relations among the boys, driving a car without a license among girls, and game violations among both boys and girls. In spite of the statistical significance of these comparisons, however, it is apparent that there is a good deal of "overlapping" between institutionalized and non-institutionalized boys and girls in the frequency of commission of our delinquency items.

In order to specify more precisely the amount of such overlapping, indexes of delinquent behavior in the form of Guttman-type scales have been constructed. Scales for 16 and 17 year old boys, consisting of seven and eleven delinquency items, have been described elsewhere.[13] These scales proved to be nearly equal in their ability to differentiate between institutionalized and non-instutionalized boys. On the seven-item scale, a cutting point is found which maximizes the difference in delinquency

11. These data are described and graphically presented in F. Ivan Nye and James F. Short, Jr., "Scaling Delinquent Behavior," *op. cit.*
12. This conclusion is based upon statistical comparison of figures presented in Tables 2.1 and 2.2, for our institutionalized and non-institutionalized western state boys and girls.
13. *Ibid.* The seven-item scale included the following delinquency items: driving a car without a license or permit, taking little things (worth less than $2) that did not belong to you, buying or drinking beer, wine or liquor (include drinking at home), skipping school without a legitimate excuse, purposely damaging or destroying public or private property, sex relations with a person of the opposite sex, and defying parents' authority to their faces. Offenses added for the eleven-item scale were: taking things of medium value, taking things of large value, running away from home, and narcotics violations. These data were rescored following the Israel "Gamma" technique in order to remove "idiosyncratic" elements, prior to scaling. For the procedure, and an exposition of its rationale, see M. W. Riley, J. W. Riley, and Jackson Toby, *Scale Analysis* (New Brunswick, N.J.: Rutgers University Press, 1954), chap. 18.

involvement between the two groups of boys at 71 percent (See Table 2.3). At this cutting point, 86 percent of the non-institutionalized boys had been accounted for, as compared with only 14 percent of the training school boys. This difference on the eleven-item scale was maximized at 67 percent.[14] The amount of overlapping between institutionalized and non-institutionalized boys is here specified more closely than has been

Table 2.3. Delinquent behavior scores of high school and training school boys aged 16 and 17

Scale Type	Delinquent Behavior score	High School		Training School	
		Frequency	Cumulative percent	Frequency	Cumulative percent
1	00	0	0	0	0
2	01	128	22	0	0
3	02	40	29	0	0
4	03	60	40	0	0
5	04	105	58	3	2
6	05	28	63	2	4
7	06	26	68	3	6
8	07	25	72	2	8
9	08	80	86	7	14
10	09	31	92	24	32
11	10	27	96	8	39
12	11	6	97	11	48
13	12	6	98	15	60
14	13	5	99	16	72
15	14	3	100	34	100
		570		125	

Note: No scores were obtained for one training school and eight high school boys.

done in previous research. We have cited only the maximum differences between the two groups. Thus, if we were to study "delinquent" and "non-delinquent" boys by comparing our institutionalized and non-institutionalized groups, on the basis of the seven-item scale we would in fact be studying a group of delinquent boys, 14 percent of whom are less

14. It is interesting to compare these findings with results of the delinquency scale of the California Psychological Inventory, as obtained by Gough. Comparing a broad cross section of delinquents (as indicated by their being institutionalized or classed as "high school disciplinary problems") and non-delinquents on this scale, he found a cutting point above which 70 per cent of his male non-delinquents fell, as compared to 20 per cent of his male non-delinquents. See Harrison Gough, "Systematic Validation of a Test for Delinquency," paper read at the annual meeting of the American Psychological Association, 1954.

delinquent than are 14 percent of the "non-delinquent" boys. Comparisons can, of course, be obtained at any point along the scale.

A nine-item scale for the sixteen and seventeen year old western high school and training school girls differentiates somewhat more clearly between the two groups.[15] On this scale a maximum difference of 80 percent is found at scale type 09 (See Table 2.4). At this point on the

Table 2.4. Delinquent behavior scores of high school and training school girls aged 16 and 17

Scale type	Delinquent behavior score	High School		Training School	
		Fre-quency	Cumula-tive percent	Fre-quency	Cumula-tive percent
1	00	135	26	1	2
2	01	72	40	0	2
3	02	21	44	1	4
4	03	74	59	1	6
5	04	61	71	0	6
6	05	52	81	0	6
7	06	15	84	1	8
8	07	11	86	1	10
9	08	22	90	0	10
10	09	10	92	1	12
11	10	23	97	6	25
12	11	9	99	4	33
13	12	2	99	7	48
14	13	5	100	25	100
		512		48	

Note: No scores were available for one high school and two training school girls.

scale 90.4 percent of the high school girls and only 10.4 percent of the training school girls are accounted for. That is, only about 10 percent of the high school girls are more delinquent than is indicated by scale type 08, while nearly 90 percent of the training school girls fall into this more delinquent category.

Sex Differences

Comparison of boys and girls within the high school sample indicates a higher proportion of boys committing nearly all offenses. With few ex-

15. The girls' scale consisted of the offenses included in the eleven-item boys' scale, with the exception of taking things of large value and narcotics violations.

ceptions such differences are statistically significant (at .01 level). This finding is similar to that revealed by official data, though the 5 to 1 ratio of boys to girls reported by the Children's Bureau [16] is not found in many cases, suggesting a bias in under-reporting female delinquency on the part of official data. Offenses for which significant differences between the sexes are not found are generally those offenses for which girls are most often apprehended, e.g., running away from home, defying parents' authority (incorrigibility), and drinking. The fact that significantly higher proportions of boys in both samples report engaging in heterosexual relations and the fact that girls are most often referred to court for such activities presumably reflects society's greater concern for the unsupervised activities of girls.

Fewer statistically significant differences are found between training school boys and girls than was the case in our samples of high school students. Significantly greater percentages of the boys report committing 11 of the 24 offenses studied, and 13 of these offenses "more than once or twice." For nine of these offenses the recorded differences are not significant. Four of the offenses are reported by larger percentages of training school girls. These include running away from home, defying parents' authority, narcotics violations, and homosexual relations. A higher percentage of girls also report heterosexual relations, though this difference is not statistically significant. With the exception of narcotics violations, these are offenses for which girls are most often apprehended. The offenses reported by the highest percentage of training school boys, with the exception of fighting, which is a part of "growing up," are also those for which boys are most often apprehended, viz., stealing and traffic offenses.

Arrest Rates

Arrest rates for the high school and training school samples described above are not available. Data from the first phase of our research program, comparing college and training school students, indicates that non-institutionalized (college) students experience arrest in a far smaller proportion of offenses which they report committing than do training school students.[17] This is especially true of girls, for college girls report arrests only for traffic offenses. These arrest data bear a close relationship to

16. U. S. Department of Health, Education, and Welfare, Social Security Administration, Children's Bureau, *Juvenile Court Statistics,* 1955, Children's Bureau Statistical Series, no. 37.

17. James F. Short, Jr., "A Report on the Incidence of Criminal Behavior, Arrests, and Convictions in Selected Groups," Proceedings of the Pacific Sociological Society, 1954, published in *Research Studies of the State College of Washington,* XXII (June 1954), 110–118. See Table 3, p. 117.

officially available data. For both training school boys and girls arrest rates are highest for offenses against the person exclusive of sex offenses. Arrest rates for property offenses are more than twice as high among boys as among girls in the training school populations, while the reverse is true of sex offenses among these groups. Arrests among college men are reported in only a small percentage of property offenses (.3 percent as compared to 13.7 percent for training school boys), behavior problem offenses (2.3 percent compared to 15.1 percent for training school boys), and "casual" offenses (1.9 percent compared to 5.2 percent).

Socio-Economic Distribution

Finally, the socio-economic characteristics associated with delinquent behavior among our high school and training school populations have been studied.[18] For this purpose analysis of delinquent behavior by individual behavior items and by scale type was made, holding constant sex categories and two age groups in the western and midwestern states. Similar analysis was made for adolescents 16 and older in the "training schools" of the western state. Few significant differences were found between socioeconomic strata. Such differences as were found indicated greater delinquent involvement within the highest socio-economic category as often as in the lowest.

Conclusions

While recognizing the limitations of our definition of delinquent behavior, in terms of the behavior categories studied, and the limitations of the samples employed, it appears that the following tentative conclusions regarding the extent of juvenile delinquency in the non-institutionalized population are warranted:

1. Delinquent conduct in the non-institutionalized population is extensive and variable;

2. Delinquent conduct as we have measured it is similar in extent and nature among non-institutionalized high school students in widely separated sections of the country;

3. Delinquent conduct *reported* by institutionalized and non-institutionalized students is similar to delinquency and crime as treated officially in the following respects:

(1) sex ratio—non-institutionalized boys admit committing virtually all delinquencies more frequently than do non-institutionalized girls,

18. F. Ivan Nye, James F. Short, Jr., and V. J. Olson, "Socio-Economic Status and Delinquent Behavior," *American Journal of Sociology*, LXIII (January 1958).

"once or twice" and "more than once or twice;" fewer differences exist, and these differences are smaller, between institutionalized boys and girls;

(2) the offenses for which boys are most often arrested are generally those which they most often admit committing, e.g., property offenses, traffic violations, truancy, destruction of property, drinking; a few offenses are reported by large proportions of boys which are not often recorded in official statistics, e.g., game violations and fist fights;

(3) the offenses for which girls are most often arrested are, with the exception of sex offenses among high school girls, generally the offenses which girls most often admit committing, e.g., sex offenses, incorrigibility, running away. A few offenses are reported by high proportions of girls which do not find their way into official statistics;

(4) significantly greater proportions of training school boys and girls admit committing virtually all delinquencies, and admit committing them more frequently, than do high school boys and girls;

(5) when training school students are compared with high school students on a composite scale of delinquency activities there is considerable overlapping between groups of both boys and girls, but training school students as a group rank significantly higher, in terms of seriousness of involvement in delinquent behavior, than do high school students;

(6) differences on the delinquency scales, and in the commission of individual delinquencies, are greater between high school and training school girls than between high school and training school boys;

(7) variation in the proportion of reported delinquencies which result in arrest are similar to variations in the "cleared by arrest" figures collected by the Federal Bureau of Investigation.

4. Delinquent conduct reported by non-institutionalized students differs from official data in the following ways:

(1) arrests—comparison of college and training school students indicates that training school students are arrested in higher proportions of all classes of delinquencies which they admit committing than college students;

(2) socio-economic status—delinquency within the non-institutionalized populations studied is distributed more evenly throughout the socio-economic structure of society than are official cases, which are found disproportionately in the lower socio-economic strata.

Further research of this nature may be expected to provide additional clues as to the extent and nature of delinquent behavior in various segments of the population. By such means the structural correlates of delinquency, together with other important etiological considerations, may be better understood. Reported delinquent behavior as a method warrants and requires further investigation. [19] The present status of research by reported behavior is regarded as still in a pioneer stage. It provides an alternative to the use of institutionalized populations and court records, with new opportunities for research in delinquent behavior and comprehension of it.

19. For a discussion of advantages, as well as methodological problems of this approach, see Short and Nye, "Reported Behavior as a Criterion of Deviant Behavior," *op. cit.*

3. The Incidence of Hidden Delinquency

FRED J. MURPHY, MARY M. SHIRLEY, and HELEN L. WITMER

MENTAL hygienists have always been concerned, on the one hand, that many a youthful violator of the law goes unprosecuted and even undetected until a delinquent pattern becomes deeply ingrained; and on the other, that many a lad receives a juvenile court record for a relatively innocent misdemeanor. Students of juvenile delinquency have long suspected that juvenile court statistics do not reflect adequately the extent of youthful misconduct and that a considerable number of violations and violators never find their way into official court records. Hitherto, research workers have been baffled as to how to get at this pool of hidden delinquency. The Cambridge-Somerville Youth Study, which has maintained an intimate contact with a large group of boys throughout their adolescent years, has afforded a unique opportunity to arrive at some measure of the amount of juvenile lawbreaking that is hidden from public view. From our case records, it is possible to make a minimum estimate of how fre-

Reprinted from *American Journal of Orthopsychiatry*, October 1946, pp. 686–695. Copyright 1946, the American Orthopsychiatric Association, Inc. Reproduced by permission.

quently the group of boys under study committed acts that *could* have brought them into court if someone in the community had wanted to register a court complaint.

This program of character-building and delinquency-prevention sponsored by the late Dr. Richard Cabot directed its efforts chiefly toward underprivileged boys who lived amidst the congestion and squalor of high delinquency areas. The plan of treatment involved close contact with the subjects and their parents by case workers who became trusted friends and were consequently afforded the boys' confidences. In the course of work the case workers acquired a great deal of information concerning misdeeds that had never become a matter of official court complaint.

Before extracting the pertinent data from the case histories, certain terms had to be understood and procedures developed and explained. The General Laws of Massachusetts define a delinquent as "A child between seven and seventeen years who violates any city ordinance or town by-law or commits an offense not punishable by death or by imprisonment for life." Our classification as to an unofficial or official delinquent depended upon whether or not a court complaint had been granted for an offense. The distinction was arbitrarily established at this point because Juvenile Court statistics are computed upon the basis of the number of court complaints issued. This step was decided upon in collaboration with an official of the Boston Juvenile Court, now Justice John J. Connelly, a recognized authority on delinquency.

Because the length of a period of probation or the term of institutional commitment for juvenile offenses do not serve as an adequate measure of the seriousness of an act, three groupings by nature of offenses were formulated with the assistance of the aforementioned authority. The three categories as developed in the order of seriousness were:

1. *Violations of City Ordinances*, such as shining shoes or vending without a license, street ball playing, hopping street cars, swimming and/ or fishing in forbidden places, and curfew laws.

2. *Minor Offenses*, of the nature of truancy, petty stealing (5 and 10¢ stores), trespassing, running away, stubborn child, sneaking into movies.

3. *More Serious Offenses*, involving such acts as breaking and entering, larceny, assault, drunkenness, sex offenses.

The comprehensive list of approximately 50 offenses was drawn up on individual work sheets which provided space for identifying material on the boy and columns for tabulating his law violations.

A group consultation with the case workers, later to be interviewed individually, was held. This was done to avoid confusion and to assure consistency in the workers understanding the procedure. The project was thoroughly explained and their advice sought particularly in reference to the tabulation of the frequency of unofficial acts wherein it did not always make for accurate enumeration. Case workers often knew that a boy had repeatedly committed a certain infraction during a given period, but they would have been at a loss to enumerate the individual occurrences. Hence, it was decided to use—*rarely, occasionally* and *frequently*—giving to each a range of numerical value which would represent the number of violations in a given year of a boy's life. *Rarely* denoted a frequency span of from one to three offenses per year; *occasionally,* from four to nine, and *frequently*, ten and over. By this method it was obvious that we would have to be satisfied in most instances with a numerical approximation of a youth's unofficial offenses. This was termed a "score" of law infractions.

In the process of tabulating a boy's offenses, the case worker and I (F.J.M.) jointly reviewed each page of the case record. Any uncertainty as to whether an offense had been committed, either because the record was vague or because it seemed possible that the boy was entertaining his case worker with a story of fantasied misdeeds, always resulted in his being given the benefit of the doubt, and no tally was recorded. Likewise, in totaling the number of misdemeanors of a boy in a given year, we conservatively employed the lowest weighting; i.e., *rarely* was given a weight of 1, *occasionally,* 4, and *frequently,* 10. When an incident might have two possible interpretations, the less serious was utilized. For example, one little culprit disturbed a theater manager no end by dropping a lighted match into his pocket. This situation never reached the court, but if it had, we speculated that one of two complaints could have been made—a charge of malicious mischief, or a more serious one of assault and battery. In this instance we used the former label. As the result of these precautions, our estimate of the number of violations and of their seriousness is a very conservative one.

In order to obtain uniformity in the delinquency scores, it was necessary to select an age span that could be consistent for all cases. From a survey of the entire case load, it was found that the majority had received service throughout the age span from 11 to 16 years. A total of 114 boys had been given service throughout this five-year period, and the present study is based upon their analyses.

To the workers' knowledge, only 13 of the boys had never committed an offense for which a complaint might have been made in court. The rest had all been more or less serious juvenile offenders; 40 designated as official delinquents because complaints were registered in court, and 61 as unofficial delinquents because they "got by" without court complaint.

The numerical scores hereafter referred to as "number of violations" represent the minimum number of law infractions committed by these boys between their eleventh and sixteenth years. At our conservative estimate, these boys had committed a minimum of 6,416 infractions of the law during the five-year period; while only 95 of their violations had become a matter of official complaint. In other words, authorities took official action in less than 1½ per cent of the infractions. Approximately 1,400 of these infractions were violations of city ordinances, none of which became a matter of court complaint. Of 4,400 minor offenses, only 27 (.60%) were prosecuted. Of 616 serious offenses, 68 (11%) were prosecuted.

Table 3.1. Comparison of violations for unofficial and official delinquents[a]

Violation	Unofficial Delinquents	Official Delinquents	Both
	N 61	N 40	N 101
City Ordinance	739	655	1394
Minor Offenses	1913	2493	4406
Serious Offenses	174	442	616
Total	2826	3590	6416

[a]Based on records of 114 boys, ages 11–15. Of 114 boys, 13 had no violations to the case workers' knowledge.

Lest the small proportion of infractions resulting in court complaints should lead to the inference that law enforcement was lax in these communities, it must be explained that during the period covered by this study there was a policy of handling a large proportion of juvenile offenders informally. Hence, many of our boys were apprehended and warned by police but no complaint was registered in court. Furthermore, lest it be thought that CSYS case workers were protecting the boys from court involvement, it must be mentioned that, in many instances the boys revealed their delinquencies months or even years after they had occurred. In reminiscing on their activities, they often owned up to earlier law violations hitherto unsuspected.

Analysis of the type of infractions for which court complaints were registered indicated that larceny, and breaking and entering were the charges of highest frequency. Truancy and school offenses were a matter of official court complaint only rarely in comparison to the frequency with which these were committed. This suggests that school authorities manifest a considerable degree of tolerance of such juvenile offenses and tend to handle them by their own methods rather than to call upon the help of the court.

In the main, the transgressions of the official offenders were more frequent and more serious than those of the unofficial group. The total scores of violations for the officials ranged from 5 to 323 with a median of 79; whereas the unofficials ranged from 0 to 266 with a median of 30. Furthermore, the median official delinquent over the five-year period scored 10 city ordinance infractions, 53 minor acts, and 6 more serious offenses; whereas the median unofficial delinquent had scored 0 on city ordinance violations, only 20 on minor offenses, and 0 on serious offenses. There were, however, a number of exceptions because 5 boys having official records had total scores less than 30, the median of the unofficials; and 13 unofficials equaled or exceeded in minor and more serious offenses the median score of the official delinquents. In computing the percentiles for the scores of delinquent acts for the two respective groups, it was found that for the most part from year to year, 11 through 16, the pattern of asocial behavior was fairly even and consistent. The amount of delinquency exhibited in the eleventh year remained surprisingly constant in the ensuing four years.

Table 3.2. Number and proportion of violations resulting in court complaints

Type of Violation	No. Court Complaints	Official Delinquents	Both Groups
City Ordinance	0	0.00%	0.00
Minor Offenses	27	1.08	.61
Serious Offenses	68	15.39	11.04
Total	95	2.72	1.47

Relevant to the bearing that intelligence might have as a differentiating factor between the two groups, we at first speculated that perhaps higher mental endowments enabled the unofficial delinquents to remain out of court. However, upon compiling the figures, it was found that there was no appreciable difference. The official offenders had IQ's on the revised Stanford-Binet ranging from a low of 59 to a high of 117 with a median of 93.25, as compared to a median of 93.70 for the unofficials who ranged from 65 to 149. Thus, our study seems to substantiate the present more

Table 3.3. Percentile scores for unofficial and official delinquents

Percentile	Unofficial Delinquents*				Official Delinquents*			
	CO	MO	SO	All	CO	MO	SO	All
First	0	0	0	0	0	0	0	5
Tenth	0	1	0	2	0	12	0	27
Twenty-fifth	0	8	0	10	0	30	1	39
Fiftieth	0	20	0	30	10	53	6	79
Seventy-fifth	14	48	0	71	24	70	16	102
Ninetieth	50	84	5	107	40	118	32	194
Hundredth	88	134	44	266	90	187	46	323

*Type of offense
CO = City Ordinance
MO = Minor Offenses
SO = Serious Offenses

or less accepted contention that law violators, known officially by the courts and authorities, do not differ markedly from the general population.

We were interested further in ascertaining what the case records revealed concerning the personalities of these boys, especially insofar as these enabled us to judge whether the delinquencies seemed to spring from a neurotic basis or whether they resulted largely from the boys' acquiescence to the prevailing juvenile pattern of their communities. It was also hoped that the records might throw light on why some relatively law-abiding boys had court records and why some of the chronic offenders escaped court action. We therefore studied the case records of the five official delinquents who had low scores and the 13 unofficial delinquents with high scores. It appeared that three of the five official delinquents were dull, passive boys, who had considerable security within their own families and were not particularly troublesome in the community. For these three, court involvement seemed to be a piece of ill luck. Two were perhaps the victims of police vigilance directed toward their entire families.

Ned, one of the boys, had always been a quiet stay-at-home, but regularly throughout Ned's childhood the father had been arrested for drunkenness and assault, and the older brother had been sent to a correctional school on a charge of larceny. Hence, when Ned was discovered with a "borrowed" bicycle, the police being aware of the hazards surrounding children in this family, brought him into court and he was placed on probation. The other two, with a small number of violations, gave the impression of being greatly disturbed, with neurotic trends springing largely from difficult home relationships. Henry's father regarded his wife as his inferior; he constantly belittled his son, and remarked openly that the boy took after his mother's family and would sooner or later end up in a penal institution. The mother was ambivalent toward the boy, occasionally indulging him but more often railing at him. As he grew into adolescence, Henry's toleration of this treatment lessened, and the case worker believed that his removal from the home would be the only way of safeguarding him from an aggressive attack upon his parents or from some serious delinquency outside. The parents were eager to have him placed out, but were not willing to have the placement go through court. The placement agency was reluctant to accept the boy without a court order. While placement negotiations were under way, Henry was summoned to a police station to give testimony concerning a sex pervert of whom he had been a victim, but he was led to believe that he would not be implicated. Upon learning of this private hearing, the placement worker, in an effort to obtain court custody, started a rumor that Henry was being protected in his delinquencies. When this rumor, much enlarged, reached the ears of the officer he was disturbed, had Henry reappear and prosecuted him on a charge of lewdness. Embittered by what he considered as "being framed," Henry walked out of court muttering "I'll show that officer what I can do"; whereupon he entered a haberdashery, stole a pair of braces from the counter, was apprehended by the store detective and again handed over to the police.

Percy, the last of these five boys, seems to have had a delinquency score that was spuriously low, due to the fact that he was in foster homes in rural villages during much of his eleventh to sixteenth years. Prior to CSYS contact he and his brothers had been sent out by their mother to steal. Her desertion led to breaking up of the home and to placement of the children in areas that either presented fewer temptations or were more tolerant of youthful misdemeanors. On the other hand, the foster mothers may have been less willing to recount to the case worker, at his infrequent visits, all of Percy's bad deeds lest their own status as worthy foster mothers be questioned. Percy was in and out of foster homes and correctional schools throughout the entire period, and his inability to settle down and accept the advantages of a good placement, when such was provided, was indicative of his general instability.

Of greater interest are the personalities of the 13 who avoided court records in spite of having committed a larger number of minor or serious infractions than the median official delinquent. These likewise could be grouped in a general way into two categories—gregarious, fairly well-adjusted boys whose delinquencies seemed free from a neurotic component; and emotionally disturbed boys whose asocial behavior seemed primarily the outgrowth of tension or friction within the home. There were five boys in the first group; eight in the second.

The four most frequent and most serious of these offenders gave no evidence of being poorly adjusted, in that their behavior reflected the mores of their particular group. Marcus whose minor infractions totaled 134 and whose 44 serious offenses included larceny from parked cars, assault, picking the pockets of a service man, and breaking and entering, was a confirmed gang member from early childhood. Although his mother was psychotic and was hospitalized a good part of the period under consideration, her illness and absence from the home seemed to have little effect on the boy's pleasant, outgoing personality and his popularity with the gang with whom he roved the neighborhood. His infractions increased from begging on the streets at age 11 and peddling Christmas wreaths stolen from front doors, to the mysterious possession of a seaman's wallet containing more than $200 at the age of 14. In this last escapade, his accomplice was a boy on probation through whom the incident became known to the probation officer. The boys declared they had found the wallet on the floor of a theater. Since no loss was reported they got by with their story, Marcus's father having first salted the money away in war bonds and hired an attorney to discuss his rights with a probation officer. On some of their other larcenies the gang's activities were known and Marcus was warned by the police. Often he tended to drop out when he believed serious mischief was in the wind. While he has never manifested particular strengths, he has maintained good standing with his friends throughout and now seems to be making an adequate adjustment in the Merchant Marine.

Denny, with a score of 84 minor offenses and 25 serious ones, manifested considerable strength and independence in the management of his own life when his home was broken up by the accidental death of his besotted stepmother. Reviewing this period of his life later with his case worker, he told how his gang had taken a bike here and there until they had so many of them they didn't know what to do. He told that he had often stolen food, and when he was ill-shod in winter he and a pal had snatched a purse containing $40. "Every now and then I see that woman on the street and it makes me feel pretty mean," he added. While some of these early larcenies seemed prompted by a desire for excitement, many seemed to the case worker to have been directed toward survival. Though only 14 when his home dissolved, Denny took things into his own hands, obtaining working papers and making his way back and forth to the home of a friendly Vermont farmer each summer. Winters, he lived either with his aunt or with his employer, an ash hauler. Denny demonstrated his ability to fend for himself at an early age, and he kept himself out of trouble with the law by being very street-wise.

Al, with a score of 96 minor infractions, seemed an independent, self-sufficient boy, with inner strengths that fortified him against the more contaminating influences of a highly delinquent neighborhood. On the whole, his family life was one of harmony and integration. During the early years, he had the companionship of his grandfather which seemed to have represented a character-building force in his life. His case worker observed that his gang membership seemed in a peripheral capacity so far as group activities went, but that he had a close enough association with each of the members to obtain a companion in a dual project—one for swimming and another for bicycle trips. Thus, the gang did not have sway over his activities for he knew what he wanted and always had command of the situation. His most frequent offenses were street fighting, sneaking into movies, swimming in forbidden places, and shining shoes without a license. Only occasionally did he engage in petty stealing, and never in more serious larceny.

Jerry, with a score of 108 minor offenses, was a passive, lackadaisical boy, who tended to go along with the gang in their less serious infractions and to avoid becoming involved in more serious episodes. This seemed a sign of weakness and cowardice, and was all of a pattern with his tendency to give up school at the slightest difficulty, and to postpone until tomorrow or next week or until he was 16, appointments for job interviews arranged for him. He was, in fact, a quitter, and his avoidance of serious law infractions was not a matter of ego strength. In spite of these signs of weakness, Jerry showed no symptoms of deep, underlying anxieties. He lived on the surface, and made as little effort as possible, following perhaps the pattern of his two ne'er-do-well brothers rather than of his steady, hard-working father.

John, the last of these five reasonably well-adjusted boys, had a score of 61 minor infractions, and was once warned by the police for trespassing during a realistic game of commandos. Temper outbursts during his early school years were perhaps suggestive of some emotional disturbance, but these had been overcome by the time he was 11. He was a favorite with his teachers and had friends among the boys in the neighborhood. John's father was given to drunken sprees, during which his mother seemed to lean on John as the eldest of her three boys. He accepted this responsibility in a rather mature way. Throughout the years, the case workers tried to draw him out on the subject of family relationships, thinking he well might feel considerable hostility toward his father. They were never able to elicit anything except matter-of-fact comments and occasional genuine admiration of his father's athletic prowess, and concluded that he felt no resentment and really took the father's drunkenness and periodic upsets in the home in his stride.

In contrast to these five, the other eight unofficial delinquents all seemed to be suffering to some degree from neurotic difficulties springing largely from discord within the home.

Between Mrs. B. and her eldest son, Herbert, a cordial hatred existed, stemming perhaps from the paternal grandparents' belief that their son had married beneath him. They compensated for their dislike of the mother by indulging Herbert, encouraging him to seek haven in their home when he and his mother came to blows, which sometimes occurred. Herbert's 104 minor offenses consisted largely of aggression and profanity directed toward the mother. His eight serious offenses were composed of occasional physical assaults on his mother and some sex play with one of his sisters. Since his infractions were for the most part confined to aggression within the home, it is understandable that they did not come to the attention of the police.

Edwin, whom the police had warned because his mother complained that he was stubborn and sometimes assaulted her, had adequate provocation for attacks on his mother. This childish widow never stopped lamenting that her only child had not been a girl, and never ceased to nag for every little fault, from failure to brush his hair to ripping a button from his shirt at play. She constantly harped on her own imaginary ailments and upon her many sacrifices for her son. She tried her best to train him into girlish behavior, and to some extent succeeded, so that he was considered a sissy by his contemporaries. Small wonder that his response to all these frustrations developed from childish pinching and pommeling of his mother to adolescent attacks with a chair, and finally, to bitter cursing and turning away. His mother often expressed to the case worker her wonderment that she, being such a good woman, could have such a bad boy. She often threatened to have him sent to a correctional school, but it was apparent that she could not part with him, nor could he emancipate himself from her.

Dan, a colored boy whose father had deserted during Dan's infancy, had close physical contact with his mother, even sleeping with her until late childhood. Many of his aggressions seemed to have a sexual basis, his most serious offense being that of assaulting white girls. In the opinion of the case worker, they were only girls who were sexually promiscuous with colored boys. The worker summarized Dan's record by saying "Certain antisocial problems exist not because of any conflict between Dan and his environment, but because Dan is so akin to his environment."

The most neurotic boy of all this group early exhibited traits suggestive of Levy's "affect hunger" cases. Andy's mother had died in his infancy. The father placed him and his much older brother in various boarding homes where they suffered a good deal of neglect and abuse. When Andy was three, the father married a rather young woman who later claimed that her love of children and the knowledge that she would never have any of her own had entered into her decision to marry Mr. T. and bring up his motherless boys. At the beginning of the study, Andy was a disturbing element in the primary grades, being unable to concentrate on his lessons and annoying the teachers and other children. His parents also found him a problem at home, and the father controlled him with very strict discipline. The stepmother worked, thus leaving the elder brother to enforce the stringent rules laid down by the father.

Andy's attitude toward his case worker was that of teasing and begging for little gifts and for trips and excursions. The worker recognized him as a very disturbed child and sought the help of a child guidance clinic. There Andy and his mother received treatment for several months, with little improvement in his behavior. Eventually, he was removed from his home, which shortly after placement was dissolved, leaving the boy entirely without anchorage. He was resentful at being sent to a boarding school for difficult children and ran away twice. Andy's delinquencies consisted mainly of truancy, school offenses, and stubborn, unruly behavior. He engaged in petty stealing only twice, and in breaking and entering once. The depth of his emotional disturbance was indicated by his failure to use the help of either his CSYS case workers or of the psychiatrist in a constructive way. He has developed into a youth that borders on the psychopathic personality.

The chief contribution of this study is that we have been able to arrive at a minimal estimate of the amount of unofficial delinquency that takes place among a sizable group of underprivileged boys. Both official and unofficial delinquents commit numerous infractions of juvenile laws which do not become a matter of official record. Although both groups differ somewhat in the frequency and seriousness of offenses, there is much overlapping between the two.

While it has not been within the scope of this paper to make a comprehensive analysis of factors which may perhaps differentiate the official and unofficial delinquents, some marked similarities between the two groups have been found. Both have a wide range in intelligence as measured by standard tests, and show no difference in this respect. Both groups contain boys who are socially well adjusted to the pattern of life within their particular subcultures and whose asocial acts could not be considered as springing from emotional conflict or turmoil within themselves. These boys seem to commit most of the violations of property rights, such as larceny, breaking and entering, and destruction of property. Both groups also contain boys whose offenses seem to arise out of deep neurotic disturbance within themselves. These boys, with a neurotic component in their delinquencies, tend to commit aggressions directed toward the home or school in greater frequency than they commit violations against property rights. This observation is consistent with the findings of other students of delinquency and is what one would be led to expect from psychological theory. It is hoped that further analysis of the material will reveal factors that differentiate between the groups of official and unofficial delinquents.

PART THREE

Delinquents and the Police

THE MAJOR role played by the police in the sifting and sorting of juveniles into our out of the population of official delinquents has already been alluded to. Some statistics on this activity of law-enforcement agencies are found in national arrest figures from 4556 police agencies in 1967. The 5 million arrests made by the police included 1,339,578, or 24.3 percent, involving persons under 18 years of age.[1] Of these, 46.2 per cent were disposed of informally within the department, so that they did not result in court referral.[2] Similarly, data from California indicate that in 1966 the police made 303,020 arrests of persons under 18 years of age, accounting for 12 per cent of the youth population of that state. These arrests involved 112,155 for major and minor law violations and 190,865 for "delinquent tendencies." Nearly three-fourths of the major law violations were handled by referral to the juvenile court, while only about

1. U. S. Department of Justice, *Uniform Crime Reports for the U. S., 1967* (Washington, D.C.: U. S. Government Printing Office, 1968), p. 121.
2. *Ibid*, p. 110.

half of the minor law violations and delinquent tendencies arrests were dealt with in this manner.[3]

The figures above, together with the preceding sections of this book, indicate that the police often react to juvenile lawbreakers in terms of the seriousness of their offenses. Those youthful deviants who carry out acts involving major financial losses or extensive damage are the ones who get sent off to court, while the offenders who carry out petty mischief are much more likely to be dismissed with a warning or admonition from the officer. Yet at the same time, the police do not send all cases of serious delinquency on to the courts, nor do they always deal informally with youths who are implicated in relatively inconsequential acts. Clearly, additional variables beyond the nature of the delinquent act are considered by police agents as they make their decisions.

What are some of the major dimensions of police work with juveniles? On this point, David Bordua has suggested that police agencies and their activities with youthful offenders ought to be approached both microscopically and macroscopically.[4] By the first he means that police dispositions are partially a response to various social characteristics of delinquents, including seriousness of the offense, the prior record of the lawbreaker, his racial and economic status, and other factors of this kind. Additionally, police officers may take account of such things as the appearance and demeanor of the lawbreaker, so that some elements of social interaction between the police agent and the youth may enter into the dispositions made of the case.

The macroscopic study of police behavior would involve a historical and comparative perspective on police organizations. Perhaps over time, police agencies change their policies regarding youthful offenders. Then too, different law enforcement organizations may be guided by different procedural rules and norms such that the handling of youthful offenders may vary from department to department. If this is the case, we may find that, while certain social characteristics of offenders are attended to by police officers generally, the varied organizational policies of specific departments have the consequence that rates of court referral vary from community to community. The individual delinquent's chances of ending up in a juvenile court may depend in part upon his social characteristics and in part upon the peculiarities of the community in which he resides.

One major investigation of police decisions, the social characteristics of offenders, and police-delinquent interaction has been conducted by Gold-

3. Bureau of Criminal Statistics, State of California, *Crime and Delinquency in California, 1966* (Sacramento: Department of Justice, 1967), pp. 180–181.
4. David J. Bordua, "Recent Trends: Deviant Behavior and Social Control," *Annals of the American Academy of Political and Social Science*, CCCLIX (January 1967), 159–161.

man, who studied a small mill-town, an industrial center, a trade center, and an upper-class residential area in Allegheny County, Pennsylvania. [5] He found that the police in these communities usually referred automobile thieves and other serious delinquents to court, but they dealt with most instances of mischief and other minor misbehavior informally. Police officers were also influenced in their decisions by their views of the juvenile court, such that those who were pessimistic about its rehabilitative potential sent fewer offenders to it. The demeanor of the juvenile violator was also taken into account by the policeman. The police referred relatively more Negro youths than white youngsters to court. However, differential referral of Nego delinquents was not a manifestation of gross racial prejudice. Instead, more of these offenders were sent to court because their social backgrounds were perceived as more disorganized than was true of white lawbreakers.

The study by Terry in Racine, Wisconsin, included here, parallels the investigation by Goldman. In it, Terry found that males, Mexican-Americans, Negroes, and lower-income youths were most likely to receive the most formal and severe dispositions by the police and other agencies. According to Terry, those social characteristics are related to police dispositions principally because of their linkage to offense-seriousness. In other words, the police sort out the most criminalistic youths for court handling and these youngsters tend to be lower-income, male, minority-group members.

The interaction processes between policemen and offenders were noted by Goldman in the investigation referred to above. Some parallel observations have been made by Sellin and Wolfgang concerning Philadelphia policemen. They reported that these officers weigh the offense, the prior record of the offender, his family background, his demeanor, and the attitude of the victim, and they also are influenced by their opinion of the juvenile court. [6] One of the most revealing studies of this matter is the one by Piliavin and Briar, reprinted in this section. They indicate that serious offenses nearly always result in court referral, but in other instances of misconduct, police officers base their actions upon the appearance of the offender, his demeanor, and other on-the-spot considerations.

The role of the demeanor of the youthful offender in the actions taken against him is complex. In one essay on this subject, Werthman and Piliavin have suggested that police officers may often call out hostile and defiant responses from certain offenders because of their own posture

5. Nathan Goldman, *The Differential Selection of Juvenile Offenders for Court Appearance* (New York: National Council on Crime and Delinquency, 1963).

6. Thorsten Sellin and Marvin E. Wolfgang, *The Measurement of Delinquency* (New York: Wiley, 1964), pp. 95–100.

toward these youngsters.[7] The policeman who looks upon most Negroes and members of certain other minority groups as "symbolic assailants," that is, as persons who have a high potential for troublesome behavior, may adopt a harsh, suspicious approach to them.[8] In this way, the demeanor of the police officer may trigger the "tough-guy" mannerisms of the juvenile offender.

Turning to the question of organizational structure of police agencies, Bordua has offered some evidence showing that referral rates to the juvenile court for various police departments in the United States in 1965 were extremely varied.[9] In some, nearly all youths who were arrested were turned over to the court, while, in others, nearly all of the delinquents were handled informally. Although some of this variation may be due to differences in amounts and patterns of delinquency in different communities, a good share of it must be the result of variations in departmental organization and policies.

Wilson's study of two urban police departments included in this volume is the most detailed and revealing investigation to date of the effects of organizational structure upon police behavior with juveniles. The reader may be surprised to find that the less "professional" of the two referred fewer juveniles to the court than did the more bureaucratic, professional department.

The papers on the police included in this volume are but a small sample of the rapidly growing literature on the social organization of law-enforcement agencies, a subject which has received scant attention form sociologists until the last decade. [10] We have learned much about the workings of the police in recent years, including police decision-making concerning juvenile offenders. Still, it ought to be noted that relatively little information is at hand concerning the behavior of police agencies in suburban communities, in relatively small towns, and in certain other areas. Accordingly, the essays in this section can be taken as indicators of some of the directions to be pursued as research on law-enforcement agencies continues within sociology.

7. Carl Werthman and Irving Piliavin, "Gang Members and the Police," in David J. Bordua, ed., *The Police* (New York: Wiley, 1967), pp. 56–98.
8. The concept of "symbolic assailant" comes from Jerome H. Skolnick, *Justice Without Trial* (New York: Wiley, 1966), pp. 45–48.
9. Bordua, "Recent Trends: Deviant Behavior and Social Control," p. 160.
10. A review of this literature on various aspects of police organization can be found in Don C. Gibbons, *Society, Crime, and Criminal Careers* (Englewood Cliffs, N.J.: Prentice-Hall, 1968), pp. 47–70.

4. Discrimination in the Handling of Juvenile Offenders by Social Control Agencies

ROBERT M. TERRY

AMONG the chief functions of agencies of social control are identifying, defining, and sanctioning individuals who violate legal norms. The application of "deviant labels" is a salient issue in the process of social control, crucial for understanding the development of deviant roles (or career deviance) and for assessing the relative merits of generalizations based on control-agency data.

Offenders and audiences act out a complementary interactive relationship. The actions taken by audiences may have significance for the offender's future behavior since audiences may (1) accord deviant statuses, (2) restrict the offender's choice of alternative roles, (3) isolate and stigmatize the offender as a deviant, and (4) take actions which lead to the offender's conception of himself as a deviant.[1]

Reprinted from *Journal of Research in Crime and Delinquency,* July 1967, pp. 218–230, by permission of *Journal of Research in Crime and Delinquency* and the author. Copyright 1967 by National Council on Crime and Delinquency.

1. This position has been developed especially by Lemert; see Edwin M. Lemert, *Social Pathology* (New York: McGraw-Hill, 1951). Also see Kai T. Erikson, "Notes

In the assessment of control-agency data, most generalizations concerning the etiology of criminal or delinquent behavior stem from research utilizing inmates of correctional institutions, parolees or probationers, clients of social and welfare agencies, or individuals contacted or arrested by the police. It is generally assumed that these subjects and their behavior provide adequate and accurate indices of a deviant population and the frequency of deviant behavior.

Students of deviant behavior generally regard three variables as highly significant in identifying, defining, and sanctioning individuals for violations of legal norms. Control agents, presumably, regard the sex of the offender, his socio-economic status, and his ethnicity as criteria in deciding (1) whether to identify the behavior as deviant, (2) whether to define the offender as a deviant, and (3) how severely to sanction offenders.

Two issues appear relevant here. First, social-control agencies are believed to discriminate against lower-status offenders, members of minority groups, and males. Second, official statistics gathered by or in the possession of control agencies thus are regarded as biased in that those discriminated against are over-represented in police records. Their over-representation is not regarded as indicating that these offenders more often engage in legal violations, but that the police are more likely to identify and define the lower-status person as a deviant.

These notions permeate the literature on crime and delinquency even though empirical research dealing with these issues is relatively sparse and poorly conceived. However, this has not prevented students of deviance from asserting that such biases *do* exist, frequently implying that a prodigious body of research exists to support the assertions.

For example, Lemert maintains: "Members of minority groups, migrants, and persons with limited economic means are often the salient objectives, if not scapegoats, of the frustrated police in our local communities." [2] Glaser states: "It has been well established that official agencies take a more punitive attitude toward misbehavior by low-status youth than toward the same behavior in higher status youths." [3] Similarly, Clinard asserts: "It is a generally established fact that Negroes, as well as Spanish-speaking peoples, on the whole, are arrested, tried, convicted,

---

on the Sociology of Deviance," *Social Problems* (Spring 1962), pp. 307–14; Howard S. Becker, *Outsiders: Studies in the Sociology of Deviance* (New York: Free Press, 1963); *The Other Side: Perspectives on Deviance,* Howard S. Becker, ed. (New York: Free Press, 1964); John I. Kitsuse, "Societal Reactions to Deviant Behavior: Problems of Theory and Method," *Social Problems* (Winter 1962), pp. 247–56; and Thomas J. Scheff, "The Role of the Mentally Ill and the Dynamics of Mental Disorder: A Research Framework," *Sociometry* (December 1963), pp. 436–453.

2. Lemert, *op. cit.* n. 1, p. 311.

3. As quoted in Richard A. Cloward and Lloyd E. Ohlin, *Delinquency and Opportunity* (Glencoe, Ill.: Free Press, 1960), p. 12.

and returned to prison more often than others who commit comparable offenses." [4] Regarding sex differences, Reckless states:

> Citizens are willing to report the behavior of males much more readily than that of females. The police are supposed to be much more lenient in their arrests of females. Judicial processes in America are supposed to be very much more lenient with women than men. Consequently, female offenders have a much better chance than male offenders of not being reported, of not being arrested, and of dropping out of the judicial process, that is, of remaining uncommitted.[5]

Nearly any criminology or delinquency text will support these statements.[6]

The research literature on which these assertions are based is characterized chiefly by (1) its highly descriptive nature, (2) use of anecdotal rather than systematic evidence, (3) the leap from statistical significance to causal determinacy, (4) failure to introduce control variables into statistical procedures, (5) a focus on selected aggregates of offenders in order to make inferences about the criteria utilized in decision-making at earlier stages in the legal process instead of on the decision-making process itself, and (6) the equation of attitudes expressed by agents of social control with their actual behavior.[7]

4. Marshall B. Clinard, *Sociology of Deviant Behavior*, rev. ed. (New York: Holt, Rinehart and Winston, 1963), pp. 550–551.

5. Walter C. Reckless, *The Crime Problem,* 3rd ed. (New York: Appleton-Century-Crofts, 1961), p. 37.

6. See e.g., Harry Elmer Barnes and Negley K. Teeters, *New Horizons in Criminology*, 3rd ed. (Englewood Cliffs, N.J.: Prentice-Hall, 1959), p. 150; Herbert A. Bloch and Gilbert Geis, *Man, Crime, and Society* (New York: Random House, 1962), p. 421; Ruth S. Cavan, *Criminology*, 3rd ed. (New York: Crowell, 1962), pp. 32, 35; Mabel A. Elliott, *Crime in Modern Society* (New York: Harper, 1952), pp. 36, 204–05, 298; Elmer H. Johnson, *Crime, Correction and Society* (Homewood, Ill.: Dorsey Press, 1964), pp. 71–91; Martin H. Neumeyer, *Juvenile Delinquency in Modern Society*, 3rd ed. (Princeton: Van Nostrand, 1961), p. 43; Harry M. Shulman, *Juvenile Delinquency in American Society* (New York: Harper and Row, 1961), pp. 72, 128; Edwin H. Sutherland and Donald R. Cressey, *Principles of Criminology*, 6th ed. (Philadelphia: Lippincott, 1960), p. 285; Donald R. Cressey, "Crime," in Robert K. Merton and Robert A. Nisbet, eds., *Contemporary Social Problems* (New York: Harcourt Brace and World, 1961), pp. 33–44; and Donald R. Taft, *Criminology*, 3rd ed., (New York: Macmillan, 1956), p. 134.

7. The usefulness of each of the following studies is limited by one or more of these difficulties: Sophia M. Robison, *Can Delinquency Be Measured?* (New York: Columbia University Press, 1936); Edward E. Schwartz, "A Community Experiment in the Measurement of Juvenile Delinquency," *Yearbook of the National Probation Association* (New York: National Probation Association, 1945), pp. 157–81; Wayne R. LaFave, "The Police and Nonenforcement of the Law—Part II," *Wisconsin Law Review* (March 1962), 188–238; Nathan Goldman, *The Differential Selection of Juvenile Offenders for Court Appearance* (New York: National Council on Crime and Delinquency, 1963); George W. Mitchell, *The Youth Bureau: A Sociological Study* (Wayne State University, unpublished master's thesis, 1957); Jack Kinney, John Klem, and Samuel Myers, "Selective Factors Involved in Differential Treatment of Youthful Offenders at

A number of studies have avoided at least some of these pitfalls, but the findings reported do not provide substantial evidence to support the aforementioned assertions. Lemert and Rosberg, for example, found that Negroes and Mexican-Americans in Los Angeles are less likely to be placed on probation than are "whites" even when other variables are controlled.[8] Eaton and Polk, however, in a study of problems of measuring delinquency in Los Angeles County, found that males receive severer dispositions than females by the probation department but that racial differences were unimportant.[9] Green's study of the sentencing of adults by the courts in Philadelphia concluded that males and Negroes are dealt with more severely but that differences in type of offense as well as in criminal record rather than sex and ethnicity account for these variations in sentences.[10] Shannon's study of the handling of juvenile offenders by the police in Madison, Wis., provides indirect evidence that the socio-economic status of the offender does not seem a determinant of dispositions accorded.[11] Piliavin and Briar observed encounters between police and juveniles and found that Negroes are dealt with more severely than whites but that this was primarily a function of the demeanor exhibited by the offenders rather than racial differences per se.[12]

In a study of the screening of juvenile offenders by the police, this writer found that sex, ethnicity, and socio-economic status were related with statistical significance to the type of disposition accorded. When control variables were introduced, however, these relationships became negligible.[13] Therefore, serious questions arise concerning the validity of the common assertions that control agencies base decisions upon the offender's sex, ethnicity, or socio-economic status. Further research should investigate intensively and systematically the possible relationships be-

---

the Juvenile Court of Cook County" (University of Chicago, unpublished master's thesis, 1951); Sidney Axelrad, "Negro and White Male Institutionalized Delinquents," *American Journal of Sociology* (May 1952), pp. 569–574: William M. Kephart, *Racial Factors and Urban Law Enforcement* (Philadelphia: University of Pennsylvania Press, 1957); Otto Pollak, *The Criminality of Women* (Philadelphia: University of Pennsylvania Press, 1950), pp. 1–7. Not all of these studies provide support for the assertions in question.

8. Edwin M. Lemert and Judy Rosberg, "The Administration of Justice to Minority Groups in Los Angeles County," *University of California Publications in Culture and Society*, II (1948), 1–28.

9. Joseph W. Eaton and Kenneth Polk, *Measuring Delinquency* (Pittsburgh: University of Pittsburgh Press, 1961).

10. Edward Green, *Judicial Attitudes in Sentencing* (New York: St. Martin's Press, 1961).

11. Lyle W. Shannon, "Types and Patterns of Delinquency Referral in a Middle-Sized City," *British Journal of Criminology*, July 1963, pp. 24–36.

12. Irving Piliavin and Scott Briar, "Police Encounters with Juveniles," *American Journal of Sociology*, September 1964, pp. 206–214.

13. Robert M. Terry, *Criteria Utilized by the Police in the Screening of Juvenile Offender* (University of Wisconsin, unpublished master's thesis, 1962).

tween these variables and the severity of sanctions accorded by control
agencies.

The Problem

This study focused on the screening of juvenile offenders by three control
agencies. Juveniles whose behavior has been identified and defined as
delinquent may become involved subsequently in the legal-judicial process, including the police, the probation department, and the juvenile
court. At each stage, decisions are made with respect to possible dispositions or sanctions of varying severity. Thus, it is possible to test hypotheses
at each stage of the screening process. For the purposes of this research,
it was assumed that the commonly held notions were accurate, and the
following hypotheses were proposed:

Hypothesis 1: The severity of sanctions accorded juvenile offenders
is positively related to the "maleness" of the offender.[14]

Hypothesis 2: The severity of sanctions is positively related to the
offender's minority status. The ethnic groupings used as measures of the
degree of minority status are (1) Anglos, (2) Mexican-Americans, (3)
Negroes.[15]

Hypothesis 3: The severity of sanctions is negatively related to the
offender's socio-economic status. Socio-economic status, as measured
by the use of the Minnesota Scale for Paternal Occupations, includes (1)
lower status, (2) middle status, (3) upper status.[16]

Police actions are ranked as follows with respect to severity: (1) release, (2) referral to a social or welfare agency, (3) referral to the county
probation department, (4) referral to the State Department of Public
Welfare. Release is the least serious type of disposition since it indicates
there will be no further action taken. by social-control agencies. Referral
to a social or welfare agency results in counseling in a "nonauthoritarian"
setting. Referral to the county probation department calls for adjudication of the offender as a delinquent by the juvenile court or, minimally,

14. This was deemed proper in view of the fact that, in the existing criminological
literature, males are regarded as being much more severely sanctioned.

15. Minority status may be viewed as an indicator of social distance between offenders
and agents of social control. "Anglos" include all Caucasians with the exception of
Mexican-Americans, whose status is regarded as higher than that of Negroes for two
reasons: (1) Several of them are members of the community's social-control agencies
while no Negroes are so employed. (2) There is less overt discrimination in the community under study against Mexican-Americans than against Negroes. During the
period under study, Negroes were not permitted to stay in the community's major
hotels or eat in a number of establishments and were more segregated in housing.

16. Lower status consists of Classes V, VI, and VII of the Minnesota Scale, middle
status consists of Classes III and IV, and upper status consists of Classes I and II.
see "The Minnesota Scale for Paternal Occupations" (Minneapolis: University of Minnesota Institute of Child Welfare, n.d.).

for action to be taken by the probation department to prevent further misbehavior. Finally, referrals to the State Department of Public Welfare represent direct calls for the institutionalization of the offender by the police.

Probation department action consists of four ranks: (1) release, (2) placement under informal supervision, (3) referral to the juvenile court, (4) waiver to the criminal court. Release is the least severe disposition made by the probation department. Somewhat more severe is placement under informal supervision (probation), in which the offender must comply with certain rules and regulations under the threat of possible further legal action. Referral to the juvenile court involves the filing of a petition and a formal court hearing. This makes commitment to an institution a distinct possibility and minimally involves adjudication of the offender as a delinquent. Finally, waiver to criminal court is a probation-department recommendation whereby the judge usually signs the waiver on the basis of information provided by the probation department. The offender whose offense is waived to the criminal court is held responsible for his actions and is subject to the same punitive sanctions as an adult.

Although a variety of dispositions are available to the juvenile court, the judge in the community in which this research was undertaken utilized only two kinds: (1) placement under formal supervision and (2) institutionalization. Institutionalization is obviously more severe than placement under formal supervision in that it removes the offender from his home and subjects him to the regimentation and discipline of a correctional institution.

Data

The study was made in a heavily industrialized Midwest community of slightly less than 100,000. Basic data included information obtained from records on file in the police Juvenile Bureau, with respect to the nature of the offense; the offender's prior record; personal, behavioral, and situational characteristics; and disposition by the police. Probation-department records were utilized to ascertain the dispositions accorded by both the probation department and the juvenile court. Since records of control agencies generally do not indicate the socio-economic status of an offender, parents' occupations were obtained from city directories for this purpose.

To include a sufficient number of offenders from the juvenile court stage it was necessary to utilize a universe rather than a sample of offenses; thus, all offenses during 1958-1962 on file in the Juvenile Bureau were included in the research. Several kinds of offenses and offenders were eliminated, including children under six years of age, nonresidents of the community, traffic offenses (subject to different handling), and "information" cases (juveniles who were victims of an offense or had information about offenses or offenders but were not otherwise involved). The resulting "universe" included 9,023 juvenile offenses which had resulted in contact with the police. Of these, 775 were referred to the probation department; only 246 appeared in the juvenile court.

The principal statistical measure used was Kendall's rank order correlation coefficient, tau. This measure seems particularly appropriate since the variables can be viewed meaningfully as ordinal and the measure can be generalized to a partial rank order correlation coefficient ($tau_{xy.z}$), thus permitting the introduction of control variables where warranted. Since this study did not utilize a sample, in the strictest sense, assessing the significance of relationships became important. Previous research indicated that relationships in this area are frequently of relatively small magnitude. This may be attributed, in part, to the fact that a large number of independent variables may be important. In view of this, hypotheses in which $+.10 > tau > -.10$ were rejected except when the matrix indicated that the direction of the relationship was consistent for each category of the independent variable despite the introduction of control variables.[17]

Adequacy of the Data

The adequacy of police records is crucial to this analysis since citation in these records is prerequisite to appearance at any of the three stages of the legal-judicial process. Recording of juvenile offenses by the police had to be such that unforeseen biases would not enter the data. Fortunately, offenses which result in police contact with juveniles appear to be recorded without bias.

First, when anyone other than the police is the complainant, the offense automatically becomes a part of the record; officers at the complaint desk attach numbers to every complaint received and fill out standard forms recording information on the nature of the offense, its location, the time reported, etc. Of the 9,023 offenses, 83.9 per cent were reported by persons other than the police, indicating that a sizable proportion had been recorded without bias.

The second grouping of offenses consists of those in which the police themselves are the complainant. In late 1957, the chief of police instituted

17. Although only significant effects will be reported, the following variables were used as controls in each of the tests of hypotheses: age of offender, seriousness of offense, number of previous offenses committed, complainant, delinquency rate of area of residence, degree of commercial or industrial development of the area in which the offense occurred, degree of involvement with adult offenders, degree of involvement with offenders of the opposite sex, and the number of individuals involved in the commission of the offense.

a "street-level" policy in which officers were encouraged to dispose of minor offenses by releasing the juveniles to their parents without undue recourse to the Juvenile Bureau; however, they were ordered to record and report *all* delinquent offenses to the Juvenile Bureau together with the usually recorded information. Juveniles were told the Juvenile Bureau would contact them and their parents if investigation or action was to be carried further. The result was an increase in the number of delinquent offenses on file in the police records in 1958, which can be attributed to the greater reporting and recording of minor offenses. While we have no way of proving that this kind of police contact is inclusive, it appears to be relatively accurate and adequate.

Results

Each hypothesis was tested three times since we were concerned with three successive and separate stages of the legal-judicial process.

SEX

Table 4.1 shows the relationships found to exist between the offender's "maleness" and the severity of the disposition. In the case of the police, the relationship, although relatively small (tau $= -.05$), was in the direc-

Table 4.1. Sex and the severity of disposition

	Female	Male
Police Disposition	(N = 1,611)	(N = 7,411)
Released	84.9%	89.7%
Referred to Social or Welfare Agency	7.4%	0.8%
Referred to County Probation Dept.	7.4%	8.8%
Referred to State Dept. of Public Welfare	0.3%	0.7%
Total	100.0%	100.0%
tau $= -.05$		
	Female	Male
Probation Disposition	(N = 119)	(N = 656)
Released	27.7%	30.0%
Informal Supervision	46.2%	28.6%
Referred to Juvenile Court	25.3%	32.9%
Waived to Criminal Court	0.8%	8.5%
Total	100.0%	100.0%
tau $= .07$		
	Female	Male
Juvenile Court Disposition	(N = 30)	(N = 216)
Formal Supervision	23.3%	40.3%
Institutionalized	76.7%	59.7%
Total	100.0%	100.0%
tau $= -.11$		

tion opposite to that which had been hypothesized. The reason appears to be that girls, much more than boys, are likely to be referred to social and welfare agencies. If we account for the disproportionate number of female referrals to social and welfare agencies, most of the relationship may be explained in terms other than sex. The data provide a plausible explanation. While girls account for only 17.9 per cent of all offenses, they represent nearly half of the sex offenses and incorrigibility cases. Nearly 70 per cent of all referrals to social and welfare agencies are in this category. Thus, the apparently greater severity in dealing with girls stems from their disproportionate commission of offenses which result in referral to social and welfare agencies. While the hypothesis must be rejected, an alternate hypothesis, suggesting a negative relationship between the severity of police action and the "maleness" of the offender, is not warranted.

Table 4.1 indicates a positive relationship (tau = .07) between the "maleness" of the offender and the severity of probation department disposition. Again, the relationship is relatively small. When the seriousness of the offense committed and the number of previous offenses committed are controlled, the existing relationship is reduced in magnitude ($tau_{xy.z}$ = .04 and .04, respectively). The relationship may be largely accounted for in terms of the influence of these two variables. First, while girls are heavily over-represented among offenses for which informal supervision is most likely to be accorded (sex offenses and incorrigibility), boys are heavily over-represented among offenses for which referral to the juvenile court is most likely (burglary, auto theft, homicide, and robbery) and among those offenses which result disproportionately in waiver to criminal court (disorderly conduct, liquor offenses, assault, violent property damage, homicide, and robbery).

In addition, boys are heavily over-represented among offenders who have committed seven or more previous offenses, which further explains the disproportionate waiver of boys to the criminal court. Girls are heavily over-represented among offenders who have committed from one to four previous offenses. This type of record is most likely to result in placement under informal supervision.

The seriousness of the offense and the number of previous offenses appear to account for most of the relationship between the "maleness" of the offender and the severity of the probation department disposition. In view of this, the hypothesis was rejected.

Finally, a *negative* relationship of significant magnitude was found between the "maleness" of the offender and the severity of juvenile court dispositions (tau = −.11), indicating that females are more likely to be institutionalized than males. When the degree of involvement with the opposite sex and with adult offenders was controlled, the existing relationship was reduced ($tau_{xy.z} = -.07$ and $-.08$, respectively), indicating that girls are more often cited for offenses involving the opposite sex and adults, both of which are more likely to result in institutionalization. When the number of previous offenses was controlled, however, the negative relationship between "maleness" and severity of juvenile-court disposition was enhanced ($tau_{xy.z} = -.18$), indicating that females are more severely sanctioned than males even though they tend to have less extensive records of prior delinquent behavior. These results led to the rejection of the hypothesis; an alternate was posited, maintaining that a negative relationship exists between the "maleness" of the offender and the severity of juvenile court sanctions.

The reasons why girls are more severely dealt with in the juvenile court (but not, apparently, at earlier stages in the process) can only be suggested. The appearance of a girl in juvenile court may be taken more seriously since it frequently indicates that she has failed to conform after previous measures have been taken or that the offense is serious enough to warrant adjudication as a delinquent; personal and situational characteristics justify the severe action the court may take.[18] Such factors perhaps are considered much more seriously in the case of girls since they may be less compatible with the female role.

DEGREE OF MINORITY STATUS

Table 4.2 presents the relationships that exist between the degree of the offender's minority status and the severity of disposition. A positive relationship was found to exist between the offender's minority status and police sanctions, although it was very small (tau = .02). The most salient difference was the over-representation of Mexican-Americans among referrals to the county probation department. A review of the data indicates that this may result from their over-representation in the commission of the offenses for which referrals to the county probation department are most common. Although Mexican-Americans commit only 7.1 per cent of all offenses, they commit 12.5 per cent of the homicide and robbery, 7.5 per cent of the auto theft, 11.6 per cent of the burglary, and 9.0 per cent of the assault and violent property damage offenses. The relationship between degree of minority status and severity of police disposition is negligible when the seriousness of the offense is held constant ($tau_{xy.z} = .00$). These results led to the rejection of the hypothesis at this level.

The severity of dispositions of offenders of varying minority status by the probation department also indicates a negligible relationship (tau = .01). Only the percentage waived to the criminal court increased as the degree of minority status increased and the differences were very small.

18. See Terry, op. cit., pp. 242–255.

Table 4.2. Degree of minority status and the severity of disposition

Police Disposition	Anglo (N = 7,282)	Mexican-American (N = 637)	Negro (N = 1,104)
Released	89.1%	84.0%	89.5%
Referred to Social or Welfare Agency	2.1%	1.4%	1.7%
Referred to County Probation Dept.	8.2%	14.4%	7.7%
Referred to State Dept. of Public Welfare	0.6%	0.2%	1.1%
Total	100.0%	100.0%	100.0%

tau = .02

Probation Disposition	Anglo (N = 598)	Mexican-American (N = 92)	Negro (N = 85)
Released	28.7%	37.0%	28.2%
Informal Supervision	32.9%	26.0%	25.9%
Referred to Juvenile Court	31.9%	28.3%	34.1%
Waived to Criminal Court	6.5%	8.7%	11.8%
Total	100.0%	100.0%	100.0%

tau = .01

Juvenile Court Disposition	Anglo (N = 191)	Mexican-American (N = 26)	Negro (N = 29)
Formal Supervision	39.3%	38.5%	31.0%
Institutionalized	60.7%	61.5%	69.0%
Total	100.0%	100.0%	100.0%

tau = .04

The hypothesis as it applies to the probation department stage of the screening process was rejected.

A positive relationship was found to exist between the degree of minority status and the severity of juvenile court sanctions, although it was again of small magnitude (tau = .04). This relationship appears to be a function of the more severe dispositions accorded Negro offenders. A review of the data reveals, however, that Negroes are under-represented among offenders who have committed two or fewer previous offenses and are over-represented among offenders having more extensive prior records of delinquent behavior. When the number of previous offenses committed is controlled, the relationship in question is reduced (tau$_{xy.z}$ = .02). In view of this, the hypothesis at the juvenile court stage of the screening process was rejected.

SOCIO-ECONOMIC STATUS

A negative relationship was posited between the socio-economic status of the offender and the severity of disposition accorded (Table 4.3). At the police level, a negative relationship was found, although it was relatively small (tau $= -.04$). While the differences exist in the hypothesized direction, the similarities are perhaps even more noteworthy. When the seriousness of the offense and the number of previous offenses were controlled, the relationship is slightly reduced (tau$_{xy.z} = -.03$), reflecting the slight tendency for lower-status juveniles to commit the more serious types of offenses as well as to have more extensive prior records of delinquent behavior. Therefore, it is doubtful that the police utilize socio-economic status as a criterion in referral. The hypothesis was rejected at this level.

The severity of the probation-department disposition is also related negatively to the offender's socio-economic status, although the magnitude of the relationship was even less than at the police level (tau $= -.02$). Variations appear to result from the prior records of the offenders. Middle- and, especially, upper-status offenders are more likely than lower-status offenders to have committed only one or two previous offenses or none at all. Lower-status offenders are much more likely to have committed seven or more previous offenses. When the number of previous offenses is controlled, the relationship between socio-economic status and severity of probation department disposition is negligible (tau$_{xy.z} = .00$). In view of this evidence, the hypothesis was rejected.

A negative relationship was found to exist between socio-economic

Table 4.3. Socio-economic status and the severity of disposition

	Lower (N = 6,415)	Middle (N = 1,861)	Upper (N = 737)
Police Disposition			
Released	88.1%	90.0%	92.4%
Referred to Social or Welfare Agency	2.2%	1.9%	0.8%
Referred to County Probation Dept.	9.1%	7.5%	6.7%
Referred to State Dept. of Public Welfare	0.6%	0.6%	0.1%
Total	100.0%	100.0%	100.0%
tau $= -.04$			
	Lower (N = 588)	Middle (N = 138)	Upper (N = 49)
Probation Disposition			
Released	29.9%	30.4%	24.5%
Informal Supervision	30.1%	32.6%	40.8%
Referred to Juvenile Court	31.8%	31.9%	30.6%
Waived to Criminal Court	8.2%	5.1%	4.1%
Total	100.0%	100.0%	100.0%
tau $= -.02$			
	Lower (N = 187)	Middle (N = 44)	Upper (N = 15)
Juvenile Court Disposition			
Formal Supervision	35.8%	43.2%	53.3%
Institutionalized	64.2%	56.8%	46.7%
Total	100.0%	100.0%	100.0%
tau $= -.09$			

status and severity of juvenile court dispositions (tau $= -.09$), consistently in the expected direction. However, when the number of previous offenses was controlled, the relationship was drastically reduced (tau$_{xy.z} =$ $-.02$), indicating that lower-status offenders are more likely to have committed a greater number of previous offenses than middle- and upper-status offenders. The large reduction in the magnitude of the relationship would seem to indicate that lower-status offenders are accorded more severe dispositions not because they are lower-status individuals, but because of differences in prior records of delinquent behavior. (The prior record of delinquent behavior appears to be the most significant criterion utilized by the juvenile court in the screening of offenders.) Therefore, the hypothesis was rejected at this level.

Conclusion

The evidence indicates that the severity of disposition is not a function of the degree of minority status of the juvenile offender or his socio-economic status. The sex of the offender was found to be directly relevant at only one of the three stages of the screening process and, in that instance, the relationship was in a direction opposite to that expected. These findings clearly contradict the assertions commonly made by students of criminal and delinquent behavior.

Obviously, generalization of this research must be regarded with caution. The findings are limited in that we have studied the disposition of offenders in a single community, utilized rather crude measures of socio-economic status, have not controlled for variations in the population which appears in the police records in the first place, and have concerned ourselves with decision-making by a limited number of control agents. However, the findings certainly warrant further research.

While males, Mexican-Americans, Negroes, and lower-status offenders are over-represented in correctional institutions, probation departments, courts, and police records, this over-representation does not, on the basis of the evidence examined in this study, appear to be a direct result of these characteristics. The over-representation of these individuals is not the result of discrimination by control agencies.

Discussion

If the findings can be generalized beyond the community studied, we may well inquire why students of crime and delinquency have assumed the opposite of what has been found and have devoted little attention to supporting their assertions empirically. A number of explanations are possible.

First, many may tend to confuse the administration of legal processes with bias in the statutes themselves. For example, some laws are applicable only to specific individuals. It is, by definition, virtually impossible for middle- and upper-status individuals to commit certain offenses, such as vagrancy. Those committing these offenses may be banished from the community or jailed, but this does not prove discrimination unless it can be demonstrated that middle- and upper-status offenders committing the same offenses are handled differently by control agents.

Second, students of crime and delinquency may be overeager to generalize on the basis of nonsystematic information presented by the news media or intuition as to what is involved in legal proceedings. To this writer's knowledge, no systematic attempts have been made to discover racial variations in the disposition of Negro and white offenders in the South by social-control agencies, although most behavioral scientists have no doubt such discriminatory treatment exists.[19]

Students of crime and delinquency also appear overeager to generalize from what may be a regionally limited phenomenon to the entire legal system. That discriminatory disposition of Negroes may exist in the South does not mean that control agents throughout the nation engage in such discrimination.

In addition, proof of bias in the handling of certain kinds of deviance does not necessarily support inferences about other kinds. For example, some evidence supports the notion that the diagnosis and treatment of mental disorders is class-related. Middle- and upper-status individuals are more likely to be diagnosed as neurotic while lower-status individuals are more likely to be diagnosed as psychotic. Lower-status individuals are more likely to receive organic types of therapy while the "talking therapies" tend to be reserved for middle- and upper-status individuals.[20] If these findings are accurate, it remains to be demonstrated whether this also applies to the practices of police, probation officers, and judges. An intriguing problem for further research consists of the delineation of variations in actions taken by different control agents.

Finally, the literature on crime and delinquency may reflect what Becker has called "unconventional sentimentality." The unconventional sentimentalist assumes "that the underdog is always right and those in authority always wrong." [21] Thus, sociologists may tend to champion the causes of males, minority groups, and lower-status individuals without consider-

---

19. A recent example of nonscientific data dealing with this issue is *Mississippi Black Paper* (New York: Random House, 1965).

20. See, e.g., August B. Hollingshead and Frederick C. Redlich, *Social Class and Mental Illness* (New York: Wiley, 1958); and Jerome K. Meyers and Leslie Schaffer, "Social Stratification and Psychiatric Practice: A Study of an Outpatient Clinic," *American Sociological Review*, June 1954, pp. 307–310.

21. Becker, *op. cit.*, p. 5.

ing (much less systematically studying) the premises on which they are operating.

Summary

This research, contradicting three time-honored hypotheses in the literature on crime and delinquency, has found that the severity of disposition accorded juvenile offenders is not a function of the offender's socio-economic status or minority status and that females are more severely sanctioned by the juvenile court although sex differences are unimportant at the police and probation department levels. Further research is needed to explicate the functioning of control agencies; meanwhile, sociologists must exercise caution in assessing the functioning of these agencies.

5. Police Encounters with Juveniles

IRVING PILIAVIN and SCOTT BRIAR

As THE first of a series of decisions made in the channeling of youthful offenders through the agencies concerned with juvenile justice and corrections, the disposition decisions made by police officers have potentially profound consequences for apprehended juveniles. Thus arrest, the most severe of the dispositions available to police, may not only lead to confinement of the suspected offender but also bring him loss of social status, restriction of educational and employment opportunities, and future harassment by law-enforcement personnel.[1] According to some criminolo-

Reprinted from *The American Journal of Sociology,* September 1964, pp. 206–214, by permission of *The American Journal of Sociology* and the authors. Copyright 1964 by The University of Chicago Press.

1. Richard D. Schwartz and Jerome H. Skolnick, "Two Studies of Legal Stigma," *Social Problems,* X (April 1962), 133–142; Sol Rubin, *Crime and Juvenile Delinquency* (New York: Oceana Publications, 1958); B. F. McSally, "Finding Jobs for Released Offenders," *Federal Probation,* XXIV (June 1960), 12–17; Harold D. Lasswell and Richard C. Donnelly, "The Continuing Debate over Responsibility: An Introduction to Isolating the Condemnation Sanction," *Yale Law Journal,* LXVIII (April 1959), 869–899.

gists, the stigmatization resulting from police apprehension, arrest, and detention actually reinforces deviant behavior.[2] Other authorities have suggested, in fact, that this stigmatization serves as the catalytic agent initiating delinquent careers.[3] Despite their presumed significance, however, little empirical analysis has been reported regarding the factors influencing, or consequences resulting from, police actions with juvenile offenders. Furthermore, while some studies of police encounters with adult offenders have been reported, the extent to which the findings of these investigations pertain to law-enforcement practices with youthful offenders is not known.[4]

The above considerations have led the writers to undertake a longitudinal study of the conditions influencing, and consequences flowing from, police actions with juveniles. In the present paper findings will be presented indicating the influence of certain factors on police actions. Research data consist primarily of notes and records based on nine months' observation of all juvenile officers in one police department.[5] The officers were observed in the course of their regular tours of duty.[6] While these data do not lend themselves to quantitative assessments of reliability and validity, the candor shown by the officers in their interviews with the investigators and their use of officially frowned-upon practices while under observation provide some assurance that the materials presented below accurately reflect the typical operations and attitudes of the law-enforcement personnel studied.

The setting for the research, a metropolitan police department serving an industrial city with approximately 450,000 inhabitants, was noted within the community it served and among law-enforcement officials elsewhere for the honesty and superior quality of its personnel. Incidents

2. Richard A. Cloward and Lloyd E. Ohlin, *Delinquency and Opportunity* (Glencoe, Ill.: Free Press, 1960), pp. 124–130.

3. Frank Tannenbaum, *Crime and the Community* (New York: Columbia University Press, 1936), pp. 17–20; Howard S. Becker, *Outsiders: Studies in the Sociology of Deviance* (New York: Free Press, 1963), chaps. i and ii.

4. For a detailed accounting of police discretionary practices, see Joseph Goldstein, "Police Discretion Not To Invoke the Criminal Process: Low Visibility Decisions in the Administration of Justice," *Yale Law Journal*, LXIX (1960), 543–594; Wayne R. LaFave, "The Police and Non-enforcement of the Law—Part I," *Wisconsin Law Review*, January 1962, pp. 104–137; S. H. Kadish, "Legal Norms and Discretion in the Police and Sentencing Processes," *Harvard Law Review*, LXXV (March 1962), 904–931.

5. Approximately thirty officers were assigned to the Juvenile Bureau in the department studied. While we had an opportunity to observe all officers in the Bureau during the study, our observations were concentrated on those who had been working in the Bureau for one or two years at least. Although two of the officers in the Juvenile Bureau were Negro, we observed these officers on only a few occasions.

6. Although observations were not confined to specific days or work shifts, more observations were made during evenings and weekends because police activity was greatest during these periods.

involving criminal activity or brutality by members of the department had been extremely rare during the ten years preceding this study; personnel standards were comparatively high; and an extensive training program was provided to both new and experienced personnel. Juvenile Bureau members, the primary subjects of this investigation, differed somewhat from other members of the department in that they were responsible for delinquency prevention as well as law enforcement, that is, juvenile officers were expected to be knowledgeable about conditions leading to crime and delinquency and to be able to work with community agencies serving known or potential juvenile offenders. Accordingly, in the assignment of personnel to the Juvenile Bureau, consideration was given not only to an officer's devotion to and reliability in law enforcement but also to his commitment to delinquency prevention. Assignment to the Bureau was of advantage to policemen seeking promotions. Consequently, many officers requested transfer to this unit, and its personnel comprised a highly select group of officers.

In the field, juvenile officers operated essentially as patrol officers. They cruised assigned beats and, although concerned primarily with juvenile offenders, frequently had occasion to apprehend and arrest adults. Confrontations between the officers and juveniles occurred in one of the following three ways, in order of increasing frequency: (1) encounters resulting from officers' spotting officially "wanted" youths; (2) encounters taking place at or near the scene of offenses reported to police headquarters; and (3) encounters occurring as the result of officers' directly observing youths either committing offenses or in "suspicious circumstances." However, the probability that a confrontation would take place between officer and juvenile, or that a particular disposition of an identified offender would be made, was only in part determined by the knowledge that an offense had occurred or that a particular juvenile had committed an offense. The bases for and utilization of non-offenses related criteria by police in accosting and disposing of juveniles are the focuses of the following discussion.

Sanctions for Discretion

In each encounter with juveniles, with the minor exception of officially "wanted" youths,[7] a central task confronting the officer was to decide what official action to take against the boys involved. In making these

---

7. "Wanted" juveniles usually were placed under arrest or in protective custody, a practice which in effect relieved officers of the responsibility for deciding what to do with these youths.

disposition decisions, officers could select any one of five discrete alternatives:

1. outright release
2. release and submission of a "field interrogation report" briefly describing the circumstances initiating the police-juvenile confrontation
3. "official reprimand" and release to parents or guardian
4. citation to juvenile court
5. arrest and confinement in juvenile hall.

Dispositions 3, 4, and 5 differed from the others in two basic respects. First, with rare exceptions, when an officer chose to reprimand, cite, or arrest a boy, he took the youth to the police station. Second, the reprimanded, cited, or arrested boy acquired an official police "record," that is, his name was officially recorded in Bureau files as a juvenile violator.

Analysis of the distribution of police disposition decisions about juveniles revealed that in virtually every category of offense the full range of official disposition alternatives available to officers was employed. This wide range of discretion resulted primarily from two conditions. First, it reflected the reluctance of officers to expose certain youths to the stigmatization presumed to be associated with official police action. Few juvenile officers believed that correctional agencies serving the community could effectively help delinquents. For some officers this attitude reflected a lack of confidence in rehabilitation techniques; for others, a belief that high case loads and lack of professional training among correctional workers vitiated their efforts at treatment. All officers were agreed, however, that juvenile justice and correctional processes were essentially concerned with apprehension and punishment rather than treatment. Furthermore, all officers believed that some aspects of these processes (e.g., judicial definition of youths as delinquents and removal of delinquents from the community), as well as some of the possible consequences of these processes (e.g., intimate institutional contact with "hard-core" delinquents, as well as parental, school, and conventional peer disapproval or rejection), could reinforce what previously might have been only a tentative proclivity toward delinquent values and behavior. Consequently, when officers found reason to doubt that a youth being confronted was highly committed toward deviance, they were inclined to treat him with leniency.

Second, and more important, the practice of discretion was sanctioned by police-department policy. Training manuals and departmental bulletins stressed that the disposition of each juvenile offender was not to be based solely on the type of infraction he committed. Thus, while it was departmental policy to "arrest and confine all juveniles who have committed a felony or misdemeanor involving theft, sex offense, battery, possession of dangerous weapons, prowling, peeping, intoxication, incorrigibility, and disturbance of the peace," it was acknowledged that "such considerations as age, attitude and prior criminal record might indicate that a different disposition would be more appropriate." [8] The official justification for discretion in processing juvenile offenders, based on the preventive aims of the Juvenile Bureau, was that each juvenile violator should be dealt with solely on the basis of what was best for him.[9] Unofficially, administrative legitimation of discretion was further justified on the grounds that strict enforcement practices would overcrowd court calendars and detention facilities, as well as dramatically increase juvenile crime rates—consequences to be avoided because they would expose the police department to community criticism.[10]

In practice, the official policy justifying use of discretion served as a demand that discretion be exercised. As such, it posed three problems for juvenile officers. First, it represented a departure from the traditional police practice with which the juvenile officers themselves were identified, in the sense that they were expected to justify their juvenile disposition decisions not simply by evidence proving a youth had committed a crime —grounds on which police were officially expected to base their dispositions of non-juvenile offenders [11]—but in the *character* of the youth. Second, in disposing of juvenile offenders, officers were expected, in effect, to make judicial rather than ministerial decisions.[12] Third, the shift from the offense to the offender as the basis for determining the appropriate disposition substantially increased the uncertainty and ambiguity for officers in the situation of apprehension because no explicit rules existed for determining which disposition different types of youths should receive. Despite these problems, officers were constrained to base disposition decisions on the character of the apprehended youth, not only because they wanted to be fair, but because persistent failure to do so could result in judicial criticism, departmental censure, and, they believed, loss of authority with juveniles.[13]

8. Quoted from a training manual issued by the police department studied in this research.

9. Presumably this also implied that police action with juveniles was to be determined partly by the offenders' need for correctional services.

10. This was reported by beat officers as well as supervisory and administrative personnel of the juvenile bureau.

11. In actual practice, of course, disposition decisions regarding adult offenders also were influenced by many factors extraneous to the offense per se.

12. For example, in dealing with adult violators, officers had no disposition alternative comparable to the reprimand-and-release category, a disposition which contained elements of punishment but did not involve mediation by the court.

13. The concern of officers over possible loss of authority stemmed from their belief that court failure to support arrests by appropriate action would cause policemen to "lose face" in the eyes of juveniles.

Disposition Criteria

Assessing the character of apprehended offenders posed relatively few difficulties for officers in the case of youths who had committed serious crimes such as robbery, homicide, aggravated assault, grand theft, auto theft, rape, and arson. Officials generally regarded these juveniles as confirmed delinquents simply by virtue of their involvement in offenses of this magnitude.[14] However, the infraction committed did not always suffice to determine the appropriate disposition for some serious offenders;[15] and, in the case of minor offenders, who comprised over 90 per cent of the youths against whom police took action, the violation per se generally played an insignificant role in the choice of disposition. While a number of minor offenders were seen as serious delinquents deserving arrest, many others were perceived either as "good" boys whose offenses were atypical of their customary behavior, as pawns of undesirable associates or, in any case, as boys for whom arrest was regarded as an unwarranted and possibly harmful punishment. Thus, for nearly all minor violators and for some serious delinquents, the assessment of character—the distinction between serious delinquents, "good" boys, misguided youths, and so on—and the dispositions which followed from these assessments were based on youths' personal characteristics and not their offenses.

Despite this dependence of disposition decisions on the personal characteristics of these youths, however, police officers actually had access only to very limited information about boys at the time they had to decide what to do with them. In the field, officers typically had no data concerning the past offense records, school performance, family situation, or personal adjustment of apprehended youths.[16] Furthermore, files at police headquarters provided data only about each boy's prior offense record. Thus both the decision made in the field—whether or not to bring the boy in—and the decision made at the station—which disposition to invoke— were based largely on cues which emerged from the interaction between the officer and the youth, cues from which the officer inferred the youth's

14. It is also likely that the possibility of negative publicity resulting from the failure to arrest such violators–particularly if they became involved in further serious crime –brought about strong administrative pressure for their arrest.

15. For example, in the year preceding this research, over 30 per cent of the juveniles involved in burglaries and 12 per cent of the juveniles committing auto theft received dispositions other than arrest.

16. On occasion, officers apprehended youths whom they personally knew to be prior offenders. This did not occur frequently, however, for several reasons. First, approximately 75 per cent of apprehended youths had no prior official records; second, officers periodically exchanged patrol areas, thus limiting their exposure to, and knowledge about, these areas; and third, patrolmen seldom spent more than three or four years in the juvenile division.

character. These cues included the youth's group affiliations, age, race, grooming, dress, and demeanor. Older juveniles, members of known delinquent gangs, Negroes, youths with well-oiled hair, black jackets, and soiled denims or jeans (the presumed uniform of "tough" boys), and boys who in their interactions with officers did not manifest what were considered to be appropriate signs of respect tended to receive the more severe dispositions.

Table 5.1 Severity of police disposition by youth's demeanor

Severity of Police Disposition	Youth's Demeanor		Total
	Co-operative	Unco-operative	
Arrest (most severe)	2	14	16
Citation or official reprimand	4	5	9
Informal reprimand	15	1	16
Admonish and release (least severe)	24	1	25
Total	45	21	66

Other than prior record, the most important of the above cues was a youth's *demeanor*. In the opinion of juvenile patrolmen themselves the demeanor of apprehended juveniles was a major determinant of their decisions for 50–60 per cent of the juvenile cases they processed.[17] A less subjective indication of the association between a youth's demeanor and police disposition is provided by Table 5.1, which presents the police dispositions for sixty-six youths whose encounters with police were observed in the course of this study.[18] For purposes of this analysis, each youth's demeanor in the encounter was classified as either co-operative or unco-operative.[19] The results clearly reveal a marked association between youth demeanor and the severity of police dispositions.

17. While reliable subgroup estimates were impossible to obtain through observation because of the relatively small number of incidents observed, the importance of demeanor in disposition decisions appeared to be much less significant with known prior offenders.
18. Systematic data were collected on police encounters with seventy-six juveniles. In ten of these encounters the police concluded that their suspicions were groundless, and consequently the juveniles involved were exonerated; these ten cases were eliminated from this analysis of demeanor. (The total number of encounters observed was considerably more than seventy-six, but systematic data-collection procedures were not instituted until several months after observations began.)
19. The data used for the classification of demeanor were the written records of

The cues used by police to assess demeanor were fairly simple. Juveniles who were contrite about their infractions, respectful to officers, and fearful of the sanctions that might be employed against them tended to be viewed by patrolmen as basically law-abiding or at least "salvageable." For these youths it was usually assumed that informal or formal reprimand would suffice to guarantee their future conformity. In contrast, youthful offenders who were fractious, obdurate, or who appeared nonchalant in their encounters with patrolmen were likely to be viewed as "would-be tough guys" or "punks" who fully deserved the most severe sanctions: arrest. The following excerpts from observation notes illustrate the importance attached to demeanor by police in making disposition decisions.

1. The interrogation of "A" (an 18-year-old upper-lower-class white male accused of statutory rape) was assigned to a police sergeant with long experience on the force. As I sat in his office while we waited for the youth to arrive for questioning, the sergeant expressed his uncertainty as to what he should do with this young man. On the one hand, he could not ignore the fact that an offense had been committed; he had been informed, in fact, that the youth was prepared to confess to the offense. Nor could he overlook the continued pressure from the girl's father (an important political figure) for the police to take severe action against the youth. On the other hand, the sergeant had formed a low opinion of the girl's moral character, and he considered it unfair to charge "A" with statutory rape when the girl was a willing partner to the offense and might even have been the instigator of it. However, his sense of injustice concerning "A" was tempered by his image of the youth as a "punk," based, he explained, on information he had received that the youth belonged to a certain gang, the members of which were well known to, and disliked by, the police. Nevertheless, as we prepared to leave his office to interview "A," the sergeant was still in doubt as to what he should do with him.

As we walked down the corridor to the interrogation room, the sergeant was stopped by a reporter from the local newspaper. In an excited tone of voice, the reporter explained that his editor was pressing him to get further information about this case. The newspaper had printed some of the facts about the girl's disappearance, and as a consequence the girl's father was threatening suit against the paper for defamation of the girl's character. It would strengthen the newspaper's

observations made by the authors. The classifications were made by an independent judge not associated with this study. In classifying a youth's demeanor as co-operative or unco-operative, particular attention was paid to: (1) the youth's responses to police officers' questions and requests; (2) the respect and deference—or lack of these qualities —shown by the youth toward police officers; and (3) police officers' assessments of the youth's demeanor.

position, the reporter explained, if the police had information indicating that the girl's associates, particularly the youth the sergeant was about to interrogate, were persons of disreputable character. This stimulus seemed to resolve the sergeant's uncertainty. He told the reporter, "unofficially," that the youth was known to be an undesirable person, citing as evidence his membership in the delinquent gang. Furthermore, the sergeant added that he had evidence that this youth had been intimate with the girl over a period of many months. When the reporter asked if the police were planning to do anything to the youth, the sergeant answered that he intended to charge the youth with statutory rape.

In the interrogation, however, three points quickly emerged which profoundly affected the sergeant's judgment of the youth. First, the youth was polite and co-operative; he consistently addressed the officer as "sir," answered all questions quietly, and signed a statement implicating himself in numerous counts of statutory rape. Second, the youth's intentions toward the girl appeared to have been honorable; for example, he said that he wanted to marry her eventually. Third, the youth was not in fact a member of the gang in question. The sergeant's attitude became increasingly sympathetic, and after we left the interrogation room he announced his intention to "get 'A' off the hook," meaning that he wanted to have the charges against "A" reduced or, if possible, dropped.

2. Officers "X" and "Y" brought into the police station a seventeen-year-old white boy who, along with two older companions, had been found in a home having sex relations with a fifteen-year-old girl. The boy responded to police officers' queries slowly and with obvious disregard. It was apparent that his lack of deference toward the officers and his failure to evidence concern about his situation were irritating his questioners. Finally, one of the officers turned to me and, obviously angry, commented that in his view the boy was simply a "stud" interested only in sex, eating, and sleeping. The policemen conjectured that the boy "probably already had knocked up half a dozen girls." The boy ignored these remarks, except for an occasional impassive stare at the patrolmen. Turning to the boy, the officer remarked, "What the hell am I going to do with you?" And again the boy simply returned the officer's gaze. The latter then said, "Well, I guess we'll just have to put you away for a while." An arrest report was then made out and the boy was taken to Juvenile Hall.

Although anger and disgust frequently characterized officers' attitudes toward recalcitrant and impassive juvenile offenders, their manner while processing these youths was typically routine, restrained, and without rancor. While the officers' restraint may have been due in part to their desire to avoid accusation and censure, it also seemed to reflect their inurement to a frequent experience. By and large, only their occasional "needling" or insulting of a boy gave any hint of the underlying resentment and dislike they felt toward many of these youths.[20]

Prejudice in Apprehension and Disposition Decisions

Compared to other youths, Negroes and boys whose appearance matched the delinquent stereotype were more frequently stopped and interrogated by patrolmen—often even in the absence of evidence that an offense had been committed [21]—and usually were given more severe dispositions for the same violations. Our data suggest, however, that these selective apprehension and disposition practices resulted not only from the intrusion of long-held prejudices of individual police officers but also from certain job-related experiences of law-enforcement personnel. First, the tendency for police to give more severe dispositions to Negroes and to youths whose appearance corresponded to that which police associated with delinquents partly reflected the fact, observed in this study, that these youths also were much more likely than were other types of boys to exhibit the sort of recalcitrant demeanor which police construed as a sign of the confirmed delinquent. Further, officers assumed, partly on the basis of departmental statistics, that Negroes and juveniles who "look tough" (e.g., who wear chinos, leather jackets, boots, etc.) commit crimes more frequently than do other types of youths.[22] In this sense, the police justified their selective treatment of these youths along epidemiological lines: that is, they were concentrating their attention on those youths whom they believed were most likely to commit delinquent acts. In the words of one highly placed official in the department:

20. Officers' animosity toward recalcitrant or aloof offenders appeared to stem from two sources: moral indignation that these juveniles were self-righteous and indifferent about their transgressions, and resentment that these youths failed to accord police the respect they believed they deserved. Since the patrolmen perceived themselves as honestly and impartially performing a vital community function warranting respect and deference from the community at large, they attributed the lack of respect shown them by these juveniles to the latters' immorality.

21. The clearest evidence for this assertion is provided by the overrepresentation of Negroes among "innocent" juveniles accosted by the police. As noted, of the seventy-six juveniles on whom systematic data were collected, ten were exonerated and released without suspicion. Seven, or two-thirds of these ten "innocent" juveniles were Negro, in contrast to the allegedly "guilty" youths, less than one-third of whom were Negro. The following incident illustrates the operation of this bias: One officer, observing a youth walking along the street, commented that the youth "looks suspicious" and promptly stopped and questioned him. Asked later to explain what aroused his suspicion, the officer explained, "He was a Negro wearing dark glasses at midnight."

22. While police statistics did not permit an analysis of crime rates by appearance, they strongly supported officers' contentions concerning the delinquency rate among Negroes. Of all male juveniles processed by the police department in 1961, for example, 40.2 per cent were Negro and 33.9 per cent were white. These two groups comprised at that time, respectively, about 22.7 per cent and 73.6 per cent of the population in the community studied.

If you know that the bulk of your delinquent problem comes from kids who, say, are from 12 to 14 years of age, when you're out on patrol you are much more likely to be sensitive to the activities of juveniles in this age bracket than older or younger groups. This would be good law enforcement practice. The logic in our case is the same except that our delinquency problem is largely found in the Negro community and it is these youths toward whom we are sensitized.

As regards prejudice per se, eighteen of twenty-seven officers interviewed openly admitted a dislike for Negroes. However, they attributed their dislike to experiences they had, as policemen, with youths from this minority group. The officers reported that Negro boys were much more likely than non-Negroes to "give us a hard time," be unco-operative, and show no remorse for their transgressions. Recurrent exposure to such attitudes among Negro youth, the officers claimed, generated their antipathy toward Negroes. The following excerpt is typical of the views expressed by these officers:

> They (Negroes) have no regard for the law or for the police. They just don't seem to give a damn. Few of them are interested in school or getting ahead. The girls start having illegitimate kids before they are 16 years old and the boys are always "out for kicks." Furthermore, many of these kids try to run you down. They say the damnedest things to you and they seem to have absolutely no respect for you as an adult. I admit I am prejudiced now, but frankly I don't think I was when I began police work.

Implications

It is apparent from the findings presented above that the police officers studied in this research were permitted and even encouraged to exercise immense latitude in disposing of the juveniles they encountered. That is, it was within the officers' discretionary authority, except in extreme limiting cases, to decide which juveniles were to come to the attention of the courts and correctional agencies and thereby be identified officially as delinquents. In exercising this discretion policemen were strongly guided by the demeanor of those who were apprehended, a practice which ultimately led, as seen above, to certain youths, (particularly Negroes [23] and boys dressed in the style of "toughs") being treated more severely than other juveniles for comparable offenses.

But the relevance of demeanor was not limited only to police disposition practices. Thus, for example, in conjunction with police crime statistics

23. An unco-operative demeanor was presented by more than one-third of the Negro youths but by only one-sixth of the white youths encountered by the police in the course of our observations.

the criterion of demeanor led police to concentrate their surveillance activities in areas frequented or inhabited by Negroes. Furthermore, these youths were accosted more often than others by officers on patrol simply because their skin color identified them as potential troublemakers. These discriminatory practices—and it is important to note that they are discriminatory, even if based on accurate statistical information—may well have self-fulfilling consequences. Thus it is not unlikely that frequent encounters with police, particularly those involving youths innocent of wrongdoing, will increase the hostility of these juveniles toward law-enforcement personnel. It is also not unlikely that the frequency of such encounters will in time reduce their significance in the eyes of apprehended juveniles, thereby leading these youths to regard them as "routine." Such responses to police encounters, however, are those which law-enforcement personnel perceive as indicators of the serious delinquent. They thus serve to vindicate and reinforce officers' prejudices, leading to closer surveillance of Negro districts, more frequent encounters with Negro youths, and so on in a vicious circle. Moreover, the consequences of this chain of events are reflected in police statistics showing a disproportionately high percentage of Negroes among juvenile offenders, thereby providing "objective" justification for concentrating police attention on Negro youths.

To a substantial extent, as we have implied earlier, the discretion practiced by juvenile officers is simply an extension of the juvenile-court philosophy, which holds that in making legal decisions regarding juveniles, more weight should be given to the juvenile's character and life-situation than to his actual offending behavior. The juvenile officer's disposition decisions—and the information he uses as a basis for them—are more akin to the discriminations made by probation officers and other correctional workers than they are to decisions of police officers dealing with non-juvenile offenders. The problem is that such clinical-type decisions are not restrained by mechanisms comparable to the principles of due process and the rules of procedure governing police decisions regarding adult offenders. Consequently, prejudicial practices by police officers can escape notice more easily in their dealings with juveniles than with adults.

The observations made in this study serve to underscore the fact that the official delinquent, as distinguished from the juvenile who simply commits a delinquent act, is the product of a social judgment, in this case a judgment made by the police. He is a delinquent because someone in authority has defined him as one, often on the basis of the public face he has presented to officials rather than of the kind of offense he has committed.

6. The Police and the Delinquent in Two Cities

JAMES Q. WILSON

THE PURPOSE of this chapter is to compare two large American police departments to discover what difference (if any) a high level of "professionalism" makes in the handling of juvenile offenders. If the object of police administration and reform is "professional" standards, it is crucial to know what difference these standards actually make—not simply with respect to honesty but with respect to the quality of justice. The police is one of the agencies that has the most extensive and continuing contact with juvenile delinquents (real or alleged), and no recommendation for the treatment of delinquency should be made without careful consideration of the important differences (if any) in the treatment of delinquents by the police, as well as of the political and organizational situation explaining the differences.

In this chapter, we shall use the terms "juvenile delinquent" and "juvenile offender" to refer to any person under the age of seventeen

Reprinted from Stanton Wheeler (ed.), *Controlling Delinquents*, New York: John Wiley and Sons, Inc., 1968, pp. 9–30, by permission of John Wiley and Sons, Inc., and the author. Copyright 1968 by John Wiley and Sons, Inc.

who commits an act that violates some ordinance or statute. There are, of course, some laws that apply to juveniles only and that, obviously, are not intended to proscribe "criminal" behavior (laws against loitering, for example, or against truancy from school); we shall, for the most part, confine our comparison to acts which, if committed by an adult, would constitute a crime.

A juvenile is arrested and tried, not for committing a "crime" but for behavior that may eventuate in his being made a ward of the court. Although laws vary from state to state, the common practice (and the practice of the states in which are located the cities that we analyze here) is not to regard proceedings before a juvenile court as criminal but, in the language of one state statute, as intended to "secure for each minor under the jurisdiction of the juvenile court such care and guidance, preferably in his own home, as will serve the spiritual, emotional, mental, and physical welfare of the minor and the best interests of the State; to preserve and strengthen the minor's family ties whenever possible, removing him from the custody of his parents only when his welfare or safety and protection of the public cannot be adequately safeguarded without removal. . . ." In the words of another state statute, delinquent children "shall be treated, not as criminals, but as children in need of aid, encouragement and guidance."

These legal considerations and the customary practices that result from them confer on the authorities considerable discretion in the treatment of juveniles.[1] The police as well as the courts need not and, indeed, do not arrest and punish every child who has committed an act which, if he were an adult, would be a misdemeanor or a felony; the police are generally free to exercise their judgment as to which acts require arrest for the protection of society or the welfare of the child and which acts can be dealt with by other means, including police reprimands, unofficial warnings, or referral to parents or welfare agencies.

The two police departments compared here are those of what we shall call Eastern City and Western City. Both cities have substantially more than 300,000 inhabitants; they are heterogeneous in population and in economic base; both are free of domination by a political machine; and both have a substantial nonwhite population. Western City generally has a mild climate, which probably contributes to rates of crimes against property that are somewhat higher than the rates of Eastern City, where severe winters assist the police in keeping thieves off the streets.

1. On the general problems of police discretion, compare Joseph Goldstein, "Police Discretion Not to Invoke the Criminal Process: Low-Visibility Decisions," *Yale Law Journal*, LXIX (March 1960), 534–594; and Herman Goldstein, "Police Discretion: The Ideal Versus the Real," *Public Administration Review*, XXIII (September 1963), 140–148.

The Meaning of Professionalism

The most important difference between the police of the two cities is that in Western City the police department is highly "professionalized." This does not mean that in Eastern City the police department is wholly corrupt and incompetent; far from it. But as any observer familiar with Eastern City will readily acknowledge, its police officers have been recruited, organized, and led in a way that falls considerably short of the standards set forth in the principal texts. Whether the standards of the texts are right is, of course, another matter. Since the meaning (to say nothing of the value) of professionalism is itself problematical, an effort will be made here to arrive at a general analytical definition and to specify the particular attributes of the police that professionalism implies and how the two police forces differ in these attributes.

A "professional" police department is one governed by values derived from general, impersonal rules which bind all members of the organization and whose relevance is independent of circumstances of time, place or personality.[2] A nonprofessional department (what will be called a "fraternal" department), on the other hand, relies to a greater extent on particularistic judgments—that is, judgments based on the significance to a particular person of his particular relations to particular others. The professional department looks outward to universal, externally valid, enduring standards; the nonprofessional department looks, so to speak, inward at the informal standards of a special group and distributes rewards and penalties according to how well a member conforms to them. The specific attributes that are consistent with these definitions include the following ones.

> A professional, to a greater extent than a fraternal, department recruits members on the basis of achievement rather than ascriptive criteria. It relies more on standardized formal entrance examinations, open equally to all eligible persons. Thus the professional department recruits not only impartially as to political connections, race or religion; it recruits without regard to local residence. Nonprofessional departments often insist (or laws require them to insist) on recruitment only from among local citizens. Educational standards are typically higher for entrants to professional departments.
>
> Professional departments treat equals equally; that is, laws are enforced without respect to person. In such departments "fixing" traffic tickets is difficult or impossible and the sons of the powerful cannot ex-

2. The following definitions are taken from, and treated in greater detail by James Q. Wilson, "The Police and Their Problems: A Theory," *Public Policy*, XII (1962), 189–216.

pect preferential treatment. Fraternal departments have a less formal sense of justice, either because the system of which they are a part encourages favoritism or because (and this is equally important) officers believe it is proper to take into account personal circumstances in dispensing justice. Concretely, we may expect to find less difference in the professional department between the proportion of white and nonwhite juvenile offenders who are arrested, as opposed to being let off with warnings or reprimands.

Professional departments are less open to graft and corruption and their cities will be more free of "tolerated" illegal enterprises (gambling, prostitution) than will cities with nonprofessional departments.

Professional departments seek, by formal training and indoctrination, to produce a force whose members are individually committed to generally applicable standards. Their training will acquaint them with the writing and teaching of "experts" (that is, of carriers of generalized, professional norms). In fraternal departments, there is less formal training and what there is of it is undertaken by departmental officers who inculcate particularistic values and suggest "how to get along" on the force.

Within the professional department, authority attaches to the role and not to the incumbent to a greater extent than in nonprofessional departments. The essentially bureaucratic distribution of authority within the professional force is necessary because, due to the reliance of achievement, young officers are often promoted rapidly to positions of considerable authority (as sergeants and lieutenants in both line and staff bureaus).[3]

By these tests Western City has a highly professionalized force and Eastern City has not. An observer's first impressions of the two departments suggest the underlying differences: the Western City force has modern, immaculate, and expensive facilities, new buildings, and shiny cars; the officers are smartly dressed in clean, well-pressed uniforms; the routine business of the department is efficiently carried out. In Eastern City, the buildings are old and in poor repair; cars are fewer, many are old and worn; the officers are sometimes unkempt; routine affairs, particularly the keeping of records, are haphazardly conducted by harried or indifferent personnel.

In Western City, three-fourths of the officers were born outside the city and one-half outside the state (this is about the same as the proportion of all males in the city who were born outside the state). In Eastern City, the vast majority of officers were born and raised within the city they now serve, many in or near neighborhoods in which they now live. In Western City, over one-third of all officers had one year or more of college education; over one-fifth have two years or more; and one-tenth

3. There is a general tendency for authority to adhere more to the person than to the office in a police force as compared to other kinds of public agencies. See Robert L. Peabody, "Perceptions of Organizational Authority: A Comparative Analysis," *Administrative Science Quarterly*, VI (March 1962), 477–480.

Table 6.1. Proportion of suspected juvenile offenders arrested or cited, by race, for selected offenses in Western City (1962)

	Total Offenses		Percentage Arrested or Cited	
Offense	White	Negro	White	Negro
Robbery	19	105	100.0	92.4
Aggravated assault	9	61	78.8	55.4
Burglary	199	331	87.9	92.8
Auto theft	124	142	93.6	86.6
Larceny	459	1119	56.2	56.6
Loitering	504	829	12.5	20.0
Drunk and disorderly	151	343	39.1	34.7
Malicious mischief	213	216	33.8	37.5
Assault and battery	93	306	58.1	65.3
Total	1771	3452	46.5	50.9

a college degree or better. In Eastern City, the proportion of officers educated beyond high school is far smaller.[4]

In Western City, there was little evidence of gambling or prostitution; Eastern City, while far from "wide open," has not made it difficult for a visitor to find a bookie or a girl. For several years at least, Western City has had a department free from the suspicion of political influence and a court system noted for its "no-fix" policy. In Eastern City, *reports* of influence and fixes are not infrequent (of course, a scholar without the power of subpoena cannot confirm such charges).

The chief of the Western City police department has been a high official of the International Association of Chiefs of Police (IACP); Eastern City's force, by contrast, has been the subject of a special comprehensive report by the IACP, contracted for by the local officials and containing recommendations for extensive reorganization and improvement. In sum, whether judged by subjective impression or objective measure, the police forces of the two cities are significantly different. The crucial question is the consequences of the differences upon the handling of juvenile offenders.

In Western City, justice, on the basis of fragmentary evidence, seems more likely to be blind than in Eastern City. Table 6.1 shows the per-

4. These differences are characteristic of entire regions and not simply of the two departments here studied. In one study it was found that almost 90 per cent of the officers in police departments in the Pacific states, but only about two-thirds of those in New England and North Atlantic states, had a high school education. Similarly, 55 per cent of those from the Pacific states, but only about 18 per cent of those from New England and North Atlantic states, had attended college. See George W. O'Connor and Nelson A. Watson, *Juvenile Delinquency and Youth Crime: The Police Role* (Washington, D.C.: International Association of Chiefs of Police, 1964), pp. 78–79.

centage of youths of each race arrested or cited in 1962 by Western City's police department for each of the most common offenses. Those not arrested or cited were disposed of, for the most part, by official reprimands. As the table indicates, Negro and white juveniles received remarkably similar treatment for all offenses but two; whites were more frequently arrested than Negroes for aggravated assault, and Negroes more frequently arrested than whites for loitering.

Table 6.2 gives similar though not precisely comparable information for Eastern City. This table is based on a random sample (1/25) of all juveniles processed by the Eastern City police over the four years since the juvenile bureau began keeping records. The data on offense and disposition were taken from cards for individual juveniles; thus, the figures in Table 6.2 show what proportion of *juveniles,* by race, were taken to court for various offenses, while the figures in Table 6.1 show what proportion of *juvenile offenses* (many juveniles being counted more than once), by race, resulted in a court disposition. Despite the lack of strict comparability, the differences are worth consideration. Although, in Western City, there was little difference in the probability of arrest for whites as compared to Negroes, in Eastern City the probability of court action (rather than warnings or reprimands) is almost three times higher for Negroes than for whites.

Table 6.2. Proportion of juveniles (in 1/25 samples of all those processed) taken to court, by race, for selected offenses in Eastern City (1959–1961)

Offense	Total Offenses		Percentage Taken to Court	
	White	Negro	White	Negro
Assaults	26	12	11.5	25.0
Burglary	34	4	11.8	100.0
Auto theft	7	3	42.8	66.7
Larceny	98	27	24.5	52.0
Drunk and disorderly	33	4	0.0	0.0
Malicious mischief	69	9	4.4	0.0
Incorrigible	20	4	40.0	100.0
Total	287	63	15.7	42.9

Handling the Delinquent

The two police departments are systematically different both in their treatment of delinquents and in the way the members think and talk about delinquents; paradoxically, the differences in behavior do not correspond to the verbal differences. Interviews with approximately half the officers (selected at random) assigned to the juvenile bureaus of the po-

Table 6.3 Number and rate of juveniles processed and arrested in Western City and Eastern City, 1962

	Western City	Eastern City
Total juveniles processed (all offenses)	8,331	6,384
Rate per 100,000 children [a]	13,600	6,380
Number of juveniles arrested or cited		
(all offenses)	3,869	1,911
Percentage arrested or cited	46.8	30.0
Rate per 100,000 children	6,365	1,910
Total juveniles processed, less those		
charged with loitering	6,685	6,384
Rate per 100,000 children	10,900	6,380
Number of juveniles arrested or cited,		
less loiterers	3,446	1,911
Percentage arrested or cited	51.6	30.0
Rate per 100,000 children	5,623	1,910

[a]Rate is based on number of children, ages six through sixteen, in population of city according to the 1960 census of population.

lice departments of Eastern and Western Cities reveal that Western City's officers have more complex attitudes toward delinquency and juveniles than their colleagues of Eastern City. The former's attitudes, at least superficially, tend to be less moralistic, less certain as to causal factors, more therapeutic, and more frequently couched in generalizations than in anecdotes. Eastern City's officers, by contrast, are more likely to interpret a problem as one of personal and familial morality rather than of social pathology, to urge restrictive and punitive rather than therapeutic measures, to rely on single explanations expressed with great conviction and certainty, and to confine discussions of juveniles almost exclusively to anecdotes and references to recent episodes than to generalizations, trends, or patterns.[5]

The behavior of the officers with respect to juveniles tends to be the opposite of what we might expect from their expressed sentiments. In Western City, the discretionary powers of the police are much more likely than in Eastern City to be used to restrict the freedom of the juvenile: Western City's officers process a larger proportion of the city's juvenile population as suspected offenders and, of those they process, arrest a larger proportion.

Table 6.3 shows the total number of juveniles processed in 1962 by the departments of Eastern and Western City, the rate per 100,000 ju-

5. Compare these dichotomous attitudes with those classified in Walter B. Miller, "Inter-Institutional Conflict as a Major Impediment to Delinquency Prevention," *Human Organization*, XVII, no. 3 (Fall 1958), 20–23; and Harold L. Wilensky and Charles N. Lebeaux, *Industrial Society and Social Welfare* (New York: Russell Sage Foundation, 1958), pp. 219–228.

veniles in the populations of the two cities, and the percentage (and rate) arrested or cited. By "processed" is meant that the youth came in contact with the police in a manner that required the latter to take official cognizance; a report was filed or a record entry made on the ground that the police had reasonable cause to believe that the youth had engaged in, or was a material witness to, acts which brought him under provisions of the state statutes. By "arrested or cited" is meant that the police brought formal action against the juvenile, either by taking him into custody and thence turning him over officially to the courts or to the probation officers or referees who can make a preliminary disposition, or by issuing an order or citation requiring him to appear before a court or official of the probation department. Such dispositions should be contrasted with all others in which the possibility of punitive action does not exist: officially reprimanding and releasing the child, referring him to another agency, returning him to his parents, and so forth. In short, the proportion arrested or cited is the proportion of all juveniles, suspected of having committed any offense, for whom the police make official punitive action a possibility—although not a certainty.

The rate of juveniles (Table 6.3) processed for *all* offenses by Western City's police was more than twice as great as the rate in Eastern City (13,600 per 100,000 as opposed to 6,380 per 100,000) and, of those processed, the proportion arrested or cited was more than 50 percent greater in Western than in Eastern City (46.8 percent as opposed to 30 percent). However, the laws of the two cities (and consequently the number of grounds on which juveniles can be processed by the police) differ, and therefore these raw figures must be modified by eliminating all juveniles processed for offenses unique to one place. The only type of offense that involved more than 1 percent of the juveniles was an anti-loitering ordinance in effect in Western City but not in Eastern City. (The fact that Western City *has* such an ordinance—that forbids persons under the age of eighteen from loitering unaccompanied by a parent in public places between 10:00 p.m. and sunrise—is, it can be argued, in itself a manifestation of the difference in the conception of justice prevailing in each city. Not only does Eastern City not have such an ordinance but the head of the juvenile bureau at the time of this research was opposed to its adoption.) Table 6.3 gives the adjusted figures after deleting from Western City's totals all juveniles processed or arrested for violation of the antiloitering ordinance; yet both the processing rate and the arrest rate remain over 50 percent higher than in Eastern City.

In short, the young man or woman in Western City is one and one-half to two times as likely to come into contact with the police and, once in contact with the police, one and one-half times as likely to be arrested or cited rather than reprimanded or referred. One explanation of the contrast might be that, because of circumstances over which the police have no control, all the people there—the old as well as the young —are more likely to commit criminal acts. The more favorable climate, for example, might well explain why there were more crimes against property in Western City than in Eastern City. It can be argued that young people who are not professional thieves are even more likely than adults to be deterred by wind, snow, and freezing temperatures from stealing cars or breaking into hardware stores. Furthermore, Western City has a higher proportion of Negroes than Eastern City. If, in fact, Western City's youths are "more criminal" or have more opportunity for criminal acts, then differences in processing and arrest rates might reveal nothing about police attitudes or community norms.

Table 6.4. Crime rates and adult and juvenile arrest rates per 100,000 population for Western City and Eastern City, 1962, by major offense

Offense	Crime Rate		Adult Arrest Rate		Juvenile Arrest Rate		Ratio[a]	
	West-ern	East-ern	West-ern	East-ern	West-ern	East-ern	Adult	Juvenile
Homicide	8	7	10	11	3	0.2	0.9	17.0
Forcible rape	17	15	14	14	36	13	1.0	2.8
Robbery	167	104	115	71	197	63	1.6	3.1
Aggravated assault	105	117	85	107	69	73	0.8	0.9
Burglary	957	566	188	118	860	334	1.6	2.6
Larceny	458	420	576	240	1,580	664	2.4	2.4
Auto theft	357	855	71	127	450	316	0.6	1.4
Total	2,069	2,084	1,059	688	3,195	1,463	1.5	2.2

[a]These are the ratios of arrest rates in Western City to arrest rates in Eastern City for adults and juveniles. The ratio was calculated by dividing the Western City rate by the Eastern City rate. Values in excess of 1.0 are measures of the degree to which Western City rates exceed Eastern City rates.

In an effort to evaluate this objection, a more detailed comparison of crime and arrest rates for both juveniles and adults is given in Table 6.4. For each of the "Part I" offenses, the seven most serious offenses as defined by the FBI, overall crime rates (that is, offenses known to the police and arrest rates for both adults and juveniles) are given for both cities for 1962. In sum, the crime rates of the two cities are remarkably similar, although some considerable disparities are concealed in the totals. As one might predict, Western City has a substantially higher crime rate for robbery and burglary; unexpectedly, Eastern City has a substantially higher rate for auto theft. Crimes against the person—homicide, forcible rape, and aggravated assault—are quite similar in the two cities, crimes of passion being unfortunately less inhibited by adverse weather, probably because so many of them occur indoors. The arrest rates are a different story: the rates for both adults and juveniles are higher in Western City than in Eastern City, but the difference is greatest for the juveniles.

Western City's police arrest a greater proportion of the population than do Eastern City's but whereas the former's rate is 50 percent higher for adults, it is over 100 percent higher for juveniles. The last two columns in Table 6.4 summarize these differences by showing, for both adults and juveniles, the ratio between Western and Eastern City rates of arrest for each offense. Only for aggravated assault were the rates for juveniles of Eastern City higher than those of Western City; for all other offenses, Western's City's rates were generally from 1.4 to 3.1 times greater. Particularly striking is the fact that, although the *auto theft rate* was over twice as high in Eastern City, the *juvenile arrest rate* for auto theft was 40 percent greater in Western City.

Thus, a juvenile in Western City is far less likely than one in Eastern City to be let off by the police with a reprimand. What the data indicate, interviews confirm. Police officers, social workers, and students of delinquency in Eastern City agree that the police there are well-known for what is called by many the "pass system." Unless the youth commits what the police consider a "vicious" crime—brutally assaulting an elderly person, for example, or engaging in wanton violence—he is almost certain to be released with a reprimand or warning on his first contact with the police and quite likely to be released on the second, third, and sometimes even on the fourth contact. It must be said that the juvenile officer who handles the case may consult a card file in his station showing previous police contacts for all juveniles in the precinct; a "pass" is not given out of ignorance.

The account of one Eastern City juvenile officer is typical of most accounts:

> Most of the kids around here get two or three chances. Let me give you an example. There was this fellow around here who is not vicious, not I think, what you'd call bad; he's really sort of a good kid. He just can't move without getting into trouble. I don't know what there is about him . . . I'll read you his record. 1958—he's picked up for shop-lifting, given a warning. 1958—again a few months later was picked up for illegal possession [of dangerous weapons]. He had some dynamite caps and railroad flares. Gave him another warning. 1959—the next year he stole a bike. Got a warning. 1960—he broke into some freight cars. [Taken to court and] continued without a finding [that is, no court action] on the understanding that he would pay restitution. Later the same year he was a runaway from home. No complaint was brought against him. Then in 1960 he started getting into some serious stuff. There was larceny and committing an unnatural act with a retarded boy. So, he went up on that one and was committed to [the reformatory] for nine months. Got out. In 1962 he was shot while attempting a larceny in a junk yard

at night. . . . Went to court, continued without a finding [that is, no punishment]. Now that's typical of a kid who just sort of can't stay out of trouble. He only went up once out of, let me see . . . eight offenses . . . I wouldn't call him a bad kid despite the record . . . the bad kids: we don't have a lot of those.

In Eastern City, there are, of course, officers who have the reputation for being "tough." The "toughness" may be manifested, however, not so much in more frequent court appearances of youths, but in the greater ease of getting information. "Tough" and "soft" officers work as teams, the latter persuading juveniles to talk in order to save them from the former. In any case, the net effect of police discretion in Eastern City is unambiguous; only 17.5 percent of the first offenders included in a 1/25 random sample of all juveniles processed over a four-year period by the police department were referred to court. Indeed, Eastern City's officers occasionally mentioned that it was their understanding that officers "in the West" made arrests more frequently than they: Western City's officers sometimes observed that they had been told that officers "in the East" made arrests less frequently than they.

Observation of the operation of the two departments provided considerable evidence of the effect of the preceding on the day-to-day practice of police work. While cruising the city in patrol cars, Western City's officers would frequently stop to investigate youths "hanging" on street corners; the officers would check the youths' identification, question them closely, and often ask over the radio if they were persons for any reason wanted at headquarters. In Eastern City, officers would generally ignore young persons hanging around corners except to stop the car, lean out, and gruffly order them to "move along." "Sweeping" or "brooming" the corners was done with no real hope on the part of the police that it would accomplish much ("they'll just go around the block and come right back here in ten minutes") but they would ask, "what else can you do?"

Technically, of course, an officer in either city who takes a person into custody on the street is required by law to bring him to police headquarters or to a station house and to initiate a formal procedure whereby an arrest is effected, charges stated, certain rights guaranteed, and, if necessary, physical detention effected. In fact, and particularly with respect to juveniles, police officers sometimes take persons directly to their homes. In Eastern City this procedure is, in my judgment (naturally no conclusive evidence is available), much more common than in Western City.

The Correlates of Discretion

If, at least in this one case, a "professionalized" police department tends to expose a higher proportion of juveniles to the possibility of court action, despite the more "therapeutic" and sophisticated verbal formulas of its officers, it is important to ask why this occurs. Many reasons suggest themselves but, since this research is limited to an intensive examination of two departments, with more cursory examination of two others, it is impossible to say how much of the variation in arrest rates can be accounted for by any single circumstance or by all circumstances together, or whether in other cities different relationships might be found. However, a rather strong argument can be made that, at the very least, the relationship is not accidental and, further, that professionalism itself in a variety of ways contributes to the result. Finally, what at first seems a paradox—the discrepancy between ideology and behavior—is not in fact a paradox at all, but simply the differing expression of a single state of affairs.

Certain structural and procedural dissimilarities undoubtedly account for some of the differences in arrests. In Eastern City the juvenile officer on the police force is also the prosecuting officer: he personally prepares and presents the case in court against the juvenile. In Western City, the juvenile officer (who, as in Eastern City, takes charge of the juvenile after a patrolman or detective has "brought him in") prepares an initial report but sends the report and, if detention seems warranted, the child himself, to an independent probation department which determines whether the suspect should be taken before the judge. In effect, Western City officers can "pass the buck," and even if the case goes to court, the officer himself only rarely is required to appear in court. In Eastern City, the police are involved right up to the moment when the judge actually makes a disposition, a police appearance being always required if there is to be a court hearing. Moreover, the probation department is not independent, but is an arm of the court which acts only *after* a court appearance. As a result of these arrangements, Eastern City's officers may have an incentive not to send the child to court because it requires more work; to Western City's officers, on the other hand, initiating a court appearance is relatively costless.

But such considerations do not explain why the *arresting* officer (who in most cases is *not* the juvenile officer who makes the ultimate disposition or the court appearance) should be less likely to make an arrest in one city than the other—unless, of course, there is some social pressure from juvenile officers in Eastern City to keep down the arrest rate. There is such pressure but, as will be shown, it does not come from juvenile officers but from the force as a whole.

It may be, of course, that the force as a whole is influenced by its perception of the probability that the court will actually punish the suspect, although it is by no means clear which way this influence might work. On the one hand, a lenient court might prove discouraging to the police, leading them to conclude that the "kid will get off anyway, so why should I go to the trouble of making an arrest?" On the other hand, a lenient court could as easily lead officers to argue that, since the kid will be "let off," there is no real danger to the suspect and, therefore, he may as well be arrested, whatever the merits of the case, as a way of throwing a harmless but perhaps useful "scare" into him.

This need not be solved, however, because the officers in both cities perceive the court, together with the probation authorities, as "excessively" lenient. And with good reason: in Eastern City, even though the police take only about 17.5 percent of all first offenders to court, only a third of these get any punishment at all and less than a tenth are sent to a reformatory. Those not committed to a reformatory are given suspended sentences or placed on probation. In sum, *only 1.6 percent* of first offenders see the inside of a correctional institution. In Western City, comparable figures are difficult to assemble. Generally speaking, however, the police are correct in their belief that only a small fraction of the youths they refer to the probation department will be sent on to court and that, of these, an even smaller fraction will be committed to a correctional institution. Of the more than eight thousand juveniles processed by the police in 1962, slightly less than half were referred, by arrest or citation, to the probation department. Of the juveniles referred, about one-third were ordered by the probation department to make a court appearance; of these, about one-sixth were sent to a public institution. In sum, *only about 2.8 percent* of the juveniles processed by the police were in some way confined. The differences in the probability of punishment in the two cities were so small as to make them a negligible influence on police behavior.

Far more important, it seems to me, than any mechanical differences between the two departments are the organizational arrangements, community attachments, and institutionalized norms which govern the daily life of the police officer himself, all of which might be referred to collectively as the "ethos" of the police force. It is this ethos which, in my judgment, decisively influences the police in the two places. In Western City, this is the ethos of a *professional* force; in Eastern City, the ethos of a *fraternal* force.

Western City's police officer works in an organizational setting which is highly centralized. Elaborate records are kept on all aspects of police work: each officer must, on a log, account for every minute of his time on duty; all contacts with citizens must be recorded in one form or another; and automatic data-processing equipment frequently issues detailed reports on police and criminal activity. The department operates out of a single headquarters; all juvenile offenders are processed in the office of the headquarters' juvenile bureau in the presence of a sergeant, a lieutenant, and, during the day shift, a captain. Dossiers on previously processed juveniles are kept and consulted at headquarters. Arresting officers bring all juveniles to headquarters for processing and their disposition is determined by officers of the juvenile bureau at that time.

In Eastern City, the force is highly decentralized. Officers are assigned to an, sometimes for their whole career, work in precinct station houses. Juvenile suspects are brought to the local station house and turned over to the officer of the juvenile bureau assigned there. These assignments are relatively constant: a patrolman who becomes a juvenile officer remains in the same station house. The juvenile officer is not supervised closely or, in many cases, not supervised at all; he works in his own office and makes his own dispositions. Whatever records the juvenile officer chooses to keep—and most keep some sort of record—is largely up to him. Once a week he is required to notify the headquarters of the juvenile bureau of his activities and to provide the bureau with the names and offenses of any juveniles he has processed. Otherwise, he is on his own.[6]

The centralized versus the decentralized mode of operations is in part dictated by differences in size of city—Eastern City has a larger population than Western City—but also in great part by a deliberate organizational strategy. Western City at one time had precincts, but they were abolished by a new, "reform" police chief as a way of centralizing control over the department in his hands. There had been some scandals before his appointment involving allegations of police brutality and corruption which he was determined would not occur again. Abolishing the precincts, centralizing the force, increasing the number and specificity of the rules and reporting procedures, and tightening supervision were all measures to achieve this objective. These actions all had consequences, many of them perhaps unintended, upon the behavior of the department. Officers felt the pressure: they were being watched, checked, supervised, and reported on. The force was becoming to a considerable extent "bu-

6. The juvenile bureau of the Eastern City police department was only created after community concern over what appeared to be a serious incident involving a juvenile "gang" compelled it. The police commissioner at the time was reported to oppose the existence of such a bureau on the revealing grounds that "each beat officer should be his own juvenile officer." The fraternal force apparently resisted even the nominal degree of specialization and centralization represented by the creation of this bureau. This, again, is also a regional phenomenon. Over 80 percent of the police departments in Pacific states, but less than 58 percent of those in New England states, have specialized juvenile units. O'Connor and Watson, op. cit., p. 84.

reaucratized"—behavior more and more was to involve the non-discretionary application of general rules to particular cases.[7] Some officers felt that their "productivity" was being measured—number of arrests made, citations written, field contact reports filed, and suspicious persons checked. Under these circumstances, it would be surprising if they did not feel they ought to act in such a way as to minimize any risk to themselves that might arise, not simply from being brutal or taking graft, but from failing to "make pinches" and "keep down the crime rate." In short, organizational measures intended to insure that police behave properly with respect to nondiscretionary matters (such as taking bribes) may also have the effect (perhaps unintended) of making them behave differently with respect to matters over which they *do* have discretion. More precisely, these measures tend to induce officers to convert discretionary to nondiscretionary matters—for example, to treat juveniles according to rule and without regard to person.

In Eastern City the nonprofessional, fraternal ethos of the force leads officers to treat juveniles primarily on the basis of personal judgment and only secondarily by applying formal rules. Although the department has had its full share of charges of corruption and brutality, at the time of this research there had been relatively few fundamental reforms. The local precinct captain is a man of great power; however, he rarely chooses to closely supervise the handling of juvenile offenders. His rules, though binding, are few in number and rarely systematic or extensive.

In Western City, the juvenile officers work as a unit; they meet together every morning for a line-up, briefing, and short training session; they work out of a common headquarters; they have their own patrol cars; and they work together in pairs. In Eastern City most, though not all, precincts have a single juvenile officer. He works in the station house in association with patrolmen and detectives; he has no car of his own, but must ride with other officers or borrow one of their cars; he rarely meets with other juvenile officers and there is practically no training for his job or systematic briefing while on it. In Western City, the juvenile officer's ties of association on and off the job are such that his fellow juvenile officers are his audience. He is judged by, and judges himself by, their standards and their opinions. In Eastern City, the relevant audience is much more likely to be patrolmen and detectives. In Western City, the primary relations of the juvenile officer are with "professional" colleagues; in Eastern City, the relations are with fraternal associates.

Eastern City's juvenile officer feels, and expresses to an interviewer, the conflicting and ambivalent standards arising out of his association with

7. Compare the causes and consequences of bureaucratization in an industrial setting in Alvin W. Gouldner, *Patterns of Industrial Bureaucracy* (Glencoe, Ill.: Free Press, 1954).

officers who do not handle juveniles. On the one hand, almost every juvenile officer in Eastern City complained that patrolmen and detectives did not "understand" his work, that they regarded him as a man who "chased kids," that they "kissed off" juvenile cases onto him and did not take them seriously, and that they did not think arresting a "kid" constituted a "good pinch." These attitudes might, in part, be explained by the patrolmen's reluctance to bring a juvenile into the station, even if they could then turn him over to the juvenile officer on duty; bringing the boy in meant bringing him in in front of their fellow patrolmen in the squad room of the station house. One patrolman's views on this were typical:

> A delinquent is not a good pinch—at least not for most officers. You get ribbed a lot and sort of ridiculed when you bring a kid in. Sort of grinds you down when you bring a kid in and the other officers start telling you, "Hey, look at the big man, look at the big guy with the little kid, hey, can you handle that kid all by yourself?" You get a little ribbing like that and finally you don't bring so many kids in for pinches.

Instead, the patrolmen or detectives often simply refer the juvenile's name to the juvenile officer and let the officer go out and handle the case from investigation to arrest. This not only places a larger work load on the juvenile officer; it places it on him under conditions that do not reward effective performance. He is given the "kid stuff" because patrolmen do not feel rewarded for handling it; at the same time, the patrolman lets it be known that he does not feel the juvenile officer ought to get much credit, either. At the same time, almost all patrolmen interviewed felt that the authorities, including in most cases the juvenile officer himself, were "too easy" on the kids. But this generalized commitment to greater punitiveness, although widely shared in Eastern City, rarely—for reasons to be discussed later—determines the fate of any particular juvenile. This being the case, the juvenile officer in Eastern City seems to allow his behavior to be influenced by associates, insofar as it is influenced by them at all, in the direction of permissive treatment.

Western City's juvenile officers, by contrast, are more insulated from or less dependent on the opinion of patrolmen and detectives. And the latter, when taking a juvenile into custody, can bring him to a central juvenile bureau staffed only by juvenile officers, rather than to a precinct station filled with fellow patrolmen and detectives. Neither juvenile officers nor arresting patrolmen are, in Western City, as directly exposed to or dependent upon the opinions of associates concerning whether a juvenile arrest is justified.

Even if Western City's officers should be so exposed, however, it is likely that they would still be more punitive than their counterparts in Eastern City. In Western City, the officer, both in and out of the juvenile bureau, is recruited and organized in a way that provides little possibility of developing a strong identification with either delinquents in general or with delinquents in some particular neighborhood. He is likely to have been raised outside the city and even outside the state; in many cases he was recruited by the representatives of the force who canvass the schools of police administration attached to western and midwestern universities. In only *one* case in Western City did I interview a juvenile officer who, when asked about his own youth, spoke of growing up in a "tough" neighborhood where juvenile gangs, juvenile misbehavior, and brushes with the police were common. There were, on the other hand, only one or two of Eastern City's officers who had *not* come from such backgrounds: they were almost all products not only of local neighborhoods but of neighborhoods where scrapes with the law were a common occurrence.

The *majority* of Eastern City's officers were not only "locals," but locals from lower or lower-middle-class backgrounds. Several times officers spoke of themselves and their friends in terms that suggested that the transition between being a street-corner rowdy and a police officer was not very abrupt. The old street-corner friends that they used to "hang" with followed different paths as adults but, to the officers, the paths were less a matter of choice than of accident, fates which were legally but not otherwise distinct. The officers spoke proudly of the fights they used to have, of youthful wars between the Irish and the Italians, and of the old gangs, half of whose alumni went to the state prison and the other half to the police and fire departments. Each section of the city has great meaning to these officers; they are nostalgic about some where the old life continues, bitter about others where new elements—particularly Negroes—have "taken over."

The *majority* of Western City's officers who were interviewed, almost without exception, described their own youth as free of violence, troubles with the police, broken homes, or gang behavior. The city in which they now serve has a particular meaning for only a very few. Many live outside it in the suburbs and know the city's neighborhoods almost solely from their police work. Since there are no precinct stations but only radio car routes, and since these are frequently changed, there is little opportunity to build up an intimate familiarity, much less an identification, with any neighborhood. The Western City police are, in a real sense, an army of occupation organized along paramilitary lines.

It would be a mistake to exaggerate these differences or to be carried away by neighborhood romanticism that attaches an undeservedly high significance to the folklore about the "neighborhood cop" walking his rounds—king of the beat, firm arbiter of petty grievances, and gruff but kind confidant of his subjects. The "oldtime beat cop," as almost all the

Eastern City's officers are quick and sad to admit, is gone forever. But even short of romanticism, the differences remain and are important. Except for the downtown business district and the skid row area, there are no foot patrolmen in Western City; in Eastern City, in all the residential areas with high crime rates, officers walk their beats. Furthermore, the station houses in Eastern City receive a constant stream of local residents who bring their grievances and demands to the police; in Western City the imposing new police headquarters building is downtown and has no "front desk" where business obviously can be transacted. Although visitors are encouraged, upon entering the ground floor one is confronted by a bank of automatic elevators. Finally, officers on duty in Eastern City eat in diners and cafés in or close to their routes; in Western City officers often drive several miles to a restaurant noted for its reasonably-priced food rather than for its identification with the neighborhood.

These differences in style between the two police departments can perhaps be summarized by saying that in Western City the officer has a generalized knowledge of juveniles and of delinquency and that, although he, of course, becomes familiar with some children and areas, that generalized knowledge—whether learned in college, from departmental doctrine, from the statute books, or from the popular literature on juvenile behavior—provides the premises of his decisions. He begins with general knowledge and he is subjected to fewer particularizing influences than his counterpart in Eastern City. In Eastern City, the officer's knowledge or what he takes to be his knowledge about delinquency, crime, and neighborhood affairs is, from the first, specific, particular, indeed, *personal,* and the department is organized and run in a way that maintains a particularist orientation toward relations between officer and officer and between police and citizens.[8]

This Eastern City ethos exists side by side with the general moral absolutism of police attitudes toward delinquency *in general.* When asked about the cause, extent, or significance of delinquency *generally,* the officers usually respond, as has been indicated, with broad, flat, moral indictments of the modern American family, overly-indulged youth, weakened social bonds, corrupting mass media of communication, and pervasive irreligion and socialism. When the same officers are asked about

8. The findings of O'Connor and Watson are consistent with this argument. They discovered that officers in Pacific police departments tended to have "tougher" attitudes toward the *means* to be employed in handling juvenile offenders than officers in New England or North Atlantic departments. The former were more likely to favor transporting juveniles in marked rather than unmarked police cars, to favor having a curfew, to oppose having the police get involved in community affairs concerning youth matters, to oppose destroying the police records of juveniles after they become adults, and to oppose having the police try to find jobs for juveniles who come to their attention. (*Op. cit.*, pp. 91–97, 115–127.)

delinquency in *their precinct,* they speak anecdotally of particular juveniles engaging in particular acts in particular circumstances, in dealing with whom they apply, not their expressed general moral absolutes, but their particular knowledge of the case in question and some rough standard of personal substantive justice.

The one striking exception arises when Negroes are involved. The white officer is not in any kind of systematic communication with Negroes; the Negro is the "invader," and—what may be statistically true—more likely to commit crimes. The officer sees the Negro as being often more vicious, certainly more secretive, and always alien. To the policemen of Eastern City, the Negro has no historical counterpart in his personal experience and, as a result, the Negro juvenile is more likely than the white to be treated, in accord not with particularist standards, but with the generalized and absolutist attitudes which express the officer's concern for the problem "as a whole."

One reason for the apparently higher proportion of arrests of Negro compared to white juveniles in Eastern City may have nothing to do with "prejudice." In addition to being perceived as an "alien," the Negro offender is also perceived as one who "has no home life." Eastern City officers frequently refer to (and deplore) the apparent weakness of the lower-class Negro family structure, the high proportion of female heads of households, and the alleged high incidence of welfare cases (notably Aid to Dependent Children). If a fraternal force is concerned as much with the maintenance of family authority as with breaking the law and if referring the child to the home is preferred to referring him to court, then the absence (or perceived absence) of family life among Negroes would lead to a greater resort to the courts.

Western City's officer, acting on essentially general principles, treats juveniles with more severity (concern with distinctions of person is less, though by no means entirely absent) but with less discrimination. Negroes and whites are generally treated alike and both are treated more severely. Because the officer in this city is more likely to be essentially of middle-class background and outlook and sometimes college educated as well, he is much more likely to be courteous, impersonal, and "correct" than the Eastern City officer.

These differences in organizational character are reinforced by the political and civic institutions of the cities. Eastern City has been governed for decades by "old-style" politics; personal loyalties, neighborhood interests, and party preferment are paramount. Western City is preeminently a "good government" community in all respects. The nonpartisan city council and administration have, by and large, made every effort to make the management of the community honest and efficient. In this, they have been supported by the press and by business and civic groups.

Western City's police chief enjoys strong support in his determined effort to maintain and extend professional standards in the force. Eastern City's chief is, of course, expected to perform creditably and avoid scandal but the whole tenor of the city's political life provides little evidence that anything more than routine competence is required or even wanted.

The differences in the ethos of both the police and the political institutions of the two communities may have a common prior cause. Even though Western City has a much larger proportion of Negroes than Eastern City, the city as a whole is slightly more "middle class" (one-fifth of the families have incomes over $10,000 a year compared to less than one-seventh in Eastern City) and significantly less "European" (less than one-fifth of the population is of foreign stock compared to nearly one-half in Eastern City). In Western City, about half the dwelling units are owner-occupied; in Eastern City, only one-third are. Three times as many households have second cars in Western City as in Eastern City.

It is not unreasonable to assume that community expectations influence the behavior of both politicians and police officers. A somewhat more middle-class community will expect more vigorous law enforcement just as—and for the same reason—it expects honest, efficient municipal management. The universalistic norms of the professional force and the particularistic norms of the fraternal force are consistent with and supported by community values.[9] (This is easily exaggerated. The differences in class composition of the two cities are not great; further, before the 1950's Western City had a lax police force and city government.)

Some Policy Implications

If this analysis is substantially correct, it will suggest several things to the policy maker. First, decisions with respect to "professionalizing" big-city police forces should not be taken without consideration of their effect on the justice meted out in discretionary cases. It is not possible—as we should have known all along—simply to make a police force "better"; these questions must first be answered: "better for what?" and "better for whom?" Students of public administration have argued long and correctly that "efficiency" or "management" can rarely be "improved" without some effect on the substantive goals of the organization. It should not be surprising that, in police departments, as elsewhere, means are almost never purely instrumental but have their consequences upon ends.

9. Differences in political ethos may parallel differences in police ethos. Compare the differences between professional, generalized norms and fraternal, particularist norms with the differences between the Anglo-Saxon middle class and the "immigrant" political ethos as described in Edward C. Banfield and James Q. Wilson, *City Politics* (Cambridge: Harvard University Press, 1963), especially Chapters 3, 11, 16, and 22.

The second implication directly concerns the problem of juvenile delinquency. The training of a police force apparently alters the manner in which juveniles are handled. A principal effect of the inculcation of professional norms is to make the police less discriminatory but more severe. As a political scientist, I cannot pretend to know whether, from the standpoint of "solving" or "treating" the "delinquency problem," this is good or bad. I find it difficult, however, to believe that the issue is settled. Plausible arguments can be advanced, I am confident, to the effect that certain, swift punishment—in this case, certain, swift referral to a court agency—is an excellent deterrent to juvenile crime. Youths are impressed early, so the argument might go, with the seriousness of their offenses and the consequences of their actions. Equally plausible arguments can no doubt be adduced that arresting juveniles—particularly first offenders —tends to confirm them in deviant behavior; it gives them the status, in the eyes of their gang, of "tough guys" who have "been downtown" with the police; it throws them into intimate contact with confirmed offenders, where presumably they become "con-wise" and learned in the tricks of the thievery trade; and, somewhat contradictorily since sentencing is rarely severe, it gives them a contempt for the sanctions open to society.

There is probably some truth in both arguments. Different strategies may work with different juveniles, and these differences may cluster along lines of class, ethnicity, or family background.

Whether Western City or Eastern City has been more effective in reducing or preventing juvenile crime is hard to say. No agency can compile statistics on crimes that were *not* committed and the police cannot, of course, specify which known but unsolved crimes were committed by juveniles. Trends in the crime rate may have more to do with population changes than with police activity. The only available comparative indicator is the clearance rate—the proportion of offenses known to the police "cleared" by arrest. These rates, however, are typically calculated differently in different cities and are based on highly subjective judgements as to how many and what kinds of offenses are "cleared" by an arrest. It would be misleading to use these rates to measure "police effectiveness."

The policy maker, searching for a way to adapt police practice to the problem of delinquency, could properly ask whether certain aspects of the professional force contribute more than others to the results described here. To that, no clear answer can be given. There is some evidence that among smaller cities, upper-class communities have police forces which *process* more juveniles but *arrest* fewer than police forces in nearby lower- or lower-middle-class communities.[10] Thus, the size of the city may

10. See Nathan Goldman, *The Differential Selection of Juvenile Offenders for Court Appearance* (New York: National Research and Information Center of the National Council on Crime and Delinquency, 1963), especially pp. 48–124.

be an important variable: perhaps in the *small* community with an upper-class, "good government" ethos, more offenses are called to the attention of the police—hence the larger number of juveniles processed—while the smaller, more intimate nature of the community encourages the police to rely more on turning offenders over to their parents. Since children of upper-class families are less likely than those of lower-class families to commit major crimes, such as burglary and larceny, their referral by the police to their parents involves less sacrifice of professional norms. On the other hand, in *large* communities with professional, "good government" standards, the greater impersonality of the police may mean that, although citizens report offenses, they do not expect—and do not get—police referral of children to the parents rather than the courts.

Another variable that may effect differences in police behavior is age. Western City's officers are, on the whole, younger than Eastern City's; further, among the latter, one can observe a tendency for the younger officers to act more like their counterparts in Western City. There is no direct evidence on this point, but further research might show that younger officers are more zealous than the older (that is, more likely to act on the basis of organizational rule than personal judgment); that they take their jobs more seriously, that they are likely to be better educated, and that all these qualities—zeal, seriousness, and education—combine to make the officer more likely to investigate suspicious circumstances, process a large number of alleged delinquents, and, of those processed, arrest a larger proportion.

The "age" of the force as a whole may further contribute to the differences. The Western City force is not only young in the average age of its members, but "young" in the sense that it was within the last ten years "reformed" and reorganized and that zealous, recently promoted officers occupy positions of authority in the department. Another big-city police department that I visited (let me call it Center City) that also has high professional standards and a record free of any major scandal involving graft or collusion did not (in comparison to Western City) process as large a proportion of the city's juveniles or arrest as large a proportion of those processed. (In Center City data are not collected in such a way as to make them exactly comparable with Western City data.) The strongest impression an observer carries away from a prolonged visit to the Center City department is that the force, while honest and competent, has lost its sense of zeal. It was "reformed" over twenty years ago after a series of major scandals. The young officers who then rose rapidly to positions of influence and who presumably for a time gave to the force a new vigor, have grown older. The tightness of supervision so characteristic of the Western City force is absent in Center City: perhaps over the years it has simply grown slack. The city remains "closed" to vice and gambling but, with respect to juveniles, there is a greater propensity to "reprimand and release" than to arrest or cite.

For these two reasons—size of city and "age" of force—and perhaps for many others as well, the conclusion that differing degrees of professionalism will everywhere produce comparable differences in police treatment of juveniles is unwarranted. Whatever the qualifications, however, the fundamental choice remains and no program of training or reorganization can escape it.

PART FOUR

The Juvenile Court in Operation

THERE IS a vast literature devoted to the juvenile court which has accumulated since its origins in the United States in Cook County, Illinois, in 1899.[1] One of the main currents of commentary in that literature centers about the court as a welfare agency, devoted to the care and treatment of youthful deviants who are in need of its tender ministrations. The advocates of the court viewed it as a fundamentally different operation from the criminal court. The juvenile court was seen as a massive child-saving device rather than a legalistic operation devoted to questions of guilt, culpability, and punishment. Juvenile courts were to operate informally, youths were to have petitions filed on their behalf, they were to be adjudicated instead of convicted, and their welfare was to be paramount. Much of the early literature on the court expressed marked enthusiasm for the welfare-oriented court, along with impatience over those legalistic aspects of court procedure which had been brought from the

1. A good, detailed summary of the literature on the juvenile court can be found in the President's Commission on Law Enforcement and Administration of Justice, *Task Force Report: Juvenile Delinquency and Youth Crime* (Washington, D.C.: U.S. Government Printing Office, 1967).

criminal courts and which lingered on in the juvenile court. Optimistic opinions about the rehabilitative potential of the court abounded, expressed by persons of stature who were guided by noble motives.

In the initial flush of enthusiasm for the juvenile court idea, few voices were heard raising questions about the possible negative effects the court might have upon some of the youths processed through it. The constitutional challenges which were raised regarding court inattention to due process and legal safeguards for juveniles were beaten back. Thus the Pennsylvania Supreme Court ruled in 1905 that juveniles had no rights of due process because the court is not a criminal court. More recently, the United States Supreme Court ruled *in re Holmes* in 1955 that juvenile courts are not criminal ones, so that constitutional rights extended to adults do not apply to juveniles.

All of these positive opinions about the court, along with disinterest in procedural standards for court operation, stem from a faith in the beneficial character of the court. Supporters of the court operated upon the assumption that since the court was designed to operate for the welfare of children, it must be beneficial in its effects. However, experience should warn us about such an assumption. Well-intentioned programs do not always turn out to work for the benefit of those to whom they are directed.

The pendulum of opinion has swung markedly over to a relatively pessimistic view in the past decade, so that critics of the juvenile court have surfaced in considerable numbers. These critics have raised a host of questions about the court and its workings, directed particularly at its loose procedural aspects and at omnibus laws which empower the court to intervene in all kinds of "behavior problems" exhibited by juveniles.

Those who would restrict the scope of juvenile court jurisdiction and who would tighten up on the due process standards of the court have noted a number of shortcomings of the youth tribunal. To begin with, courts rarely have the resources with which they are supposed to be equipped, so that relatively unqualified judges preside over them, probation officers are not well-trained and there are not enough of them, and other components which are supposed to characterize the ideal court are lacking in practice.

Juvenile court philosophy is based upon the assumption that reliable knowledge exists concerning techniques for the rehabilitation of offenders, and these only await implementation in the court. But skeptics have observed that few tested techniques for resocializing offenders are at hand. Then too, treatment agents who are currently employed in the field of corrections do not share any common body of understandings about the nature of delinquency and its treatment.

A third concern of those who are critical of the court centers about the unintended stigmatization of offenders that may go on there. This is the argument which we have examined earlier, that juvenile courts may unwittingly contribute to delinquent careers by singling youths out for attention. Perhaps the experience of appearing in court has the result in some cases of hardening the offender's image of himself as a deviant, as well as crystallizing community opinion that he is a "bad" boy.

These criticisms of the youth tribunal have had important effects in recent years. In the case of *Kent* vs. *United States,* heard before the Supreme Court in 1966, the court ruled that when juveniles are remanded to criminal courts for prosecution, they must be provided a hearing, legal representation, and the judge must provide written reasons for waiving juvenile court jurisdiction. An even farther reaching Supreme Court decision was delivered in 1967 in the case *in re Gault.* In this instance the court ruled that juveniles must be given formal notice of charges against them, they must be provided access to legal counsel, the right of confrontation and cross examination of witnesses must be given them, they must be guaranteed protection against self-incrimination, a transcript of court proceedings must be made, and the right of appeal must be provided. These decisions are not designed to reverse the treatment and protective philosophy of the court, but they do go a long way toward insuring that due process will be given to all those youngsters who appear before the juvenile tribunal. In the long run, these Supreme Court rulings will probably reduce the number of youths who turn up in court charged with loosely defined acts of misconduct, as well as having the effect of compelling courts to pay closer attention to procedural and evidential matters.

The first reading by Lemert in this section bears upon these trends in the direction of due process-oriented courts. This selection deals with two important matters. First, his paper presents an incisive discussion of the criticisms that have been levied at welfare-oriented juvenile courts, so that it is an excellent summary of this line of thought. In addition, Lemert's paper deals with changes which were introduced into California law in 1961, in the direction of increased due process for juvenile offenders. These modifications anticipated the revised standards which are demanded by the *Gault* decision. Lemert observes that these legislative revisions have not been fully implemented in California courts. The message from his research is clear, that it may be some time before the full impact of the *Gault* decision is felt throughout the United States. The articulation of new rules is one thing, but their implementation is another. Individual juvenile courts may be laggardly in responding to the directives of the Supreme Court.

Some additional comments regarding the juvenile court are in order in this introductory discussion. To begin with, procedures and facilities for detention of juveniles before and after court hearings is another area where the court has come under criticism. In many smaller jurisdictions throughout the country, youthful offenders are held in jails or other facilities commonly regarded as unfit places for children. In large metropolitan communities, some kind of juvenile hall or detention facility often exists in which juvenile referrals are detained and in which other court operations are also conducted. In many of these juvenile halls, physical separation of dependent from delinquent subjects is not maintained because of overcrowding; physical separation of younger from older offenders breaks down; the facilities are lacking in educational and recreational programs; and other glaring deficiencies characterize them.

One thing is known about detention facilities—many of them fall far short of standards for adequate juvenile halls. However, there are a number of facets of juvenile detention which cry out for investigation. Almost nothing is known about the decision processes which result in some referrals being held in detention while others are released to their parents pending court appearance. No detailed sociological investigation of the organizational structure or social life within detention facilities has been carried out. For these reasons we have not been able to include here an essay on detention halls.

Juvenile courts are supposed to be equipped with a range of alternative dispositions that they can utilize in dealing with juvenile offenders. Facilities should be available for outpatient psychiatric treatment of some wards; foster homes are in order for others; probation supervision is called for in some cases; and commitment to an institution is to be used for the most intractable and difficult wards. But in point of fact, psychiatric services, foster homes, and a variety of private agencies for youthful offenders are rarely encountered in juvenile courts. Instead, in most of them, adjudicated offenders are either placed on probation or sent off to a training school.

The activities of probation officers are the subject of attention in Part V of this book. However, it ought to be noted here that probation agents are in short supply in many courts. As a result, these officers are plagued with huge case loads and are able to give only cursory and superficial attention to youths who are under their care. Several time-and-motion studies of juvenile probation officers are available which show them to be engaged in routine administrative tasks, report writing, and other maintenance tasks which have little to do with juvenile rehabilitation.[2] These in-

2. Lewis Diana, "Is Casework in Probation Necessary?" *Focus*, XXXIV (January 1955), 1–8; Gertrude M. Hengerer, "Organizing Probation Services," *National Probation and Parole Association Yearbook, 1953*, pp. 45–59.

vestigations add further details to the picture of the juvenile court as a rusty and underpowered piece of social machinery.

One indication of the gap between the actual and the ideal in the juvenile court is shown in a nationwide study of juvenile court judges conducted in 1963.[3] That survey dealt with 1564 judges, about half of all juvenile court magistrates in the nation. Nearly all of the judges were males, 93 per cent were married, and their average age was 53.

About three-fourths of the judges had completed two years of college, but only 51 per cent had obtained bachelor's degrees. Nearly three-fourths had law degrees, but 24 per cent of them had no legal education whatever! The average amount of legal experience before taking judicial office was nine years, but one-fourth of the judges had no prior legal experience. Of the 1298 full-time judges in the sample, 72 per cent spent less than one-fourth of their time on juvenile court matters. The mean income for the judges was $12,490; rural magistrates earned considerably less than this figure and judges in metropolitan areas earned more than the overall average. The mean salary of $12,490 was less than that of judges of general trial-courts and lawyers in private practice.

Clearly, the statistics above do not show juvenile court judges to be the well trained figures one would desire in an ideal juvenile court. Along the same line, one-third of these judges asserted that they had no probation officers to aid them.

One part of this study of juvenile court judges dealt with their attitudes and orientations. This research is included as the second paper in this section. In general, it shows juvenile court judges to be less punitive and more social service-oriented than other law enforcement and correctional workers with whom they were compared.

3. Shirley D. McCune and Daniel L. Skoler, "Juvenile Court Judges in the United States. Part I: A National Profile," *Crime and Delinquency*, XI (April 1965), 121–131.

7. The Juvenile Court—Quest and Realities

EDWIN M. LEMERT

"Better a snotty child than his nose wiped off."

Roscoe Pound called the juvenile court one of the great social inventions of the 19th century. But the enthusiasms heralding its birth and early history have dampened considerably with the slow stain of passing time. Its later years have been those of unmet promise and darkened with growing controversy. Evidence that it has prevented crime or lessened the recidivism of youthful offenders is missing, and dour sociological critics urge that it contributes to juvenile crime or inaugurates delinquent careers by imposition of the stigma of wardship, unwise detention, and incarceration of children in institutions which don't reform and often corrupt. The occasional early voice of the dissenting judge and of the frustrated lawyer has grown to a heavy swell of modern contention that the juvenile court under the noble guise of humanitarian concern and scientific treatment of the problems of children too often denies them the elements of justice and fair play.

Reprinted from the President's Commission on Law Enforcement and Administration of Justice, *Task Force Report: Juvenile Delinquency and Youth Crime* (Washington, D.C.: U.S. Government Printing Office, 1967), pp. 91–106.

Even more impressive than the mounting volume of polemic literature and responsible criticism arraigning the court are the concrete actions taken by a number of leading States, such as New York and California, Minnesota, and indeed, the State of its origin, Illinois, which in years immediately past have substantially or drastically revised their laws dealing with the form and operations of the juvenile court. Other States have seen the appointment of committees of inquiry and new legislation introduced to amend significant aspects of their juvenile or family courts. Events as well as the literature of protest compel thoughtful persons to a searching reconsideration of the makeup and purposes of the juvenile court in a society dominated by large-scale social organization, aggressive public welfare ideologies, and mass-produced justice.

The Philosophy and Function of the Juvenile Court

Much has been said of the philosophy of the juvenile court and little that is definitive can be added to it, other than to note that the very preoccupation with its philosophy sets it apart from other courts. In general, American courts created for children were given broad grants of power by legislatures to protect and help children, depart from strict rules of legal procedure, and utilize kinds of evidence ordinarily excluded from criminal and civil adjudication. There have been attempts by some writers to discover historical continuity between the juvenile court and courts of equity or chancery following guardianship proceedings. But these have been held to be dubious excercises at best, and in the words of a wry English judge, little more than spurious justifications for the sometimes "highhanded methods of American judges." As he and others have noted, equity procedure clearly requires evidentiary findings within specifiable limits conspicuously lacking in our early juvenile court statutes.

It is less profitable to speculate on the philosophy of the juvenile court than to examine its historical development and the variety of its adaptations to regional and local necessities. Such an examination will benefit by heuristically distinguishing the official goals of the court from its functions, particularly those which sociologists call unintended or unanticipated consequences of purposeful action. In so doing it becomes apparent that the functions of the juvenile court in reality are several, dictated by its peculiar sociolegal characteristics. Thus while it is well known to sociologists of law that regular courts may serve a number of extralegal or nonlegal ends, such as, for example, an action for damages brought solely to embarass a business competitor, the anomalous design of the juvenile court has made its extraneous, nonlegal functions paramount.

In historical retrospect the juvenile court has the look of an agency of social control directed to raising and maintaining standards of child care, protection, and family morals, a purpose currently reinforced by its close association with social welfare organizations. At the same time the juvenile court by virtue of its inescapable identity as a court of law is an agency of law enforcement seeking to reduce and prevent crime, but also protecting legal rights. Finally, it serves purposes derived from its essentially local nature as an arena of conflict resolution, in which conflicts within and between families, between individuals, and between organizations (not excluding those within the court itself) are aired, dramatized, and sometimes turned into cold war compromises.

Despite their insular character and the cloak of independence given juvenile courts by their connection with the regular courts, they tend to reflect patterns of values and power alinements within the community or areas they service. When this is joined with the fact that there are 50 federated States, these States having from 5 to 58 more or less autonomous juvenile courts each, it is painfully clear that efforts to outline the distinctive philosophy and function of the juvenile court are feckless. It is, however, possible to state that juvenile courts in action generally reveal variations in the order in which values falling within the three areas of function of the court are satisfied. This permits questions to be raised as to whether and how the juvenile court should be restructured so that certain value orders do not occur, or further, so that some of the values currently satisfied will be excluded from its decisions and patterns of action.

There are some social science propositions which can serve well enough as guides for those seeking to install new forms and methods in the juvenile court. A salient one is that the family, even though badly attenuated or disturbed by conflict, morally questionable, or broken by divorce or death, continues to be the institution of choice for the socialization of children. Neither the Spartan gymnasium, nor the Russian creches, nor the Israeli Kibbutz nurseries, nor scientifically run childrens' homes have been found to successfully duplicate the sociopsychological mystique which nurtures children into stable adults. Explicit recognition of this might very well preface the juvenile court codes and statutes of the land. At the same time it would be well to delete entirely from such laws pious injunctions that "care, custody and discipline of children under the control of the juvenile court shall approximate that which they would receive from their parents," which taken literally becomes meaningless either as ideal or reality. Neither the modern state nor an harassed juvenile court judge is a father; a halfway house is not a home; a reformatory cell is not a teenager's bedroom; a juvenile hall counselor is not a dutch uncle; and a cottage matron is not a mother. This does not mean that the people referred to should not be or are not kindly and dedicated, but rather that they are first and foremost members of organizations, bound by institution controls and subject to its exigencies; they are enforcers of superimposed rules. Where conflicts arise between the interests of a youth and those of the organization to which these functionaires are bureaucratically responsible there is no pattern of action which can predict that they will observe an order of value satisfaction favorable to the youth's interest.

Stigma

Social scientists familiar with the juvenile court and its problems in the main agree that one of the great unwanted consequences of wardship, placement, or commitment to a correctional institution is the imposition of stigma. Such stigma, represented in modern society by a "record," gets translated into effective handicaps by heightened police surveillance, neighborhood isolation, lowered receptivity and tolerance by school officials, and rejections of youth by prospective employers. Large numbers of youth appearing in juvenile court have lower class status or that of disadvantaged minorities, whose limited commitments to education already puts them in difficulties in a society where education increasingly provides access to economic opportunity. Given this, the net effect of juvenile court wardship too often is to add to their handicaps or to multiply problems confronting them and their families.

Lest these seem like animadversions or imprecise charges, consider the hard facts that social welfare agencies can be identified which as a matter of policy, without delving into the facts of the case, arbitrarily refuse to accept as clients youth who have been wards of the juvenile court. The reality of stigma due to wardship is also borne home by the firmed policy of the Armed Forces, which may make it the grounds for rejection, or most certainly the bar to officer candidacy. The paradoxical expression of stigma often colors the statements of probation and correctional officers, even judges, who at certain stages of a youth's progress through juvenile court and beyond, openly label him as a type destined for failure.

Proposals, laws, and administrative action to preserve the anonymity of juvenile court proceedings through closed hearings, sealing case records, and expunging records are probably worthy moves, but it is vain to expect them to eliminate the stigma of wardship and contacts with the juvenile court. In smaller communities, as one judge observed, "Everyone knows about juvenile court cases anyway." In larger communities strongly organized police departments can be expected to resist rigorous controls over delinquency records detrimental to their efficiency, and will search for ways to circumvent them. Employers denied information from juvenile courts often get the desired facts from the police.

Expunging records is not the simple operation it may seem. In California it requires initiative from the party concerned and usually the assistance of an attorney; the procedure necessitates a hearing, and it may be complicated or impossible if a person has been a juvenile ward in more than one county. Private and public organizations can and do protect themselves by including questions about a juvenile record on application forms for employment or for occupational licenses, indicating that perjured replies will be grounds for rejection. The applicant has the unpleasant "damned if you do, damned if you don't" choice of lying or revealing damaging facts about himself. Finally, it is doubtful whether total anonymity of juvenile court hearings and records is in the public interest.

While the successful management of stigma by individuals is not impossible, the necessary insights and social skills are not given to many people, least of all immature youth or those struggling with other status handicaps. A number of social psychologists, including the author, believe that social rejections provoked by such stigma may reinforce a self-image held by the individual that he is no good or that he can't make it on the outside. They may feed a brooding sense of injustice which finds expression in further delinquency, or they may support, strengthen, and perpetuate ideological aspects of delinquent subcultures. In this sense the juvenile court may become a connecting or intervening link of a vicious circle in which delinquency causes delinquency.

Preventing Delinquency

The indiscriminate way in which stigma embraces juvenile court wards raises the most serious questions about an important part of the rationale for state intervention into the lives of youth and parents through the juvenile court. Reference here is to the idea that delinquency can be or will be thereby prevented. This belief rests upon uncritical conceptions that there are substantive behaviors, isometric in nature, which precede delinquency, much like prodromal signs of the onset of disease. The viability of these ideas probably can be traced to their lineal ties with older, repressive Puritan philosophy; they received new life from early 20th century propaganda of the mental hygiene movement, which helped to birth child guidance clinics, school social work, and establish juvenile courts in many areas. Quaint examples of these views were the 19th century convictions that smoking or drinking by youth, shining shoes, selling newspapers, or frequenting poolrooms insidiously set them on a downward path toward a life of crime. Their contemporary survivals can be seen in unproved concepts like predelinquent personality, or delinquency prone, and in laws of a number of States which make truancy, running away from home, or refusal to obey parents or school officials jurisdictional bases for juvenile court control.

Social science research and current theory in social psychology refute the idea that there are fixed, inevitable sequences in delinquent or criminal careers. As yet no behavior patterns or personality tendencies have been isolated and shown to be the antecedents of delinquency, and it is unlikely that they will be. Furthermore, youthful actions conventionally regarded as delinquent tendencies in a number of jurisdictions, such as truancy, curfew violations, incorrigibility, and running away from home on close examination are found to correspond to no behavior entities, but rather to arbitrary definitions by school authorities, parents, and police. Truancy is defined variously, depending on the area, by anywhere from 3 to 10 days of unexplained absences. An older New York investigation into a large number of cases of truancy disclosed little or no similarity in the contingencies associated with school absences. Indeed, to a degree they were simply a measure of the willingness or availability of parents to write excuses for their children. Runaways found in juvenile court cases cover departures from home ranging from a few hours to 2 months, and incorrigibility may mean anything from refusing a mother's order not to see a boy friend to attacking a parent with a knife. While curfews are useful administrative devices for policing communities, there are attorneys who argue that the associated ordinances are questionable law because they leave violations incapable of definition.

The allegation of incorrigibility often is difficult to distinguish from that of parental neglect or unfitness, and both kinds of allegations at times arise in a welter of accusations and counteraccusations which are quieted by arbitrary fixing of the blame by a probation officer assigned to investigate the case.

The brave idea that the juvenile court can prevent delinquency is further deflated or even reduced to absurdity by sociological studies of unreported or hidden delinquency. These have brought to light that the majority of high school and college students at some time or another engage in delinquencies, not excluding serious law violations. The main difference which emerged from comparisons of delinquencies, by college students and those by youths who had been made wards of juvenile courts was the greater recidivism of the latter group. While these data admit of several interpretations, on their face they demand explanation as to why the large population of youth committing delinquent acts and made court wards commit more rather than fewer delinquencies. The conclusion that the court processing rather than the behaviors in some way helps to fix and perpetuate delinquency in many cases is hard to escape.

There are other data which suggest that formal efforts by the juvenile court to shape the course of childhood and adolescent development away from hypothetically dire directions in the large may be gratuitous or self-defeating. The reference is to facts or common knowledge that most youth pass through epochs in their lives when they engage in activities definable in other than their contexts as delinquency. Children normally play hookey, help themselves to lumber from houses under construction, snitch lipstick or other items from 10-cent stores, swipe some beer, get a little drunk, borrow a car, hell around, learn about sex from an available female or prostitute, or give the old man a taste of his own medicine. Transitional deviance not only is ubiquitous in our society but universal to all societies, especially among boys turning into men—Margaret Mead's droll observations on adolescence in the south seas to the contrary notwithstanding.

Most youth phase out of their predelinquency, so-called, and their law flaunting; they put away childish things, ordinarily as they become established in society by a job, marriage, further education, or the slow growth of wisdom. Maturation out of the deviance of adolescence is facilitated by a process of normalization in which troublesome behavior, even petty crimes, are dealt with by parents, neighbors, and law people as manifestations of the inevitable diversity, perversity, and shortcomings of human beings—in other words, as problems of everyday living calling for tolerable solutions short of perfection. This means the avoidance whenever possible of specialized or categorical definitions which invidiously differentiate, degrade, or stigmatize persons involved in the problems. The costs of "muddling through" with children who become problems have multiplied with the rising plateau of mass conformities needed for a high-energy society but they must be absorbed in large part where the alternatives are even more costly.

The 3-Minute Children's Hour

The ideology of delinquency prevention is much more urban than rural. Handling problems of youthful disorders and petty crime in rural areas and small towns, characteristically by sheriffs' deputies, town police, the district attorney, and probation officer in the past and even yet today in many places has been largely informal. Sharp distinctions are drawn between less consequential moral and legal infractions—"mickey mouse stuff"—and serious delinquencies, with no implications that one conduces to the other. This is reflected in the reluctance of elective officials and those beholden to them to make records of their action, but at the same time for action in serious misdemeanors and crimes by youth to be swift and punitive. The juvenile court usually reserves formal action for real problems of families and the community; the functional context of youthful misconduct ordinarily can be realistically gauged and its consequences dealt with in a number of different situations.

A major difficulty in the large bureaucratic urban juvenile court is that the functional context of child problems directed to it easily gets lost; it has to be reconstructed by bits and pieces of information obtained through investigations and inquiries conducted under highly artificial circumstances, and communicated in written reports which easily become stereotyped as they pass from person to person. There is little or no direct community feedback of criticism and reaction which might put individual cases into a commonsense context which would encourage normalization. This plus the rapidity with which cases are heard in large courts (3 minutes per case in Los Angeles circa 1959) explains why the distinction between mild and serious child problems breaks down or disappears. A notorious illustration of the tendency came to light in Orange County, Calif., in 1957 when a private attorney put his own investigator to work on a case of an 8- and 9-year-old boy and girl accused of a sex crime against a 7-year-old girl. It was discovered that the probation officer presenting the case in court had not even investigated, and the private investigator's report swiftly pared down the charge to an imputed incident witnessed by no one and reported 2 days after it supposedly occurred.

While it would push facts too far to insist that the ideology of preventing delinquency is used deliberately by juvenile courtworkers and judges to justify slipshod operations which bring cases of benign youthful misbehavior before them under the duress of formal allegations, nevertheless it has allowed them to change the basis of jurisdiction from one problem to another. The practice is baldly indicated in the statement of a California judge arguing for retention under juvenile court jurisdiction of simple traffic violations by juveniles:

> Moreover it seems to have been demonstrated that the broad powers of the juvenile court can be helpfully invoked on behalf of children whose maladjustment has been brought to light through juvenile traffic violations. A girl companion of a youthful speeder may be protected from further sexual experimentation. Boys whose only amusement seems to be joyriding in family cars can be directed to other more suitable forms of entertainment before they reach the stage of borrowing cars when the family car is unavailable.

Police and Community Delinquency Prevention

The ideology of delinquency prevention and statutes incorporating special laws for regulating the conduct of children have not been ill adapted to the needs and problems of police in large cities, and to some extent have been their outgrowth. It needs to be emphasized, however, that police generally are less concerned with the prevention of delinquency in individual cases than in its prevention and control as a communitywide problem variously manifested in gang violence, disturbances of public order, a rise in crime rates, or mounting property losses. The special utility to police of specious legal categories describing delinquent tendencies is most obvious when they seek to break up youthful gang activity, quell public disturbances, such as occur at drive-ins or public parks, gain access to witnesses or sources of information to solve a crime series or to recover stolen property. While the arrest and detention of youth to clear up other crimes may be efficient police tactics, abuses may arise at the expense of individual youths if such methods can be pursued under diffuse charges. Unfortunately there have been and are judges willing to allow juvenile detention to be used for these purposes. It was for reasons such as these that the Juvenile Justice Commission of California, following a statewide survey, in 1960 recommended legislation to encourage the use of citations for minor offenses by juveniles, and to require that detention hearings be held within specified time limits to act as a check on overzealous police action.

Lest a picture be left of police as ruthless manipulators of juveniles of law enforcement ends, be it noted that in a number of areas they have sought to aid juveniles avoid clashes with the law through setting up recreation programs, Big Brother assignments, informal probation, and even police social work. However, such undertakings have declined in recent years and tend to be looked upon as too widely divergent from essential police functions. This also may point to growing disillusionment with more generalized or communitywide delinquency prevention programs. Police in some cities sharply disagree with community organizers of such projects over the issue of maintaining the autonomy of neighborhood gangs; they tend to take a jaundiced view of proposals and attempts to divert such groups from law breaking into more compliant pursuits.

Research assessments of community programs to prevent delinquency, such as the Chicago area project, the Harlem project, and the Cambridge-Somerville youth study, have been disappointing; results either have been negative or inconclusive. Possible exceptions are community coordinating councils, especially in the Western United States where they originated. However, they seem to work best in towns between 2,000 and 15,000 population; it remains unclear whether they can be adapted successfully to large urban areas. Significantly, they work chiefly by exchanging agency information, and referrals of cases to community agencies, with full support and cooperation of the police. In effect they represent concerted action to bypass the juvenile court, and it might be said that their purpose if not function is prevention of delinquency by preventing, wherever possible, the adjudication of cases in the court.

Treatment of Child Problems and Delinquency

Much of what has already been said about preventing delinquency by means of juvenile court intervention is equally applicable as criticism of intervention by the court to treat youth problems and delinquency by therapeutic means. The ideal of therapeutic treatment found its way into juvenile court philosophy from social work and psychiatry, its pervasiveness measurable by the extent to which persons educated and trained in social work have indirectly influenced the juvenile court or moved into probation and correctional officer positions. An underlying premise of therapeutic treatment of children is that scientific knowledge and techniques exist making possible specific solutions to individual and family problems. It seeks to impose the positivism of hard science upon individual behavior.

Scientific social work, whose tenets were originally laid down by Mary Richmond in her early work, "Social Diagnosis," eventually came to lean heavily upon theories of Freudian psychiatry, taking over its psychobiological orientation and the medicinal idea that childhood problems and delinquency are symptoms of unresolved Oedipal conflicts. Updated versions of socially applied psychoanalysis conceive of delinquency as an acting out of repressed conflicts in irrational, disguised forms. Accent in treatment is laid upon the internal emotional life rather than upon external acts; the social worker or the psychiatrist is a specialist who understands the problems while the client does not; the specialist knows best, studies, analyzes, and treats, much in the manner of the authoritative medical practitioner.

A divergent, competing line of thought in social work repudiates scientific treatment in favor of a more simple conception of its task as essentially a helping process, in which problems are confronted in whatever terms the child or youth presents them; responsible involvement of the client is a sine qua non of success in this process. Needless to say, this conception of the nature of social work is much more compatible with a philosophy of democracy.

Generally speaking, social workers advocate a more curtailed dispositional function for the juvenile court and advocate assigning to other agencies many of the tasks it has assumed. Some social workers seriously doubt wether the helping process can be carried on in an authoritarian setting, and to emphasize their stand refuse as clients children who have been wards of the court. Other social workers believe that judges go beyond their competence, and should use their power solely for adjudication, after which determination of treatment should pass on to social work agencies. A smaller number of social workers hold to a more sanguine view of reconciling personal help and authority within the role of the probation officer. Finally, there are some social workers who are not beyond using juvenile court power as a tool for getting access to clients, or prolonging their contacts with them because they will benefit from treatment. Experience showed that this pattern became aggravated in Utah during the period when juvenile courts there were under the administrative control of the State department of welfare.

A long-standing, ubiquitous problem of social workers and psychiatrists of whatever theoretical persuasion has been that of the noninvolvement of their clients or patients. Clients are either disinclined to seek their services or they break off contacts after they have been established, or they respond superficially without showing interest in changing their personal values or life styles. Much of the difficulty stems from the identification of social workers with middle-class values and the invidious moralistic implications of imputing defective personalities to those they try to assist. As a result, barriers to communication often become insurmountable.

Actually, comparatively few juvenile court cases are referred to social workers for treatment and many juvenile court judges and probation officers are inhospitable toward social workers. According to a U. S. Children's Bureau study some years ago, the most frequent disposition of juvenile court cases was dismissal, followed by informal or formal supervision under a probation officer. Dismissals can scarcely be called treatment even though the associated court appearance before an admonitory judge may have a chastening effect upon some youths. At most, such cases have a brief exchange with an intake or investigating officer who asks some questions, issues a stern warning, and says he hopes he will not see the boy again.

The consequences of supervision of delinquents by probation officers either in parental homes or in foster homes have been little studied and the outcome, even when successful, little understood. Probation practices with juveniles have little in common if the Nation is taken as a whole, and often they consist of a bare minimum of office interviews and phone or mail reports. The frequent claim of probation officers that they could give more help to their charges if they had more time for supervision must be scouted as an occupational complaint rather than an accurate prediction of treatment possibilities. What little research there is on the subject has shown that mere reduction of the size of caseloads of probation and parole officers does not in itself lower rates of recidivism of those supervised.

If the results of probation supervision of delinquents on the whole are disappointing or inconclusive, even less can be said in behalf of the treatment of juvenile offenders undertaken under institutional commitments. Sociological analysis and evaluations of correctional programs in institutional settings tend to be uniformly negative, with some writers taking a position that the goals of correctional programs in prisons and reformatories are inherently self-defeating. This follows from the very fact of incarceration, which by necessarily posing a series of problems of personal deprivation for inmates, generates a more or less antithetical subculture which negates and subverts formal programs of rehabilitation. The logistics of processing delinquents or criminal populations brings large numbers of recidivists to the institutions, where they control informal communication and face-to-face interaction which importantly shapes the course of inmate socialization.

The problems of correctional institutions for delinquents have been highlighted in the popular press and literature as those of poor physical plants, niggardly appropriations and underpaid, undereducated personnel, but to the social scientist they lie far deeper. At this writing it remains doubtful whether the generously funded and well-staffed California Youth Authority has neared its original purpose of providing individualized treatment for youthful offenders. This has not been due to a lack of dedication of its leadership, but rather has resulted from having to assume the task of institutional administration, in which sheer numbers of commitments, contingencies, conflicting values of staff and custody people, and organizational inertia daily conspire to defeat the purpose of treatment. The top people of CYA have not been unaware of its dilemmas, which accounts for recent moves to establish large-scale community treatment projects and a probation subsidy program devised to stimulate local innovations in the supervision or treatment of juveniles as alternatives to commitment.

The less-than-sanguine remarks here directed to the ideology of delinquency treatment do not exclude the possibility that clinically trained and humanly wise people cannot help youth solve problems which have brought them athwart the law. Rather the intent is to leaven professional contumely with humility, to place the notion of treatment into a more realistic perspective, and to point out denotative differences between dealing with problems of human relationships and treatment as it has evolved in the practice of medicine. The treatment of delinquency is best regarded as a kind of guidance, special education, and training, much more akin to midwifery than medicine, in which hopeful intervention into an ongoing process of maturation is undertaken. Objective criteria for the use of methods of intervening, and controlled conditions necessary for predictable outcomes are neither present nor likely to be. Hence the actions of a judge, probation officer, correctional counselor, or an institutional psychiatrist at most can be small influences brought to bear among many simultaneously affecting child development and emergence of youth into adulthood. Although the power and the authority of the juvenile court can determine that certain intervenings will take place in a prescribed order in the process of socialization they cannot control the meanings and values assigned to such occurrences.

Judicious Nonintervention

The aims of preventing delinquency and the expectation of definitively treating a profusion of child‧ and parental problems have laid an impossible burden upon the juvenile court, and they may be seriously considered to have no proper part in its philosophy. If there is a defensible philosophy for the juvenile court it is one of judicious nonintervention. It is properly an agency of last resort for children, holding to a doctrine analogous to that of appeal courts which require that all other remedies be exhausted before a case will be considered. This means that problems accepted for action by the juvenile court will be demonstrably serious by testable evidence ordinarily distinguished by a history of repeated failures at solutions by parents, relatives, schools, and community agencies. The model should be derived from the conservative English and Canadian juvenile courts, which in contrast to the American, receive relatively few cases.

This statement of juvenile court philosophy rests upon the following several propositions:

1. Since the powers of the juvenile court are extraordinary, properly it should deal with extraordinary cases.
2. Large numbers of cases defeat the purposes of the juvenile court by leading to bureaucratic procedures antithetical to individualized treatment (guidance).
3. The juvenile court is primarily a court of law and must accept limitations imposed by the inapplicability of rule and remedy to many important phases of human conduct and to some serious wrongs. Law operates by punishment, injunction against specific acts, specific redress, and substitutional redress. It cannot by such means make a father good, a mother moral, a child obedient, or a youth respectful of authority.
4. When the juvenile court goes beyond legal remedies it must resort to administrative agents, or itself become such an agency, which produces conflicts and confusion of values and objectives. Furthermore, it remains problematical whether child and parental problems can be solved by administrative means.

It may be protested that the conception of the juvenile court adumbrated here is so narrow as to emasculate it or take away any distinctive purpose. However, if it can be accepted that many acts termed delinquent in reality are not equatable with adult crimes, and that many situations called dangerous for youth on close examination turn out to be functions of moral indignation by persons and groups who, to paraphrase Maitland, "Screw up standards of reasonable ethical propriety to unreasonable heights," then organized nonintervention by the juvenile court assumes a definite protective function for youth. It has become equally or more important to protect children from unanticipated and unwanted consequences of organized movements, programs and services in their behalf than from the unorganized, adventitious "evils" which gave birth to the juvenile court. America no longer has any significant number of Fagans, exploiters of child labor, sweatshops, open saloons, houses of prostitution, street trades, an immoral servant class, cruel immigrant fathers, traveling carnivals and circuses, unregulated racetracks, open gambling, nor professional crime as it once existed. The battles for compulsory education have long since been won and technological change has eliminated child labor—perhaps too well. The forms of delinquency have changed as the nature of society has changed; social and personal problems of youth reflect the growth of affluence in one area of society and the growth of hostility and aggression in a nonaffluent sector. Current sociological theories of delinquency stress drift and risktaking as causes on one hand and on the other deprivation and dilapidated opportunity structures.

The basic life process today is one of adaptation to exigencies and pressures; individual morality has become functional rather than sacred or ethical in the older sense. To recognize this at the level of legislative and judicial policy is difficult because social action in America always has been heavily laden with moral purpose. However, if the juvenile court is to become effective, its function must be reduced to enforcement of the ethical minimum of youth conduct necessary to maintain social life in a high energy, pluralistic society. Given this lower level of function, it can then proceed to its secondary task of arranging the richest possible variety of assistance to those specially disadvantaged children and youth who come under its jurisdiction.

Structuring the Juvenile Court

A philosophy of judicious nonintervention demands more than verbal or written exhortation for implementation. Action is needed to research and redefine the jurisdiction of the court, the nature of the roles assigned to its personnel, and its procedures. Ideally it will be so structured that it will have built-in controls, feedback mechanisms, and social scanning devices which make it self-regulating and adaptive. This by no means signifies that the juvenile court should or will become inner directed; if anything, contacts and interaction with the community and its agencies will have more importance, if for no other reason than to guard its stance of nonintervention.

It follows that relationships between juvenile courts and policing agencies probably will become more critical with a shrinkage in juvenile court functions. However, it can be hoped that this will be an irritant means whereby more police departments develop juvenile bureaus and upgrade their competence for screening and adjusting cases within their own cognizance. Even now it is common practice for many police departments to dismiss large numbers of juvenile arrests or adjust them within the department. More and better trained juvenile officers and rationalizing of their procedures can greatly decrease referrals to juvenile courts. This does not mean that police should develop their own probation or social work service, but rather will parsimoniously utilize contacts with relatives and referrals to community agencies, or at most, engage in brief, policeman-like counseling with youths where they believe it may do some good. One way to answer the cry of American police for public support is to funnel grants of aid into juvenile officer training and police consultation services.

Since police probably always will to some extent seek to employ the juvenile court for their own special purposes of keeping law and order or preventing crime in the large, the second line of defense protecting jurisdictional boundaries of the juvenile court must be manned by intake workers of the juvenile court or the probation department serving it. These ideally should be organized into an intake, referral, and adjustment division, where the maximum effort of the court is made by its most competent personnel. Organizational considerations suggest that it should have a good deal of autonomy, assuming that a high caliber of staff is reached, and be oriented toward the social welfare agencies of the community. Denial of applications for petitions should be its clear-cut prerogative.

In some large probation departments it may be possible to erect a still higher level of screening by a special division of the workers who file petitions for assuming jurisdiction by the court. Again, some organizational independence would be needed to reject petition applications sent forward by intake people. To an extent such screening already exists in many probation departments but tends to be overshadowed by functional specialization due to the heavy volume of investigations and placements in overworked courts. If probation departments were so empowered that investigations of the factual basis of law violations were a mandatory police function, more time and energy could be allocated to screening, referrals, and dispositions work.

As Paul Tappan and others have noted, referral of cases from juvenile courts to social work agencies is complicated by unwillingness of the latter to expand their resources on hostile or unco-operative clients. Believing that contact with the juvenile court fosters unco-operativeness in youth, many agencies, as previously stated, refuse their referrals. Juvenile courts which take on the treatment of children with small difficulties, which often are indistinguishable from those daily being handled in large numbers by welfare agencies, forego their opportunities to make use of referrals at a later date. For this reason, it appears that referrals should be made immediately, prior to detention, minus confrontations with youth and parents, or without investigations which go beyond the reasons for their referral to the court. Intake interviews and citation hearings should not turn into fishing expeditions to uncover and record problems to justify further action by the court.

JURISDICTION

Action to narrow and refine the functions of the juvenile court will need much greater precision than now holds in setting the jurisdictional limits to its authority, explicitly with reference to problem categories and minimum age of cases accepted. Statutes conferring jurisdiction over children on the juvenile court generally differentiate four categories: (1) Those lacking care due to contingencies of family life—death, absence of a parent or parents, or their inability to provide the care, (2) those who are neglected or mistreated, (3) those who disregard, defy, or disobey authority of parents, guardians, custodians, or teachers, (4) those who violate laws. Popularly, administratively, and to some extent legally, these categories are status attributions designating the dependent child, the neglected child, and the delinquent. Although the early and primary aim of the juvenile court was to abolish the stigma of such statutes, this has not occurred, and the pall of moral questionability continues to settle over all children made wards in these categories.

It is difficult or impossible in the face of facts known about modern society to defend the locus of jurisdiction over dependent children in the juvenile court on any grounds other than convenience. Just why, for example, a child whose mother must be committed to a mental hospital should be made the ward of a court whose latent structure is criminal is not readily explainable. The same is true for children whose parents' problems stem from deficient income, or unemployability due to disability or illness; likewise for orphaned and illegitimate children. Granted that some person or agency other than parents must take custody, and that this needs legal sanction, there is no irrebuttable proof that this cannot be done by civil courts, with welfare agencies receiving custody, so long as a time limit is placed upon its duration and the rights of child and parents presumptively kept by law.

Probation officers are apt to defend juvenile court jurisdiction over dependent children by referring to cases in which a delinquent child and a dependent child are in the same family and to contend that duplicate supervision should be avoided. They also have defended placing dependent children in the same institution with delinquent children on these grounds and the additional one that families should not be broken up. Yet in a number of areas welfare agencies carry a large share of the supervision of dependency cases for the juvenile court, and on the whole they are probably better prepared than probation officers to supervise such cases. Unless a child presents the most serious kind of delinquency or unless welfare agencies refuse to do the job, less delinquent and dependent children in the same family should be under welfare supervision.

The arguments for retaining juvenile court jurisdiction over neglected children are somewhat stronger but still questionable, for if the child's problem is truly the fault of his parents why should he receive the stigma of wardship? The suspicion is strong that juvenile court procedure has been invoked to gain control over children where it would be troublesome or impossible to prove neglect in an adult criminal court, borne out by the fact that statutes in some States allow such cases to be tried in juvenile courts. Admittedly a knotty problem exists, but it is a problem of court procedure and law for which children should not pay the costs. If it is necessary to put parents on probation it should be done by regular legal procedures, and if a child must be removed from their custody let it be placed through a welfare agency, and as with dependent children, a time limit set to such custody carrying the presumption that parents will have mended their ways at its termination.

A less obvious but more pervasive reason why juvenile court people wish to retain jurisdiction over dependent and neglected children lies in persistent beliefs that the roots of delinquency and crime are discoverable in dependency and parental neglect. These ideas, descended from hoary biblical notions and 19th century, middle-class moralism, and outmoded by modern sociology, still have their partisans. A 1959 annual report of a probation department strongly oriented in a psychiatric direction and serving a heavily middle-class population, speaks of the function of its separate dependency and neglect unit:

> Implicit in the function of this unit is the concept that it is very probable that the basis for delinquent acting out has been laid in the children and that delinquency prevention is, therefore, a prime concern.

Sociological research has discovered little durable evidence to support the contention that poverty, broken homes, and many of the chrages of parental unfitness—alcoholism, sexual immorality, or cruelty—are in themselves causes of delinquency. Most delinquents come from intact homes, and various studies comparing the incidence of delinquents with broken and with unbroken homes show differences to rangé from 7 to 24 percent. Furthermore, for every child in a broken home who is delinquent there are on the average two or more brothers or sisters who are non-delinquent. Cruelty or alcoholism in a father can contribute to the growth of serious problems for his children, but nothing in sociological research demonstrates that they will necessarily take the form of breaking laws. The rationale for bringing dependent and neglected children under juvenile court aegis to prevent delinquency rests upon small statistical pluralties which are categorical or group differences, not predictable individual differences.

DELINQUENT TENDENCIES

Truancy, runaways, and incorrigibility already have been shown to be diffuse categories whose conversion into statutory foundation for jurisdiction by the juvenile court is made superficially plausible by unexamined assumptions that they are precursors to delinquency. If the juvenile court is to proceed with approximate uniformity which is a central attribute of law, the weakness of such statutes either as substantive law or as legislative directives for the development of administrative rules is patent. The reasons may be summarized as follows: (1) They lack common meaning from one jurisdiction to another, or between different judge's rulings in the same jurisdiction, (2) they are not derived from any fixed criteria, (3) they assign criminal responsibility to children in many instances where blame or responsibility cannot be determined or where closer investigation would reveal their actions to have been reasonably normal responses to highly provocative or intolerable situations.

If the image of the juvenile court is to be changed from that of a multifarious problem-solving agency, and its functions circumscribed to be more consistent with available means, then its statutory jurisdiction cannot be allowed to rest upon subjective definitions. Furthermore, if it is to avoid the risk of making delinquents by a labeling process, statutes whose vagueness in some localities allow almost any child, given compromising circumstances, to be caught up in the jurisdictional net of the court, must be altered.

Highly important is the fact that when such specious legal grounds as incorrigibility and associated terms are written into statutes as warrants for juvenile court action they invite its use for extraneous conflict resolution. They allow parents, neighbors, school officials, and police—even the youth themselves—to solve their problems by passing them on to the court. No better illustration of this is at hand than the lengthy history of conflict between juvenile court workers and school officials, in which the former accuse the school people of foisting off their own failures onto the court, and the latter replying heatedly that the court is unreceptive or does nothing about really mean kids. Probation officers rue-fully discover in some countries that sheriff's deputies expect them to settle all neighborhood quarrels in which juveniles are involved, and parents or relatives in juvenile court many times leave it clear that they desire their child to be punished for highly personal reasons, or that they have abdicated responsibility for no defensible reason. So long as the court allows itself to be used in these ways it creates its official prob-lems largely by definition.

Runaways must be understood in the same interactional context as incorrigibility, with the added difference that they are proportionately more numerous among girls than boys. Often runaways have the quality of dramatic demonstrations, a little like suicide attempts by adult women, or bids for partisans in an unequal battle with parents. California girl runaways sometimes demand to be placed in detention in order to expose the "hatefulness" of their home situation, or to embarrass their parents. While police action often is clearly indicated in runaways, action by the court is decidedly not. If drama is needed it should be staged under some other auspices.

A depressing sidelight is that the juvenile court itself can be a cause of incorrigibility when in effect it holds a child in contempt. Thus failure to obey an order of the court can be an official reason for a more severe disposition—even commitment to an institution. Runaways from camps may be treated in this way, without any need to inquire into the condi-tions or situation which led to the boy's flight. Inasmuch as the original cause for taking jurisdiction may have been minor, it can be seen how problems of children grow and aggravate in interaction within the court. It might be said that in such cases the ego of the court causes incor-rigibility.

A net conclusion is that incorrigibility, truancy, and running away should not in themselves be causes for assuming juvenile court jurisdiction over children. There is much reason to believe that the bulk of such prob-lems can be handled successfully by referrals, demonstrated by an inquiry in the District of Columbia where it was found that noncourt agencies took responsibility for 98 percent of the total identifiable or reported runa-ways, 95 percent of truancies, 76 percent of sex offenses, and 46 percent of youth termed ungovernable. If disobedience, truancy, and running away are retained as bases for juvenile court jurisdiction, statutes should be rigorously drawn to require a showing of their material relevance to serious law violations, or a showing that other agencies have been incapable of con-taining the problems.

TRAFFIC

The heavy rise in the volume of juvenile traffic offenses in past decades and the large portion of total juvenile arrests for which they account have produced much confusion of procedures and stirred hot debates over the subject of jurisdiction. There are those who contend that ordinary traffic violations of juveniles are no different from those of adults, and since the State in licensing juveniles assumes them capable of ordinary care and caution in operating automobiles, their violations should be processed by regular courts. Opposition to removing jurisdiction over juvenile traffic offenses from the juvenile court has been strong, even fervent, among judges and others who see such proposals as part of a militant campaign to cripple or eliminate the juvenile court. Some of their arguments have validity, namely that juveniles under regular traffic courts would be liable for large, and for them, excessive fines, and that they could be sentenced to jails or road camps in the company of petty criminals and drunkenness offenders. The further claim that juveniles should not be exposed to the routinized, "cash register" justice of adult traffic courts is less convincing, and the argument that the end justifies the means—adjudication in the juvenile court of traffic offenses allows more serious problems to be detected and treated—is from the point of view here presented least defensible of all.

While separate juvenile traffic courts with limited punitive and administrative powers are well enough justified, safeguards are needed to preclude their use as formal or informal catch places to funnel youth into juvenile courts. Organization along the lines of 1959 Minnesota legislation, which spells out that traffic offenses are not to be construed as delinquency, is preferable to placing them within jurisdiction of the juvenile courts. The strongest sanction which juvenile traffic courts can apply is revocation of drivers' licenses, which they must share with State motor vehicle departments. Methods and procedures inevitably bring them closer to those of administrative hearing officers dealing with adult cases there than to those of the juvenile court. Juvenile traffic courts, of course, should be able to make referrals to juvenile courts, but there they should be screened with the same rigor intake people apply to other types of cases presumed less serious. One added protection should be that no social report can be required on juveniles who disobey traffic rules.

AGE

Discussion of the minimum age for juvenile court jurisdiction is muddled by the fact that a specialized, technologically geared society generates functional concepts of age rather than chronological. Thus, in our society, persons as young as 15 years can be licensed to drive automobiles in some States, leave school for adult employment by the time they reach 17 years, yet be unable to marry without parental permission until they are 21. As civilians persons may be unable to purchase alcoholic beverages until past their 21st birthdays yet as members of the Armed Forces may enjoy the right at 18. Moreover, private organizations and community usages conceive responsible age in ways different from those of the law. Insurance companies select 25 years as a cutoff point for assigning high-risk premiums to automobile drivers, and many communities exist where parents see no reason why high school age boys should not be learning to drink. Automobile salesmen are not loath to sell to underage youth, or stores to issue credit to juveniles where legally there is no presumption of financial responsibility.

From such facts it must be concluded that setting a sociologically realistic minimum age for bringing youth under authority of the juvenile court is difficult or impossible if its substantive jurisdiction is pushed too far beyond law violations. Hence any discussion of age limits of jurisdiction must return to the question of the age at which responsibility for criminal actions can be assumed. Most States have settled on age 18 as the minimum below which children cannot be tried in criminal courts. However, this is qualified by statutory exceptions covering such offenses as murder or armed robbery. In highly punitive States the list of such offenses may be quite long.

Any age limit for juvenile court jurisdiction has to be arbitrary because maturation is an uneven process and varies from individual to individual. Furthermore, violation of laws symbolizing highly important social values of life, person and property are likely to arouse public demands for formal demonstration trials and punishment even though the offender involved is below the age limit. For example, cattlemen are apt to take it for granted that no child over 12 years raised by a rancher will be ignorant of or fail to understand the implications of rustling or shooting and butchering stray cattle. More generally the same assumption can be made about the taking of human life by any child who is over 8 or 9 years. The insistence on formal airing and publicity of homicides is likely to be both urgent and widespread, although with child offenders disposition can be greatly mitigated once such needs are met. The point is often missed by more sentimental juvenile court propagandists, for although history shows that a number of very young children have been tried and convicted for murder, harsh sentences seldom have been carried out.

The problems of jurisdiction and age to some extent are met by establishing concurrent jurisdiction in which offenses committed by youth in marginal age categories may be tried in either juvenile or criminal courts. California, for example, establishes 16 years as the minimum age for exclusive jurisdiction by the juvenile court, but shares jurisdiction over 17- through 21-year-old offenders with the superior court. In practice few 18-year-olds are retained by the juvenile court and very rarely those of 19 and 20. Considering that youth of 17 years coming before the courts usually have committed more serious violations and are more likely to have a lengthy juvenile court record, their retention in juvenile court in most cases is immaterial.

As a matter of fact, a youth in these borderline age groups may receive a more lenient disposition as a first time offender in an adult court than as a last resort offender in juvenile court. The most important requirement in concurrent jurisdictions are statutory safeguards to insure that the decision as to where cases in concurrent age categories get heard be made by the juvenile court. This guarantees that the occasional immature youth of 18 or 19 years will not get lost in routine processing by prosecutors and judges in adult courts, who have less experience to make such decisions.

If age is to be an effective means of limiting the authority of the juvenile court it may be as important to tie it to dispositions as jurisdiction. This should be observed closely for children of younger ages, whose offenses while chargeable as law violations qualitatively are seldom comparable to crimes. Here it may be worth recalling a Polish law of the 1920's which forbade sending any youth under 13 years of age to a correctional institution. Statutes in this vein to be meaningful would have to incorporate definitions of correctional institutions to distinguish them from those with educational or training aims, and also exclude assignment of administrative responsibility for the latter to departments of corrections. Full realization of the intent of such laws would hinge upon innovations and new means for controlling the untoward acts of administrative officials and of judges acting in administrative capacities.

PROCEDURES

The wide powers assumed by juvenile courts were more or less inherent consequences of their loose design. The origins of the juvenile courts in humanitarian social movements disposed legislators to see them primarily as child welfare agencies, with the result that early statutes specified few procedures. Subsequent statutory evolution and the growth of "living law" of juvenile courts proved to be extremely divergent, and little in the way of generally accepted case law developed to supply procedural guides, among other reasons because relatively few cases were appealed, and none of these reached the U. S. Supreme Court.

Narrowing the scope of juvenile court functions to avoid what have been its less desirable features calls for new procedures designed to modify and better fix the roles of judges and probation officers, to augment the probabilities of dismissals of cases where indicated, and to change the order of values dominant in dispositions. First and foremost are hard rules governing the number, forms, and timing of hearings, which in many courts have tended to become attenuated, ex parte or even nonexistent. The minimum essential can be no less than provision for hearings in every instance in which the freedom of children is abridged, curtailed by detention or commitment, changed from lesser to greater restraint or custody renewed according to law. Ordinarily this will mean a special hearing if a child is to be placed in a detention facility pending investigation, and a subsequent hearing or hearings when adjudication and disposition are made.

Significant changes in the direction of greater conservativism in juvenile courtwork can be achieved by introducing bifurcated or split hearings, in which adjudication is sharply set apart from dispositions. The first hearing should be devoted to findings of fact rich enough to authorize court jurisdiction, the second to ascertain what should be done with the child, equally rigorous in procedure, but admitting the soft data and evaluations which customarily make up the so-called social report.

Split hearings have had some limited use in civil (auto accident) litigation, and research on their results disclose a large and significant increase in findings for defendants over plaintiffs. A criticism has been made that such hearings may distort the balance of substantive rights between plaintiffs and defendants, but note that this claim has yet to be advanced against criminal prosecutions of adults in which probation investigations and hearings are regularly held after trial and conviction.

The aim of bifurcated hearings in juvenile cases is to make certain that impressionistic, diagnostic, purely recorded, hearsay type evidence will not be received by the court at the time of adjudication. However, the introduction of such hearings alone may go wide of their target if rules concerning admissibility of social reports are not also clarified. Bifurcated hearings were made mandatory in California in 1961 as part of a wholesale revision of its juvenile court law, but according to a 1965 survey by the author, a majority of judges (67 percent) continue to read the dispositional (social) report before jurisdictional hearings. A 1957 survey of New York judges showed about the same proportion of family court judges in that State read social reports before or during adjudication hearings.

California judges seem to take the position that the special work of the juvenile court could not be done without prior reading of the social report, and appellate wisdom in the State has decreed that the social report shall be received in evidence. In contrast, an older New York appellate decision struck directly at the practice as inconsistent with the rights of juveniles and parents. While dogmatic conclusions are out of place here, nevertheless the issue to a sociologist as well as to a civil rights advocate is highly critical, and needs enlightenment by research rather than by opinions. It may be crucially important to learn how the one-third minority of judges in the 2 States, as well as English juvenile court judges, who postpone hearing dispositional evidence, manage to get their work done, and whether its quality or results are any less effective than of judges who proceed into adjudication with knowledge of the social report.

If the contents of the social report continue to be admitted during adjudication hearings or are part of the materials on which the judge makes a finding, then the social report should be open to scrutiny by persons who are its subjects or to their representatives. Authors of statements contained therein should on request be summoned as witnesses to cross-examination in either jurisdictional or dispositional hearing if they are separated in time. As the tenor of the language here implies, the knowledge and skills of competent counsel are prerequisites to the fullest exploitation of such procedural rights and controls.

THE RIGHT TO COUNSEL

Much of the discussion of the right to counsel in juvenile court has been cast in legalistic terms, sifting through appellate decisions to uncover constitutional arguments to vindicate attorneys' claims to a place in the court procedure. The state of legal opinion seems to be that in actuality juveniles and their parents have always had the right to engage counsel to appear in court if they so desire, but that the absence of counsel per se does not imply unfairness and lack of due process; such must be demonstrated to be true on appeal. The differences of opinion lie in questions as to whether the court has a positive obligation to apprise juveniles and parents of their right to counsel and under some circumstances appoint counsel to represent their interests. The 1959 Standard Juvenile Court Act answered these questions in the affirmative, and a number of States now have statutes fixing the right to counsel.

A more generic issue underlying the legal debates revolves about the compatibility of the presence of counsel with the special philosophy of the juvenile court, which ideologically has charged the judge and the probation officer with protection of the child's interests. Rhetorical questions are posed as to whether the presence of counsel will not rob the court of its informality and open it to the possibility of regular adversary proceedings, and whether such a change does not risk converting the juvenile court into little more than a miniaturized criminal court.

The arguments that children as well as adults are entitled to full protection of constitutional rights are quite powerful when considered in the context of a society radically changed since the juvenile court was born. However, it must be heeded that the nature of law has been changing rapidly, hence it may be more informative to examine immediate questions, such as how and to what extent traditional advocacy and adversary interaction can be synthesized with a court which, although more circumscribed in function, must remain a children's court. Beyond this, a hard look must be taken at consequences of the introduction of counsel where it has occurred to see if it does engineer more constraint, preclude unnecessary wardships, or enlarge the range of alternatives for dispositions.

Research on the presence of counsel in the juvenile court has barely begun, so that any conclusions must be tentative. Research by the author in California juvenile courts has shown that advising juveniles and their parents of their right to counsel, as ordered by 1961 legislation, has indeed increased the use of counsel, but that the rate of increase and of current use varies tremendously from county to county. For all counties of the State the gain has been from about 3 percent of the cases to 15 percent. In some counties appearance of attorneys in court has risen from 0 to 1 or 2 percent, in others from a low of 15 percent to highs of 70 or even 90 percent. Generally speaking, the factors found to affect the use of counsel are the existence of a public defender's office and the attitudes of judges and probation officers at the time they advise juveniles and parents of their rights. In assigning counsel, courts tend to favor dependent and neglected children and those in which serious offenses are alleged, likely to be followed by commitment to the California Youth Authority. Thus far there is no evidence of any discrimination in assignment of counsel on the basis of social class or race.

Problems have emerged because private attorneys without experience or knowledge of the juvenile court are unsure as to what their roles should be, and often do little for their clients. Moreover public defenders tend to be co-opted by the court and may simply stipulate to the allegations by the probation officer in order not to make his workload excessive, or even because they think a youth needs some chastening experience or punishment by the court. These tendencies are likely to be pronounced where judges indiscriminately assign counsel and assume that rights of juveniles are thereby fully protected. This leads to a conclusion that mere introduction of counsel into juvenile courts without corresponding strengthening of their intake functions to cut down the sheer numbers of cases processed may be self-defeating. They also suggest that the independent private attorney may be preferable for representing juveniles over public defenders, although the latter have fuller knowledge of the workings of the court.

Another kind of problem develops where youth deny the allegations of the petition and transform hearings into adversary proceedings. The burden of presenting the case or protecting the interests of the public tends to fall most heavily on the probation officer, who is neither legally trained nor temperamentally inclined to play what is in essence a prosecutor's role. Often he resents the assignment because it alienates the youth or parents he is expected to help subsequently—often impossible. Where judges intervene to take over the interrogation, attorneys are at a painful disadvantage because they must object to the judge's questions and then hear the judge rule on the objections.

There are those, especially in police associations, who believe that prosecuting attorneys should enter the juvenile court and present contested cases, but prosecutors show little enthusiasm for the task, and judges are not yet disposed to permit hearings to become all-out adversary struggles. Their attitude is not ill-considered to one who has seen an attorney attempt to impugn the credibility of a 15-year-old girl witness by referring to her CYA record and to sexual experiences for which she received money.

Despite the problems coming with the appearance of attorneys in juvenile court and a trend toward more formal, adversary-type hearings, the author's research on one intensively studied California juvenile court indicates that attorneys do their clients some good. A comparison of cases with and without attorneys showed that the former had a higher percentage of dismissals, fewer wardships declared, and more sentences to the California Youth Authority suspended. However, dismissals were not proportionately numerous, and moreover they clustered among cases alleging neglect by parents or unfit homes. Hence the main conclusion reached was that the major contribution of attorneys in the juvenile court lay in their ability to mitigate the severity of dispositions rather than disproving allegations of the petitions.

Attorneys often successfully challenged the precision of allegations in the jurisdictional hearings, causing them to be reduced in number and seriousness. This then became grounds to argue for a more lenient disposition of the cases. Specific dispositions were influenced when attorneys found relatives to take a child in preference to a foster home placement, or when they proposed psychiatric treatment or psychological counseling as an alternative to commitment to a ranch school. Sometimes they gave emphasis to reasons why a boy should be given another chance at home, and swayed an otherwise uncertain judge. Finally, attorneys sometimes protected the client, especially a parent, against himself, by persuading him to accept a condition of probation in order to avoid a more draconic order by the court.

Not all of the good work of attorneys was reflected in the outcomes of hearings; some of it was done before and after the court sessions, through convincing probation officers to change a recommendation or make some administrative modification of an order. If California findings are indicative, the adversary function of the emerging role of the attorney in juvenile court is likely to be marginal; more important is his role as a negotiator, interpreter of court decisions to child and parents, and as a source of psychic support in a new kind of court where there is greater social distance between probation officers and juveniles. Finally, the very presence of an attorney or the possibility of his entry into cases has a monitory value reinforcing the new consciousness of judges and probation officers of rights of juveniles. For this reason it may be that the New York State concept of the attorney in juvenile court as a law guardian is a most fitting description of his role.

Commentaries on the New York system for bringing counsel into family courts have been sensitive to the problem of his possible cooptation by the court, and the need to preserve his independence of action. To make him an agent of the court raises a real question as to where his loyalties would lay. Yet total independence may mean disruption and loss of informality in the court proceedings. A recent proposal seeks to solve this dilemma by moving delinquency hearings from the juvenile court into the probation department where defense officers would be assigned to juveniles, leaving the court in a supervisory or appellate position. However, administrative justice has its own unsolved problems in which the use or function of adversary contention is clouded by uncertainties as to where and how findings are made. Loyal opposition is the desideratum, but opposition remains the social mechanism which compels total and critical assessment of facts.

LEVELS OF PROOF

The clashing views over the propriety of adversary hearings in juvenile court are not dissociated from disagreements as what kind of evidence should be mandatory for its findings. When the California juvenile court law was altered in 1961, civil rules of evidence were designated for hearings in all save most serious offenses, i.e., those which would be felonies if committed by an adult. An attempt was made at the time to institute criminal rules of evidence in such cases, but legislators qualified the original recommendation of the Juvenile Justice Commission to a "preponderance of evidence legally admissible in the trial of criminal cases." This was a concession to the fears of those who felt that the juvenile court would otherwise be made into a criminal court.

Many California judges have met the thorny problem of hearsay evidence in juvenile court hearings by admitting everything, on the assumption that they can cull out that which is not competent. This tack has some support from law scholars who argue that the hearsay rule was intended for gullible juries rather than judges. However, this misses an important point, that much juvenile court evidence is in the form of reports which often are little more than compilations of professional hearsay. Whether the ordinary run of judges and referees are qualified to sift this kind of evidence is questionable; many juvenile court judges appear remarkably naive about psychiatric diagnoses and the true nature of that which is easily called psychiatric treatment. Their knowledge of social science and its critical evaluations of psychiatry and social work at best are rudimentary.

An attractive solution to evidentiary problems of the juvenile court in the majority of its cases may be to require clear and convincing proof, which the lawbooks denote as more than a 'preponderance of evidence but less than proof beyond doubt demanded in criminal procedure. Clear and convincing proof is the highest order of civil evidence, which admits of only one reasonable conclusion.

For the most grievous juvenile law violations, in which protection of public interests becomes a dominant value, the canons of criminal proof should prevail. However, their seriousness can be defined more meaningfully in operational terms by making them contingent upon legally possible dispositions rather than on formal allegations that the offense is analogous to a felony. By this is meant that if the youth against whom the allegations are found to be true can be committed to an institution jointly used for adult criminals, or to an institution whose correctional or security features are equal to or greater than the least correctionally oriented adult institution, then criminal rules of evidence must obtain.

One difficulty with this kind of proposal is that judges, subjected to heavy public pressures or confronted with difficulties due to lack of resources for dispositions, may simply find that for the purposes at hand a given institution is noncorrectional or otherwise meets statutory requirements. If appellate courts are unwilling to look behind such findings and evaluate the evidence rather than merely determining that the judge's finding was based on evidence, other remedies, perhaps administrative, would be necessary.

Social Action to Change the Juvenile Court

Juvenile courts evolve and change in several ways: by legislation, rulings on appeals, administrative policy formation by regulatory agencies, and the cumulative, day-to-day actions of judges, probation officers, and correctional workers. Because the court either is a local or ecologically contained institution, the interaction within the court and between the court and the community is the most important area for studying the processes by which it changes. Legislation, appellate decisions, and administrative programs for this reason need formulation with recognition that the corpus of juvenile court practice to be changed is highly diverse and that outcomes of intervention will not be so much the result of selected causes as products of interaction.

While law represents a striving for uniformity, it must be heeded that similar ends may be reached by a variety of means, administrative as well as legislative. The juvenile court is a prime example of an agency in which the connection between legal action and administrative action, traditionally neglected in American jurisprudence, must be coordinated. Nowhere is this more readily seen than in sparsely populated areas and resource-poor counties, or counties with unique problems, such as a large ethnic population. A more circumscribed juvenile court means that counties which previously have relied upon the court as a receptacle for child problems of all kinds must find or develop new agencies and forms of organization for their purposes. This calls for a high order of administrative ingenuity to facilitate the working juvenile court laws without provoking resistance or destroying local initiative.

On the whole, appellate court decisions have not been effective means for shaping the course of juvenile court evolution, although they may become more so with passing time. One recent exception was the supreme court decision in Utah which removed juvenile courts from control by the department of public welfare and gave them status as an independent judiciary. The history and background of this action throws considerable light on the weaknesses of vesting administrative control over juvenile courts in a State welfare agency, which in this instance had made some notable improvements but had stirred strong dissatisfaction among judges by more or less pre-empting their right of judicial review.

Historical materials accumulated by the author on the period during which the State department of welfare supervised juvenile probation services in California indicate, that its record of achievements was not impressive. Supervisory control of juvenile probation under the regime of the California Youth Authority has been more productive of innovations in juvenile court practices, but these have had to be secured almost entirely by cooperative means. Although this agency supported the action, the impetus for the major revision of the juvenile court law came from the director of the department of corrections, a small number of dedicated private attorneys, a few judges, and several law school professors. A goodly number of judges and probation officers throughout the State resisted this change. This was in decided contrast to the Utah scene, where judges seemingly played the yeoman roles in action to change their juvenile court law.

Ordinarily bar associations may be expected to take the lead or strongly support others seeking to better adapt the juvenile court to its contemporary social setting, and this has been true for New York State and to a degree in other States. However, the California State bar has shown a singular lack of interest in problems of the juvenile court. Obviously, then, action to legislate change in the juvenile court will have to work through limitations imposed by the nature of the values or commitments of elite groups in professional associations and State power structures.

An issue which complicates any action to modify juvenile court procedures is the old one as to whether the legislature or the courts should make rules for courts to follow. Since the juvenile court is a peculiar type of court, with direct policy implications, the scales get weighted in favor of legislative action. However, legislative action pushed without a sense of full participation by judges and their probation officers risks subversion of changes by judicial indifference or noncompliance, and judges are a notoriously hard lot to discipline by direct means.

Modifying the structure and procedures of the juvenile court through legislative channels in such a way to make it part of the living law, the implicit as well as the explicit rules of the game, is contingent on complementary communication and opinion change among judges. Such processes can be encouraged by such organizations as the National Council of Juvenile Court Judges, the National Probation and Parole Association, National Council on Crime and Delinquency, and the U. S. Children's Bureau, but differences between States make imperative some type of State administrative or regulatory agency for juvenile courts. It is probably too early to tell whether such organization should be part of judicial councils or commission with autonomy of their own. Changes which make the fate of the juvenile courts the proprietary interests of judges should be avoided, because the police, probation officers, prosecutors, public defenders, and social workers all have solid stakes in the workings of the juvenile court.

The most important objective, so far as administrative action is concerned, is that some State body exist to continuously oversee juvenile court operations, to promote the organic growth and advise application of legal procedures, to accumulate data, and contract for research on the court as needed. Such an agency could not review the decisions of juvenile court judges but it might conceivably be given some power to review the acts of administrative officials in juvenile correctional institutions or some inquisitorial and injunctive power to compel them to desist from practices inconsistent with juvenile court objectives. Hopefully this might begin to establish long-needed liaison between work of the juvenile court and ministrations of State institutions for juveniles. Even more, its very existence might discourage commitments to State institutions and speed a trend toward community centered forms of guidance and training of errant juveniles, not unlike the shifts which are occurring in treatment of mentally disordered persons.

The Place of Research

Although there is a great volume of impressions, opinions, and speculative discussion published about the juvenile court, the amount of carefully designed, relevant empirical research is pitifully small. Much of the data available on the juvenile court must be culled from surveys or study reports made by State agencies or community groups attempting to document the need for new programs. While studies of the U. S. Children's Bureau to some extent have been an exception, even its publications have been colored by long-time goals of raising standards in juvenile courts. Granted that most research on the juvenile court should be action research, nevertheless it can benefit from the wider employment of social science design and methods for gathering data comparable to those put to use in sociological studies of industries and mental hospitals. There is a pressing need for some basic ethnographic or descriptive studies to discover in greater depth what are the patterns of actions in juvenile courts, and then proceeding from these, to make more comprehensive studies of the modalities and dispersions in its patterns.

Our society now has both the surplus energy and trained social science personnel to do this job; the problem is one of their reallocation. Whether this will or can occur through the research funding methods and policies of the National Institutes of Mental Health is debatable. Research into juvenile delinquency and the program innovation for juvenile courts are of sufficient importance to merit their separate husbandry by the Federal Government. Furthermore, it does not appear that the strong appeal of health or mental health auspices is a prerequisite to securing needed research funds, for Congress already has shown its willingness to support special research and developmental programs on delinquency and the juvenile court.

The Federal Government is in a much better position that State governments to stimulate and fund the independent type of inquiry needed to clarify the nature of the anomaly which has been the juvenile court. Whatever mechanisms it devises for this purpose should be sufficiently flexible to catch up the marginal, lone wolf investigators whose detachment from organizations and wariness towards their values may be especially fitting for studying the problems of the juvenile court in modern society.

In concluding, the author freely admits to his omission of any other than incidental discussion of the kinds of adaptations in the fields of public welfare, private social work, special education and community organization which a more conservative construction of the juvenile court would entail. The changes taking place in these areas are many and rapid but their overall directions are not easy to make out in a more general atmosphere of conflict and confusion of goals. New ways of looking at things are badly needed by social workers and educators, with a recognition that differentiation and flexibility are collateral requirements of organizational advances towards common ends.

Meantime sufficient consensus on new goals for the juvenile court has accumulated to make the times propitious for its change through social action.

Sources

1. "The California Juvenile Court," *Stanford Law Review*, X (1958), 471–524.
2. Richard Cloward, "Social Control in Prison," *Theoretical Studies in Social Organization of the Prison*. (New York: Social Science Research Council, 1960), pp. 20–48.
3. *Comparative Survey of Juvenile Delinquency—Part I: North America* (United Nations, N.Y., 1958).
4. Bernard Fisher, "Juvenile Court: Purpose, Promise, and Problems," *Social Service Review*, XXXIV (1960), pp. 75–82.
5. Margaret Greenfield, *Juvenile Traffic Offenders and Court Jurisdiction* (Bureau of Public Administration, University of California at Berkeley, 1951).
6. Tadeuz Grygier, "The Concept of a State of Delinquency—an Obituary," *Journal of Legal Education*, XVIII (1965), pp. 131–141.
7. Joel Handler, "The Juvenile Court and the Adversary System: Problems of Function and Form," *Wisconsin Law Review*, LIV (1965), pp. 7–51.
8. Jacob Isaacs, "The Role of the Lawyer in Representing Minors in the New Family Court," *Buffalo Law Review*, XII (1962), pp. 501–521.
9. Alfred Kahn, *A Court for Children* (New York: Columbia University Press, 1953).
10. Orman Ketcham, "Legal Renaissance in the Juvenile Court," *Northwestern University Law Review*, LX (1965), pp. 585–598.
11. Edwin Lemert, "Legislating Change in the Juvenile Court, MNS" Center for the Study of Law and Society, Berkeley, Calif., 1966).
12. ———, "Revisionism and the Juvenile Court Law, MNS" (Center for the Study of Law and Society, Berkeley, Calif., 1964).
13. David Matza, *Delinquency and Drift* (New York: Wiley, 1964).
14. Henry Nunberg, "Problems in the Structure of the Juvenile Court," *Journal of Criminal Law and Criminology*, XLVIII (1957), pp. 500–515.
15. Lloyd Ohlin, "Conflicting Interests in Correctional Objectives," *Theoretical Studies in Social Organization of the Prison* (Social Science Research Council, New York, 1960), pp. 111–129.
16. Maynard Pirsig, "Juvenile Delinquency and Crime: Achievements of the 1959 Minnesota Legislation," *Minnesota Law Review*, XLIV (1959), pp. 363–410.
17. Austin L. Porterfield, *Youth in Trouble* (Fort Worth: Leo Potishman Foundation, 1946).
18. Roscoe Pound, "The Limits of Effective Legal Action," *22nd Annual Report of the Pennsylvania Bar Association*, XXII (1916), pp. 221–239.
19. "Report of the Minnesota Legislative Interim Commission on Public Welfare Laws" (Minneapolis, 1959).

20. "Report of the New York Joint Legislative Committee on Court Reorganization," II (Albany, N.Y.: The Family Court Act, 1962).
21. "Report of the Special Committee on Juvenile Courts of the Utah State Bar" (Salt Lake City, May 1962).
22. "Report of the Wisconsin Legislative Council, Conclusions and Recommendations of the Child Welfare Committee," vol. VI, part I. (Madison, 1955).
23. Margaret Rosenheim, ed., *Justice for the Child* (New York Free Press, 1962).
24. I. J. Shain and Walter Burkhart, "Report of the Governor's Special Study Commission on Juvenile Justice," I, II (Sacramento, 1960).
25. William H. Sheridan, "Juvenile Court Intake," *Journal of Family Law, II* (1962), pp. 139–156.
26. James Short, Jr., and F. Ivan Nye, "Extent of Unrecorded Juvenile Delinquency," *Journal of Criminal Law and Criminology, IL* (1958), pp. 296–302.
27. Eugene E. Siler, Jr., "The Need for Defense Counsel in Juvenile Court," *Crime and Delinquency, XI* (1965), pp. 45–58.
28. Paul Tappan, *Delinquent Girls in Court* (New York: Columbia University Press, 1947).
29. R. Weiss, "The Illinois Family Court Act," *University of Illinois Law Forum* (1962), pp. 533–549.
30. Glenn Winters, "The Utah Juvenile Court Act of 1965," *Utah Law Review*, IX (1965), pp. 509–517.

8. Juvenile Court Judges in the United States: Working Styles and Characteristics

REGIS H. WALTHER and SHIRLEY D. McCUNE

THE GROWTH of the juvenile court movement has produced a new breed of judicial officer. Part legal expert, part administrator, part community organizer, and part politician, the juvenile court judge has developed distinctive styles and strategies that enable him to discharge his complex responsibilities. The "who" and the "what" of the juvenile court judiciary—professional background, academic training, job functions, jurisdictional responsibilities, and court-related matters—have been previously outlined.[1] Here we are concerned with the "how" and the "why"—the working styles and characteristics of juvenile court judges. As we shall see, a juvenile court judge working style has been developed which is unique, though in some ways similar to that of the other professions that are concerned with delinquent and dependent youth.[2]

Reprinted from *Crime and Delinquency*, October 1965, pp. 384–393, by permission of *Crime and Delinquency* and the authors. Copyright 1965 by National Council on Crime and Delinquency.

1. S. D. McCune and D. L. Skoler, "Juvenile Court Judges in the United States—Part I: A National Profile," *Crime and Delinquency*, April 1962, pp. 121–131.
2. Both parts of the article are based on research conducted by the Center for Behavioral Sciences for a demonstration training project of the National Council of

The method used to measure working styles and characteristics is the JAIM (Job Analysis and Interest Measurement), a self-description inventory. The JAIM has been used successfully both to differentiate one occupation from another and to differentiate between superior and weak performers within an occupation.[3] The elements measured by the JAIM include behavioral styles (the consistent ways in which a person organizes and directs his mental, physical and energy resources to accomplish his goals), work preferences (the explicit choices that represent the anticipation of intrinsic satisfaction from the performance of certain types of tasks), and values (the criteria against which the performer judges the "goodness" or "badness" of his work).

Judges Compared with Lawyers

The JAIM was completed by 292 juvenile court judges while they were attending some of the institutes and work conferences that were included in the demonstration training program sponsored by the National Council of Juvenile Court Judges. This group of judges differed from the nation-wide survey of juvenile court judges [4] in several important dimensions.

Over 90 per cent of the judges completing the JAIM had been trained as lawyers. Forty-five per cent had obtained the job of juvenile court judge through election, 33 per cent had been given an interim appointment and were subsequently elected, and 22 per cent had been appointed. Forty per cent served jurisdictions with populations of less than 50,000, and 30 per cent served jurisdictions of more than 200,000 population. Twelve per cent devoted full time to juvenile matters; of the remainder, 23 per cent spent one-half time, 37 per cent one-quarter time, and 28 per cent less than one-quarter time on juvenile matters. Forty-eight per cent had served over five years as a juvenile court judge.

Thus, compared with the total group of judges discussed in the previously published part of the article, this group of judges were more likely to have been trained as lawyers, to be serving an interim appointment or be an appointed judge, to serve larger jurisdictions, to devote large portions of time to juvenile matters, and to have had considerable experience as a juvenile court judge.

Juvenile Court Judges, supported by a grant of the National Institute of Mental Health, U. S. Department of Health, Education, and Welfare (Grant MH–00998). The research upon which this article is based is reported in detail in a monograph available through the Center.
    3. The JAIM is distributed for research purposes by the Educational Testing Service, Princeton, N.J. Over thirty occupations or professions have been studied, including Foreign Service, business administration, physics, engineering, and social work. Summaries of these studies are contained in the *JAIM Manual.*
    4. McCune and Skoler, *op. cit.*

In addition to JAIM scores for the juvenile court judges, we obtained comparable scores for 89 Michigan lawyers, attending various meetings and training programs, who had not become judges; and for a group of "superior" judges. We secured names of "superior" juvenile court judges by having the list of JAIM scored judges reviewed by officers and staff of the National Council of Juvenile Court Judges and by officials of the U. S. Department of Health, Education, and Welfare who had knowledge of juvenile court operations throughout the country. Each reviewer nominated juvenile court judges whom he considered "superior," and the twenty judges receiving the most nominations were so identified. This procedure resulted in three sets of JAIM scores: scores for lawyers, for "average" juvenile court judges, and for "superior" juvenile court judges [5]

The most striking difference among these three groups was the significantly higher score of "superior" judges on Social Service, or the value of helping others (Figure 8.1).

Figure 8.1

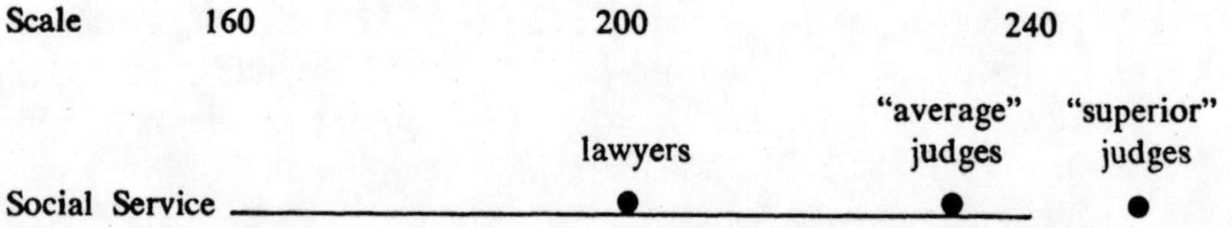

Scale	160		200		240
				"average"	"superior"
		lawyers		judges	judges
Social Service		●		●	●

The "superior" judges were also more likely than the "average" judges or lawyers to say that a supervisor gets best results by having the work group participate in decision making (Participative Leadership) rather than by making the decisions himself (Directive Leadership). In addition, the "superior" judges were less likely to emphasize punishment as a motivational strategy (Figure 8.2).

Judges and lawyers were found to have different styles for reacting to aggressive behavior. Judges tend to "pour oil on troubled waters" (Move toward Aggressor) when someone acts belligerently or aggressively, while lawyers were more likely to fight back (Move against Aggressor). On this characteristic, there were no significant differences between "superior" and "average" judges (Figure 8.3).

5. The scores reported for the JAIM are based on the average scores of candidates who took the U. S. Department of State Foreign Service Officer examination in September 1963, with the mean designated at 200 and the standard deviation, 40. Thus, a score of 240 in a particular scale is one standard deviation higher than, a score of 160 is one standard deviation lower than, and a score of 200 is the same as the average score of the Foreign Service Officer candidates. In the above example the "average" judges received a score of 238, which is approximately one standard deviation above that for Foreign Service Officer candidates.

A further difference between judges and lawyers was in their attitudes toward authority. The judges tend to identify with authority; the lawyers tend to be independent and autonomous (Figure 8.4).

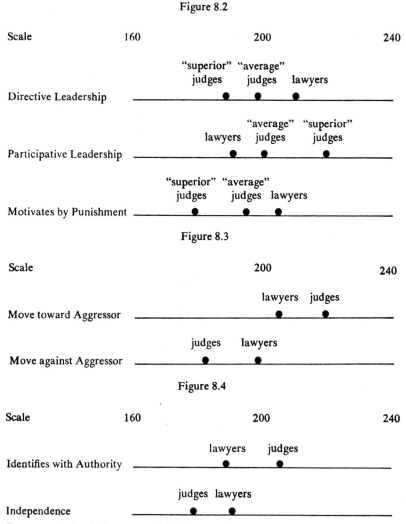

Figure 8.2

Scale   160   200   240

"superior" "average"
judges   judges lawyers

Directive Leadership

"average" "superior"
lawyers judges   judges

Participative Leadership

"superior" "average"
judges   judges lawyers

Motivates by Punishment

Figure 8.3

Scale   200   240

lawyers   judges

Move toward Aggressor

judges   lawyers

Move against Aggressor

Figure 8.4

Scale   160   200   240

lawyers   judges

Identifies with Authority

judges lawyers

Independence

In general, the judges scored higher on the scales relating to service and a supportive relationship with people, while the lawyers scored higher on the scales relating to individualism and personal achievement. Analysis of the individual items helps to clarify the differences:

The judges more often said they liked to be considered helpful, understanding, and considerate, while the lawyers more often said they liked to be considered effective, successful, brilliant, and imaginative. The judges are more likely to prefer work which is socially useful and gives them an opportunity to be helpful to others, while the lawyers prefer work which gives them an opportunity for personal accomplishment and permits them to be creative and original. When they watch games or other competitive activities, judges more often than lawyers support the "underdog" or the one who is losing rather than the champion or the skillful performer. If a person behaves toward them in a dictatorial or domineering fashion, judges are more likely to say that they would try to win him over, while lawyers were more likely to say that they would seek an occasion to have it out with him and that the best defense is a good offense.

The judges more frequently report that, as adolescents, they were obedient and eager to please their parents or guardians rather than independent, rebellious, or resentful. Their political, religious, and social views are closer to those of their parents, and they are more inclined to believe that laws and social conventions are seldom or never useless and do not hamper individual freedom. They also much more frequently say that moral principles come from an outside power higher than man rather than that moral principles are relative and depend upon circumstances.

Comparisons with Other Court Personnel

The dual responsibility of the juvenile court—rehabilitation of the delinquent and interpretation of the laws—closely links the juvenile court judge to the other court system personnel. The effectiveness of the judge's work is influenced by the quality of the job done by police, correctional, educational, welfare, recreational, probation, and other personnel concerned with imposing social control and providing therapeutic services. The court and these related community services make up a juvenile court system. A major factor in the success of any juvenile court program is the degree to which these various socializing agents are integrated and coordinated to provide the particular types of services and controls needed by dependents or delinquents.

Probation officers, welfare workers, and police youth officers were selected as the occupational groups having the most interaction with the juvenile court, and arrangements were made for a sample of each group to complete the JAIM.

Of the 161 probation officers who completed the JAIM, approximately one-half did so while attending one of four work conferences or institutes of the NCJCJ Program in Ohio, Maryland, Utah, and Arizona. The other half, employed in court systems in Michigan, Minnesota, and Washington, completed the JAIM at the request of their supervisors.

The 33 welfare workers who completed the JAIM were attending various institutes and work conferences in connection with the demonstration training program. About 50 per cent of the sample were experienced welfare workers in supervisory positions attending a work conference designed to consider the neglect and dependency jurisdiction of the court. The others were attending various institutes at the invitation of the judge of the court in which they were serving.

Three-quarters of the sample of 77 police youth officers were serving in two large metropolitan centers, and the arrangements to take the JAIM were made through their superior officers. The rest came from a number of jurisdictions of various sizes.

SIMILARITIES IN WORKING STYLES AND VALUES

All four groups (juvenile court judges, probation officers, welfare workers, and police officers) were remarkably similar in their social service orientation, their tendency to be nonpunitive, and, when confronted with aggressive behavior from others, their tendency to "move toward" rather to "move against" the aggressor. The scales differentiated police youth officers from a sample of 115 police serving as patrolmen, as shown in Figure 8.5.

Figure 8.5

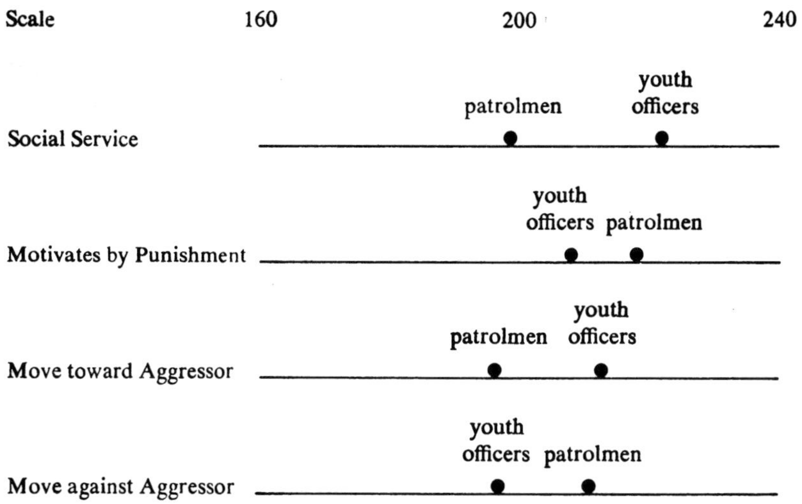

DIFFERENCES IN WORKING STYLES AND VALUES

The three major professions with which court system personnel identify are the law, police work, and social work. For the most part, probation officers and welfare workers were found to be similar in their working styles and values, and the similarity was even more marked when welfare workers were compared with probation officers trained as social workers.

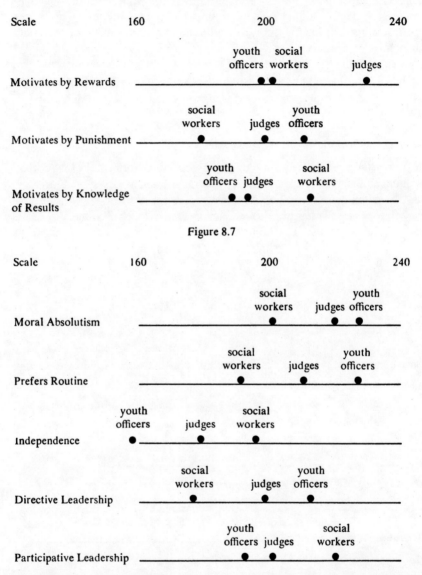

Figure 8.6

Figure 8.7

It was, therefore, possible to combine the data for social workers serving as probation officers (49 persons) and those serving as welfare workers (33 persons).

The major differences among the three professions are in their motivational strategies and attitudes toward authority. With respect to motivational strategies, judges and lawyers emphasized rewards, police youth officers emphasized punishment (though not as much as other police officers), and social workers emphasized showing people the consequences of their actions (Figure 8.6).

Other differences among the three professions relate to their preferred style for relating to authority and the degree to which they view moral principles as absolute or relative. Police youth officers were most likely, and social workers least likely, to prefer routines; to believe that moral principles come from an outside power higher than man and are not relative and dependent upon circumstances; and to believe that a supervisor gets the best results by making decisions himself rather than by having the work group participate in making them (Figure 8.7).

These results suggest a significant difference among court system personnel in the degree to which they emphasize control through authority as opposed to controls within the individual. On each of these scales the judge occupies a position between the police youth officer and the social worker.

Summary and Conclusions

This study has identified distinctive characteristics of the juvenile court judge and other professions working within the court system. The data suggest that the highly regarded judge tends to be supportive and sympathetic, rather than punitive, in his relationship with other persons; with respect to motivational strategies, he tends to emphasize rewards rather than punishment or knowledge of results; when dealing with aggressive behavior, he is more likely to "move toward" rather than "move against" the aggressor; and he tends to identify with authority and endorse moral absolutes.

The results of this study suggest clues to why some lawyers become juvenile court judges and others do not.[6] The differences between the two groups are found primarily in their values and, to a lesser extent, in their relationship to people and their attitude toward authority. Lawyers who become judges value social service, while other lawyers place greater value on status attainment and intellectual achievement. Judges react to aggressive behavior with diplomacy, while lawyers are more likely to fight back. Finally, judges identify more with authority, while lawyers tend to be more individualistic.[7]

6. Since no study was made of the behavioral styles and values of judges in other jurisdictions, we do not know whether the same differences found between lawyers and juvenile court judges would also emerge from a comparison of lawyers with judges in general.

7. A question which the data in this study cannot answer is the degree to which the working styles and values caused certain lawyers to become juvenile court judges or the degree to which occupying the role of a judge changes a lawyer's style and values. Data from other studies indicate that a person's style and values are relatively fixed and are influenced only slightly by job assignments. See R. H. Walther, *Orientations and Behavioral Styles of Foreign Service Officers* (New York: Carnegie Endowment for International Peace, in press).

The three major professions who work within the court system (lawyers who become judges, policemen who become youth officers, and social workers who become probation officers or welfare workers) were found to share some important characteristics and to differ significantly on others. They shared an orientation toward social service rather than status attainment and intellectual achievement, and a preference for "moving toward" rather than "moving against" an aggressor. The additional finding that judges scored higher than lawyers, police youth officers scored higher than patrolmen, and "superior" judges scored higher than "average" judges on the Social Service and Move toward Aggressor scales suggests that concern for other people and a supportive attitude toward them are important characteristics of all the participants in the work of the juvenile court system. These similarities can be shown graphically by combining scores, with a positive value given to Social Service and Move toward Aggressor and a negative value to Status Attainment and Move against Aggressor (Figure 8.8).

Figure 8.8

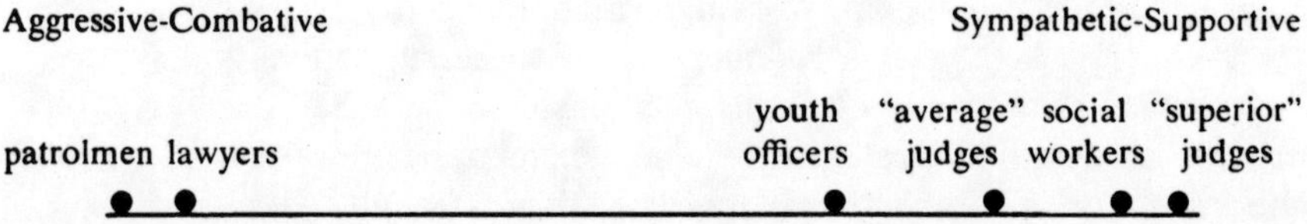

Aggressive-Combative   Sympathetic-Supportive

                                      youth   "average" social "superior"
patrolmen lawyers   officers judges workers judges
● ●   ●   ●   ● ●

The difference among the court system personnel lies in the emphasis they put on the maintenance of external controls as opposed to establishing internal controls. The police youth officers favored external controls, although to a lesser extent than other police officers. The scales on which they scored high were Moral Absolutism, Directive Leadership, Motivate by Punishment, and Prefers Routines. On each of these scales a high score indicates a reliance on external authority.

The social workers favored internal controls. The scales on which they scored high were Participative Leadership, Motivate by Knowledge of Results, and Independence. A high score on each of these scales indicates a reliance on self-development and self-control.

The judges scored between the youth officers and social workers on all of the above scales.

Police youth officers scored higher on Motivate by Punishment, while the judges and lawyers scored higher on Motivate by Reward. Each of these is an external control strategy in which one person influences the behavior of another. It is certainly no surprise that police officers tend to emphasize punishment. The nature of the policeman's job requires the use of force to control behavior, and it can therefore be expected that policemen will believe in the efficacy of punishment. The high score of judges and lawyers on the Motivate by Rewards scale probably reflects a philosophy of social control. Knowledge of results provides the possibility for strengthening internal controls; since the training of social workers focuses on the development of the individual, it is understandable that they emphasize this strategy.

Societies require both the maintenance of external controls and the development of internal controls, and these two orientations can be viewed as paralleling the legal and the rehabilitative responsibilities of the juvenile court. Effective performance of a judge probably requires an appropriate balance of the two. It is impossible to determine from the data of this study just where this balance should occur. The evidence suggests that the "superior" judge is somewhat more oriented toward the development of internal controls than the "average" judge (Figure 8.9).

Figure 8.9

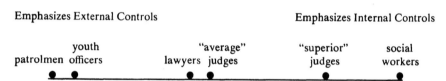

The key findings of this study have been the identification of common orientations and the description of possible points of conflict among the professions participating in the work of the juvenile court system. Work styles and values have a significant influence on performance, and it would be desirable in future studies to learn more about the nature of this relationship. Such information could be useful for curriculum development and for in-service training designed to increase the effective cooperation of the professions concerned with the problems of delinquent and dependent children.

PART FIVE

Probation and the Offender

IN EARLIER sections of this book, we have seen that large numbers of youths are screened out of the correctional machinery before being adjudicated as a "delinquent." But among those who survive this sifting and sorting, assignment to probation supervision is a common experience. For example, in 1965 in the United States a daily average of 62,773 youths were found in custodial institutions for delinquents, while 285,431 children were in community supervision, mostly on probation.[1] In general, juvenile courts tend to place first offenders and the least serious cases on probation, so that they send youths off to an institution as a "last resort."

What goes on in juvenile probation? What kinds of persons are engaged in this work? On what bases do they make decisions about offenders? How successful is probation as a form of correctional handling? These are the kinds of questions with which this section is concerned.

In the past, probation officers were often untrained, punitively-oriented

1. The President's Commission on Law Enforcement and Administration of Justice, *The Challenge of Crime in a Free Society* (Washington, D.C.: U. S. Government Printing Office, 1967), p. 161.

persons with little or no interest in rehabilitative notions. However, in recent years many juvenile and adult probation agencies throughout the nation have become staffed with college educated, treatment-oriented probation agents. A goodly number of these individuals have been recruited from social welfare backgrounds, so that they are persons who are imbued with a treatment philosophy toward offenders. According to some investigators, these social welfare-trained officers frequently experience a good deal of role conflict when they are called upon to enforce rules and to engage in other coercive tactics with lawbreakers. Then too, it has been argued that many of these welfare workers are ill-prepared by their educational training for working with the special problems posed by hostile, defiant correctional "clients," so that they experience a good deal of discomfort in the role of probation officer.[2]

One subject about which much recently has been heard concerning probation officers centers about the attempt to "professionalize" this group of workers. Probation officers have increasingly been hired from the ranks of the college educated, so that it has frequently been argued that these agents are representatives of a correctional profession. However, the skeptic is quick to point out that workers do not become professionals simply upon their own declaration. Sociologists and laymen alike restrict the label of professional to those persons in a field of endeavor who are specially and uniformly trained, who are the sole possessors of a body of complex knowledge and skills, and who share a code of ethics.[3] Measured in this way, probation agents or other correctional employees cannot be said to be incumbents of a profession. They do not all derive out of a common educational experience, nor do they share a body of techniques and knowledge. Instead, they constitute a hodge-podge of persons with diverse educational backgrounds and with varied perspectives on criminality and its treatment.

One indication of trends in probation work can be seen in a study by Seymour Gross, dealing with most of the juvenile probation officers in Minnesota.[4] He sent out questionnaires to all 84 juvenile probation officers in that state and received responses from 70 (85.3 per cent) of them. Nearly all of these workers had some college training, about 90 per cent of them had received the B.A. degree, and sixteen of them had master's degrees.

Gross reports that *Federal Probation,* a correctional journal, was most

2. Lloyd E. Ohlin, Herman Piven, and Donnell M. Pappenfort, "Major Dilemmas of the Social Worker in Probation and Parole," *NPPA Journal,* II (July 1956), 211–225.

3. The problems of professionalizing corrections are discussed in Don C. Gibbons, *Changing the Lawbreaker* (Englewood Cliffs, N.J.: Prentice-Hall, 1965), pp. 1–20.

4. Seymour Z. Gross, "Biographical Characteristics of Minnesota Probation Officers Who Deal with Juvenile Offenders," *Crime and Delinquency,* XII (April 1966), 109–116.

widely subscribed to by the officers; 56.5 per cent of them received this publication, which is available free of charge. Only a few of the officers subscribed to other journals, including social welfare publications. Gross also indicates that over 80 per cent of the officers said they read *Federal Probation,* while less than half of them read any other social work or correctional publication. In short, most of these workers read relatively little, so that their claim to professional status would seem to be shaky on these grounds. Judging by their reading habits, most apparently defined themselves as correctional workers rather than social welfare workers. However, those probation officers who had master's degrees did subscribe to and read social welfare journals, so that they apparently saw themselves primarily as welfare workers.

The first and second essays in this section deal with probation officer decision making. In a companion paper to the report cited above, Seymour Gross indicates that the officers he studied weighed the offender's attitude toward his offense, his family background, and his delinquency history most heavily. These probation agents were also of the opinion that judges accorded about the same emphasis to these factors. Cohn's study has to do with the factors taken into account by probation officers in recommending probation, institutionalization, psychiatric examination, or discharge from custody.

How effective is probation as a form of treatment? The third paper in this section by Scarpitti and Stephenson deals with this question. It arrives at conclusions similar to those of other investigators of probation. These researchers find that the probation agency studied in Essex County, New Jersey, received less delinquent, "easier" cases than did the nonresidential group-interaction program or the institutions examined. In addition, a significant number of probationers were "in-program failures" who were sent back to court before completing their program. The boys who did not complete their probation program were more delinquent and less tractable than those who finished the probation period. In this sense, they resembled the youths who were in the other programs. Among those boys who complete one or another program (probation, nonresidential treatment, institutionalization), the probationers had the highest postrelease success rate. What all of this adds up to is a picture of probation working with youths who have relatively favorable social backgrounds and short delinquency histories. The high success rate for these boys is probably an indicator that they are "self-correctors" who need minimal treatment, and not that probation per se is responsible for their favorable behavior.

9. The Prehearing Juvenile Report: Probation Officers' Conceptions

SEYMOUR Z. GROSS

THE MAIN function of the prehearing report in juvenile court proceedings is to present the sociocultural and psychodynamic factors which influenced the juvenile's alleged delinquent behavior. The prehearing report is supposed to give an objective, integrated, and perceptive evaluation so that the court can arrive at an individualized and rehabilitative disposition. Authorities generally agree on the necessity and importance of the prehearing report in juvenile court proceedings without seeking any objective verificaton of its predictive validity.[1]

Reprinted from *Journal of Research in Crime and Delinquency,* July 1967, pp. 212–217 by permission of *Journal of Research in Crime and Delinquency* and the author. Copyright 1967 by National Council on Crime and Delinquency.

1. George Everson, "The Standard of Children's Court Work," *Journal of Criminal Law and Criminology,* May 1918, pp. 105–113; Herbert H. Lou, *Juvenile Courts in the United States* (Chapel Hill: University of North Carolina Press, 1927); Paul L. Schroeder, "Minimum Standards for Social Investigation," *Proceedings of the American Prison Association,* 1932, pp. 99–110; Richard M. Eddy, "The Investigation for the Court," *Federal Probation,* August-October 1940, pp. 26–29; Ben S. Meeker, "Analysis of a Presentence Report," *Federal Probation,* March 1950, pp. 41–46; Ben S. Meeker, "Probation and Parole Officers at Work," *NPPA Journal,* April 1957, pp. 99–106; Harold Povill, "The Investigation Process," *Focus,* January 1951, pp. 75–79; Paul

Some social scientists have expressed the belief that, in determining disposition, intuition and experience should be used cautiously.[2] This position was summarized by Shannon:

> It is here [juvenile court] that we may attempt to determine something about the factors that influence the decision to define a juvenile as a serious delinquent or the decision to deal with a juvenile in one manner rather than another. How important, for example, is family status as contrasted with economic status in influencing a judge's decision? [3]

Review of Previous Research

In published literature of criminology, law, and probation, only one objective study focuses exclusively on the prehearing report; however, presentence and prehearing reports have been evaluated in connection with other research subjects. In an extensive examination of juvenile courts in New York City, Eddy found that "a small but significant group of judges ignores completely, or almost completely, the costly and time-consuming probation investigation." [4] Rumney and Murphy conducted a ten-year followup study of one thousand consecutive cases, including 137 juveniles, placed on probation in 1937. Their findings seriously challenged the utility of the prehearing report for persons placed on probation:

> Our studies failed to disclose any significant difference with respect to outcome as between those who were released on probation following investigation by a probation officer and those who were released on probation by the court without preliminary investigation.[5]

Lottier attempted to determine which kinds of data have predictive significance.[6] In his study, twenty-eight clinical judges ranked twenty-five

W. Keve, *The Probation Officer Investigates* (Minneapolis: University of Minnesota Press, 1960); Paul W. Keve, "The Message in Mr. Piyo's Dream," *Federal Probation*, December 1961, pp. 11–15; Paul W. Keve, "The Presentence Report," *Creative Thinking in Corrections*, mimeo. (Minneapolis: Minnesota Corrections Association, 1961), pp. 1–11.

2. William Healy, "Study of the Case Preliminary to Treatment," *Journal of Criminal Law and Criminology*, May 1922, pp. 74–81; Elio D. Monachesi, "Can We Predict Probation Outcomes?" *Federal Probation*, August 1939, pp. 15–18; Elio D. Monachesi, "Predicting Probation Success," *Probation*, June 1939, pp. 70–74; Stanley D. Porteus, "Setting the Sights for Delinquency Research," *Federal Probation*, June 1953, pp. 43–47; Daniel Glaser and Richard F. Hangren, "Predicting the Adjustment of Federal Probationers," *NPPA Journal*, July 1958, pp. 258–267.

3. Lyle W. Shannon, "The Problem of Competence to Help," *Federal Probation*, March 1961, pp. 32–39.

4. Alfred J. Kahn, *A Court for Children: A Study of the New York City Children's Court* (New York: Columbia University Press, 1953).

5. Jay Rumney and John A. Murphy, *Probation and Social Adjustment* (New Brunswick: Rutgers University Press, 1952).

6. Stuart Lottier, "Predicting Criminal Behavior," *Federal Probation*, October-December 1943, pp. 8–12.

social-psychological variables for predictive significance. After eliminating the less experienced raters, he found that twenty ranked as most predictive the category labeled "criminality, present and past arrests, and sentences," followed in importance by "work record, economic adjustment"; "family background, parents and siblings"; and habits, recreation, drinking." Glaser and Hangren used an actuarial approach to combine statements made by the probation officer in presentence reports expressed in subjective but fairly specific classifications.[7] They found higher predictive efficiency using these statements in contrast to objective items such as work record, residence stability, and age at first arrest. This author knows of only one study which deals objectively with the prehearing report. This recent study by Cohn attempted to determine the criteria by which a probation officer recommended four types of disposition: probation, institutionalization, psychiatric examination, and discharge.[8] The results were not reported in terms of statistical significance, although trends were discussed. The findings indicate that differential behavior and status were the determinants of each of the four types of disposition recommended by the probation officer. For example, juveniles who were more cooperative with the probation officer had a better chance to be placed on probation; the less cooperative child was recommended for institutionalization.

Present Study

The comparative lack of objective studies of presentence and prehearing reports suggests a need for further investigation. The present study was to determine how the probation officer handling juvenile offenders conceived the importance of the various sections of the report in terms of usefulness for appropriate or accurate recommendation of disposition. The officers were asked to rank the various sections of the prehearing report. A rank of *one* indicated the data *most* useful in making disposition recommendations; a rank of *ten* indicated the data *least* useful. The ranking task was then repeated to determine how they thought the court would react to the data.

The sample comprised seventy Minnesota probation officers handling juvenile offenders.[9] The seventy officers represented 85.3 per cent of the officers who returned questionnaires sufficiently complete to be tabulated. This relatively large response to a mail questionnaire indicates this report

7. Glaser and Hangren, *op. cit.*

8. Yona Cohn, "Criteria for the Probation Officer's Recommendation to the Juvenile Court Judge," *Crime and Delinquency*, July 1963, pp. 262–275.

9. For a detailed report of the biographical characteristics of the officers, see Seymour Z. Gross, "Biographical Characteristics of Minnesota Probation Officers Who Deal with Juvenile Offenders," *Crime and Delinquency*, April 1966, pp. 109–116.

covers a representative sample of Minnesota probation officers handling juvenile offenders.

Results

The probation officers ranked as *most* important (1) the child's attitude toward the offense, (2) family data, and (3) previous delinquency problems. The three sections the officers felt the court would consider *most* important were (1) present offense data, (2) previous delinquency problems, and (3) the child's attitude toward the offense. In both rankings, the probation officers considered the *least* important sections to be the data on interests, activities, and religion. The largest gap between the officers' personal evaluations and their apperception of the court's view was in regard to "present offense data." The officers perceived the court would consider this section the *most* important, while they ranked it *fourth*. Table 9.1 presents the results.

Table 9.1. Median ranks of probation officers' personal rankings of pre-hearing report sections and their apperception of the court's view

Report Sections	Officer's Personal Ranking	Apperception of Court's Ranking
Child's attitude toward the offense	2.33	3.02
Family data	3.28	4.70
Previous delinquency problems	3.36	2.50
Present offense data	4.00	1.96
Interview impression	4.43	5.90
School data	5.77	5.96
Psychological test data	6.03	6.06
Psychiatric examination data	6.57	6.07
Interests and activities data	9.00	9.38
Religious data	9.42	9.20

The Spearman Rank-Order correlation, used to determine the extent of agreement between each officer's personal ranking and his anticipation of the court's reaction, reveals that fifty-one officers (72.8 per cent) obtained significant agreement ($p < .05$) between their two rankings. (At the 0.05 level of statistical significance a correlation coefficient of 0.564 is required.) The remaining nineteen officers did not exhibit statistically significant Rank-Order correlation between their two rankings; in fact, five of these officers had negative correlation coefficients. This suggests that these nineteen officers represent an interesting subgroup of persons who, since they evidently disagreed significantly with the court, apparently were dissatisfied with their job or with certain aspects of it.[10]

10. Professor Robert D. Wirt suggested this interpretation.

The differentiating descriptive characteristics of the subgroup of nineteen officers (Group I) are summarized to compare with the fifty-one officers (Group II) who agreed with the court. Compared with Group II, the officers in Group I averaged two years older (mean age 33.9, standard deviation 5.9), had higher formal education with master's degrees (43.5 per cent of the total group of seventy), more frequently worked exclusively with juveniles (72 per cent), indicated a greater number of professional journals subscribed to and read, and placed greater importance on the results of psychological tests and psychiatric examination for recommendations for disposition. When asked how much they liked their work, all Group I officers responded in the "strongly like it" and "like it" categories. In a similar questionnaire item, they answered with a 95 per cent median value concerning their agreement with the court on specific dispositions of dismissal, probation, commitment, and continuance. If the answers of officers in Group I to direct questions about job satisfaction and agreement with the court were very similar to the majority of the officers, in what way did they disagree in the task of ranking their personal choices and their apperception of the court's opinion?

Table 9.2. Median ranks of two groups of probation officers in personal ranking of prehearing report sections

Report Sections	Group I N = 19	Group II N = 51	p
Child's attitude toward the offense	2.66	2.19	n.s.
Family data	2.33	3.58	n.s.
Previous delinquency problems	6.00	3.07	.001
Present offense data	6.75	3.00	.001
Interview impression	3.75	4.60	n.s.
School data	5.13	5.78	n.s.
Psychological test data	4.38	6.20	.001
Psychiatric examination data	5.33	6.82	n.s.
Interests and activities data	8.56	8.98	n.s.
Religious data	9.55	9.16	n.s.

Note: The level of statistical significance was obtained by the Median Test.

Table 9.2 reveals three highly significant differences between Groups I and II (p<.001). Group I did not give as much importance to the relatively objective data usually contained in the categories of "previous delinquency problems" and "present offense" data. They also considered psychological test data more important than the majority of the officers. Group I officers also indicated that "family data," "interview impression," "psychiatric examination data," and "interests and activities" data were more important for disposition than Group II officers held them to be.

Table 9.3 shows one statistically significant difference between Group I and Group II: Group I officers thought that the court gave greater importance to psychological test data than did the officers in Group II. The trends in the comparison in Table 9.3 were not as clear as for the officer's

Table 9.3. *Median ranks of two groups of probation officers' apperception of the court's opinion of prehearing report sections*

Report Sections	Group I N = 19	Group II N = 51	p
Child's attitude toward the offense	3.42	2.71	n.s.
Family data	4.33	4.75	n.s.
Previous delinquency problems	2.08	2.71	n.s.
Present offense data	2.00	1.94	n.s.
Interview impression	7.13	5.42	n.s.
School data	6.00	5.85	n.s.
Psychological test data	5.20	6.61	.05
Psychiatric examination data	5.00	6.65	n.s.
Interests and activities data	9.29	9.19	n.s.
Religious data	9.29	9.19	n.s.

Note: The level of statistical significance was obtained by the Median Test.

own perceptions. The groups were essentially in agreement concerning the court's use of the information in the prehearing report, although personal weighting of the various sections of the prehearing report demonstrated significant subgroup differences among the two groups of probation officers.

Discussion

The subgroup of Minnesota probation officers who disagreed with the way that the court generally was believed to view the prehearing report sections appeared to be oriented toward a psychodynamic or broader social casework approach than the majority of the officers. They placed more importance on report sections dealing with the less precise area of personality and family relationships and had considerably less faith in the use of relatively objective data, such as the description of present and previous delinquencies. In their apperception of the court's view of the prehearing report, however, they agreed essentially with the majority of the officers.

The biographical characteristics which differentiated Group I from the majority (Group II) now appear consistent with the way that they use the prehearing report. The officers in Group I had more graduate degrees and read a greater number of professional journals. The Group I officers identified primarily with the broader field of social casework rather than with the probation officer role.[11] Analysis of the majority of the officers (Group II) indicates that their professional identification was primarily that of a probation officer. Their primary concern was community protection; service to the offender was secondary. Since Group II included almost three-fourths of the total number of officers, it may be that Group I officers feel frustrated in dealing with the court as well as with a majority of their fellow officers. It would be interesting to know how active, if at all, the Group I officers are in trying to promote stronger social casework orientation. Whatever the merits of their disagreement with the court and fellow workers, the officers in Group I may present a problem in terms of supervision and communication.

Summary

Seventy probation officers in Minnesota who deal with juvenile offenders ranked sections of the prehearing report on the basis of their own conception of the relative importance of the various sections of the report. They repeated the ranking in terms of how they anticipated the court would view the prehearing report. The three sections ranked in order of importance for the officers' own perceptions were (1) the child's attitude toward the offense, (2) family data, and (3) previous delinquent problems. The three sections the officers felt the court would view as most important were (1) present offense data, (2) previous delinquency problems, and (3) the child's attitude toward the offense. A subgroup of nineteen officers who had higher formal education, subscribed to and read more professional journals, and, in general, appeared to have a broader social casework orientation gave significantly less importance to the more objective types of data. However, there was little disagreement between the subgroup and the majority of officers in their apperception of the court's view. This difference in orientation between social casework and probation may create communication and supervision problems.

11. Walter C. Reckless, "Training Probation and Parole Personnel," *Focus*, January 1948, pp. 44–48.

10. Criteria for the Probation Officer's Recommendation to the Juvenile Court Judge

YONA COHN

THE PURPOSE of this study is to analyze the underlying criteria used by the probation officers of the Bronx (N.Y.) Children's Court in recommending dispositions to the judge at the end of their presentence investigation reports. In other probation settings where the officer's basic assumptions about the delinquent child, the court's philosophy about the role of the probation officer, the officer's professional background, and the community's attitude toward juvenile delinquency may vary, the criteria will, of course, differ from the ones we shall present.

Although a probation officer's recommendation is common practice in the juvenile court, it is not always a formal part of the presentence investigation report. Williamson refers to the formal recommendation in her statement that "the report may or may not contain a recommendation. Some judges desire recommendations; others do not permit them, or else do not request them." [1]

1. Margaretta A. Williamson, *The Social Worker in the Prevention and Treatment of Delinquency* (New York: Columbia University Press, 1935).

Much has been written about the causes of delinquency, but whether these writings focus on the delinquency itself, on the individual juvenile, his social background, or on any combination of the three, a suitable disposition is required. For example, as far back as 1922, John W. Houston considered it inappropriate to give probation treatment to juveniles who had committed serious delinquent acts.[2] Other authors investigated the child's previous convictions, his intelligence, personality make-up, and seriousness of emotional pathology as elements to be considered in recommending probation. Dressler conducted special research on the "probation risk" presented by the "lone wolf" as compared with the gang member.[3] Many, such as Flexner and Baldwin[4] and Teeters and Reinemann,[5] stressed family cohesiveness; while early prediction tables like Monachesi's emphasized interaction of the various social, psychological, and legal criteria as a means of foretelling the successful outcome of a probation period. One of Monachesi's findings was that "no single factor may be important in determining probation behavior" and that "outcome of probation depends upon the accumulative effect of all pre-probation factors."[6]

The Study

Our study analyzes the broad background information presented by the probation officer in his presentence investigation report, with concentration on the four major recommendations he may make: probation, institutionalization, psychiatric examination, or discharge. As a means of obtaining a picture of some general trends, we shall try to isolate the criteria on which his investigation and recommendations are based.

For our study, we examined, in chronological order, 175 presentence investigation reports presented to the judge of the Bronx Children's Court from January 1, 1952 to about the middle of that year. Of these 175, fifty recommended probation, fifty recommended institutionalization, fifty recommended psychiatric examination, and twenty-five recommended dis-

2. John W. Houston, "The Right Selection of Probation Cases," *Journal of Criminal Law and Criminology*, February 1922, p. 577.
3. David Dressler, *Probation and Parole* (New York: Columbia University Press, 1951).
4. Bernard Flexner and Roger N. Baldwin, *Juvenile Courts and Probation* (New York: Century, 1914), p. 73.
5. Negley K. Teeters and John Otto Reinemann, *The Challenge of Delinquency* (New York: Prentice-Hall, 1950).
6. Elio D. Monachesi, *Prediction Factors in Probation* (Minneapolis: Sociological Press, 1932), p. 110. The Gluecks also stress a multidimensional interpretation: Sheldon and Eleanor Glueck, *Unraveling Juvenile Delinquency* (New York: Commonwealth Fund, 1950), p. 281.

charge. (This last group was limited to twenty-five because relatively fewer such recommendations are made to the court. In the tables that follow, these twenty-five cases were multiplied by two to make comparison with the other groups more convenient.) In addition to the 175 cases selected, another 500 cases were reviewed—about one-third of the yearly total. The following factors were tabulated for each case:

1. sex
2. age
3. religion
4. race
5. type of delinquent act
6. seriousness of delinquent act
7. child's role in delinquent act
8. number of previous prosecuted offenses
9. number of previous unprosecuted offenses
10. number of parents or guardians
11. economic situation
12. type of neighborhood
13. father's personality
14. mother's personality
15. degree of marital stability of parents
16. mother's relationship with child
17. father's relationship with child
18. church attendance
19. school/job attendance
20. school/job conduct
21. school/job performance
22. personality difficulties (including physical handicaps)
23. child's relationship with father
24. child's relationship with mother
25. child's relationship with sibling
26. child's relationship with peers
27. child's relationship with neighbors
28. child's group affiliation
29. child's cooperation with probation officer
30. parents' cooperation with probation officer

The statistical results for cases in each recommendation group were then tabulated and compared with the results for the other groups.

Let us examine the major tables—the distributions for sex, race, and personality of the child and the type and seriousness of his delinquent act —so that we may compare the characteristics of each recommendation group with the others in order to determine the criteria used by the probation officers in selecting these groups.

Distribution According to Sex

Table 10.1 shows a large number of girls recommended for institutionalization and a small number of girls recommended for discharge and probation. While girls made up only one-sixth of the total, they constituted nearly half the group recommended to an institution; restated as a proportion, this means that three times as many girls as boys were recommended for institutionalization.

For 30 out of 35 girls, the probation officer recommended psychiatric examination (diagnosis) or institutional treatment. Cross-tabulation of data for the 21 girls recommended to an institution reveals that most of them had committed delinquent acts against sexual taboos—acts which were generally considered decisive factors in arriving at the recommendation they received.

Table 10.1. Distribution according to sex

	Male	*Female*	*Total*
Probation	47	3	50
Institutionalization	29	21	50
Psychiatric examination	41	9	50
Discharge	48	2	50
Total	165	35	200

Distribution According to Race

The racial distribution of the total group of 200 was three white children to one Negro child. Of these, fewer Negroes were recommended for psychiatric examination or discharge than for institutionalization. The number

Table 10.2. Racial distribution

	White	*Negro*	*No Record*	*Total*
Probation	36	13	1	50
Institutionalization	25	20	5	50
Psychiatric examination	36	8	5	50
Discharge	44	6	–	50
Total	142	47	11	200

of Negro children who were recommended for institutional commitment was cross-tabulated with the kind and seriousness of delinquent act committed, the number of parents or guardians in the home, the mother's relationship with the child, the child's school attendance and personality difficulties, and parental cooperation with the probation officer. The only significant correlation found from this cross-tabulation referred only to the type and seriousness of the delinquent acts committed, which, for these Negro children, were primarily acts against sexual taboos.

The eleven unrecorded cases refer mainly to Puerto Rican children whose race the probation officer could not identify.

Personality as a Criterion

The following classifications of the child's personality were inferred from examination of a number of investigation reports: "No Difficulties," "Disturbed Behavior," "Neurotic Symptoms," "Undiagnosed Symptoms," and "Psychotic Symptoms."

A child was classified under the "No Difficulties" heading under the following three conditions: (1) when the probation officer merely said so, (2) when the officer indicated that the child's behavior problems were not attributed to any emotional disturbance, and (3) when the officer discussed a rehabilitation plan, implying that the child had no personality difficulties.

A child was classified as having "Disturbed Behavior" when the probation officer stated it in his report or when he expressed agreement with the school report's description of disturbed behavior. This classification was also used when the rehabilitation plan set forth by the probation officer seemed to suggest the presence of disturbed behavior. The probation officer's report never contained a clinical description of a child's behavior disorder.

The classification "Neurotic Symptoms" was listed in those instances where the probation officer was quoting from the psychiatric examination report.

"Undiagnosed Symptoms" were reported when the probation officer did not expressly state that the child evidenced neurotic symptoms but merely implied that certain undiagnosed personality difficulties existed. The following descriptions were illustrative of this group: "an occasionally enuretic, nervous, high-strung youngster"; [has] fear of school boys, unexpressed hostility to mother, [is] not facing responsibility, depressed"; "sullen, uncooperative, unreliable, uncommunicative, [has] temper tantrums, [is] enuretic"; "a quiet child, thumbsucker . . . mixed up, could use psychiatric help", "a nervous bedwetting hoodlum"; "the girl seems dazed, sad, hysterical, giggles constantly."

A child was classified as "Psychotic" when a psychiatric diagnosis of psychosis was quoted by the officer.

Personality criteria were recorded by probation officers in slightly more than two-thirds of 200 cases (see Table 10.3). The high number of unrecorded descriptions of personality for the group recommended to an institution may indicate either the officer's indifference or his hesitation in attaching diagnostic labels to the child when recommending referral to an institution.

Table 10.3. The personality of the child

	No Difficulties	Disturbed Behavior	Neurotic Symptoms	Un-diagnosed Symptoms	Psychotic Symptoms	No Record	Total
Probation	25	5	1	5	—	14	50
Institutionalization	8	5	5	11	1	20	50
Psychiatric examination	2	10	7	16	1	14	50
Discharge	32	—	1	1	—	16	50
Total	67	20	14	33	2	64	200

The discharge group showed a clear picture of "No Difficulties." In the probation group, two-thirds of those recorded were also classed under this heading; only one was described as showing neurotic symptoms, and none as showing psychotic symptoms. Probation was recommended, however, not only in cases having no difficulties, but also in cases with disturbed behavior or undiagnosed symptoms.

This picture is reversed in the group recommended to an institution, where only one-fourth of the recorded cases were classified under "No Difficulties" and one-third under "Undiagnosed Symptoms." The *same* number of cases with disturbed behavior appeared in the group recommended for institutionalization as well as in the group recommended to probation; but *more* cases with neurotic symptoms were recommended for institutionalization than for probation. The proportional difference is striking: of the 36 recorded cases recommended to probation, only one was diagnosed under "Neurotic Symptoms"; but of the 30 recorded cases recommended for institutionalization, five were so diagnosed.

The "Psychiatric Examination" group contained the highest number of children with undiagnosed symptoms and only two children with no difficulties. But even this particular group shows a smaller number of recorded judgments than the probation and discharge groups. Half of the "Disturbed Behavior" cases, half of the "Neurotic Symptoms" cases, half of the "Undiagnosed Symptoms," and one of the two "Psychotic Symptoms" cases were recommended for psychiatric examination, thus leading to the conclusion that the probation officer recommended psychiatric examination on general grounds—the presence of some sort of personality problem —rather than on the presence of a specific sort of personality problem. He tended to throw all difficult personality cases into the psychiatrist's lap instead of examining each case individually.

From the tabulation it is evident that personality difficulties were important criteria in the probation officer's recommendations; yet the relatively high number of cases in which no personality assessment had been recorded indicates some lack of perceptiveness on the probation officer's part.

The Delinquent Act as a Criterion

Delinquent acts were classified according to whether they were committed against life or property, against sexual taboos, and against parents. Delinquent acts against parents usually were reflected in petitions made by parents or guardians against "ungovernable" children—children (especially girls) accused of such acts as running away from home, stealing from home, or destroying furniture. Often, cases of truancy were included in this group (the accusation being that the child was refusing his parents' *legal* demand to go to school).

Table 10.4. Kind of delinquent act

	Against Life or Property	Against Sexual Taboos	Against Parents	Total
Probation	44	0	6	50
Institutionalization	17	6	27	50
Psychiatric examination	30	7	13	50
Discharge	42	2	6	50
Total	133	15	52	200

Type of delinquent act committed was a significant factor in the probation officers' recommendation. Among the three types of acts designated, those against life or property constituted 88 per cent of the recommendations to probation and 84 per cent of the recommendations for discharge. Sexual delinquencies, which constituted a very small number in all groups, were completely absent from the group recommended for probation.

Delinquent acts against parents are usually referred to the court by the parents. The conflict in the home, evidenced by both the child's delinquent act and his parents' referral, seemed to lead the probation officer to the decision that removal of the child to an institution would be the best solution to the problem. In these "Delinquency against Parents" cases, the officer recommended a psychiatric examination only half as often, and probation or discharge only one-quarter as often, as he did institutionalization. The recommendations for probation and discharge show many similarities on this table. Although the "Institutionalization" and the "Psychiatric Examination" groups are similar in their high number of sexual delinquencies, they are dissimilar in their distribution of delinquent acts against parents and against life or property. Only one-eighth of all children committing delinquencies against life or property were recommended for institutionalization, but one-half of those committing delinquent acts against parents were so recommended.

Seriousness of Delinquent Act

The following acts against life or property were regarded as serious delinquencies: a robbery with an assault which resulted in the victim's death, a serious stabbing in a gang fight, sodomy, possession of loaded firearms, an attack on a girl that caused a fracture of her skull, an armed robbery, an auto theft, a forcible rape. Serious delinquent acts against parents included suicide attempts and severe damage of the home; illegitimate births constituted a serious violation of sexual taboos (among girls), when the babies' whereabouts were unknown.

Table 10.5. Seriousness of the delinquent act

	Serious	Moderate	Mild	Total
Probation	5	35	10	50
Institutionalization	9	39	2	50
Psychiatric examination	14	34	2	50
Discharge	10	26	14	50
Total	38	134	28	200

Moderate delinquency included burglary with forced entry into a building; purse-snatching; participation, in a minor role, in a group car theft; minor thefts; assembling for a gang fight; forced entry into a school and theft of valuables there; forgery. Girls' delinquencies against their parents involved staying away from home a few nights.

Mild delinquency included kicking a boy during a fight and attempts at thefts. Delinquency against parents in this category included some truancy cases and cases of coming home late in the evening.

The seriousness of the delinquent act appears to have been of only secondary significance to the probation officer in making his recommendation. The officer who may have hesitated in putting on probation a child who committed a serious delinquent act often did not hesitate at all in recommending a discharge or a psychiatric examination.

The Child's Family Relations

Most mothers of children recommended for probation and psychiatric examination had treated them with "some rejection," as recorded by the probation officers. In the discharge group, the majority of mothers were classified as evidencing "no rejection" of the child, while those children recommended to an institution suffered from "severe rejection" by their mothers.

A similar pattern can be discerned in the less frequently recorded relationship of father and child. (While the maternal relationship was recorded in 157 of the 200 cases, the paternal relationship was recorded in only 96 instances.)

Children in each of the four recommendation groups showed distinctively different types of relationships with their parents. The children recommended to an institution usually had tense relations with both parents; the children recommended for discharge usually had good relations with both; and those recommended for probation or psychiatric examination had fair relations with them. But despite the rather distinctive differences in those cases where such information was recorded, a high number of presentence investigation reports completely omitted this information. Of the 200 reports studied, 86 did not include information on the child's relationship with his mother, and 116 did not include information on his relationship with his father.

A similar trend can be observed when one studies the factor of marital stability of the parents, which was recorded in only about half the 200 presentence reports (104 cases). The highest number of stable marital relations was recorded for parents of the discharge group, the next highest for parents of the groups recommended to probation and psychiatric examination (the figures for both of which were only slightly less than those for the first group), and the lowest number for parents of those in the institution group.

The large number of unrecorded cases—three-quarters of the 200—indicates that the probation officers did not consider the personality of the parents an important factor in arriving at a recommendation for the child. Hence, no pattern could be traced because of the limitations of the sample.

Economic level affected the officers' recommendations in much the same manner as did the familial relationships; high economic level appeared most often among those in the discharge group, least often among those in the institution group.

All data about a child's family background should be significant in determining one or another recommendation. The probation officers in our study, however, were not completely aware of this and so they only partially investigated the family background of the children, frequently omitting some vital information. As noted above, the child's personality difficulties were also frequently ignored in the investigation report.

Description of Each Group

CHILDREN RECOMMENDED FOR PROBATION

What kinds of children were most likely to be recommended for probation? Rarely were they girls. Girls who appeared before the court usually had committed delinquent acts against their parents or against sexual taboos —acts which the probation officer generally considered products of social background and personality make-up beyond the range of effective probation treatment. Indeed, sexual delinquents were *never* recommended to probation. Racial or religious affiliation was not considered a factor in recommending, or not recommending, probation. The child most often recommended to probation was the one with no personality difficulties; a child with behavior difficulties or undiagnosed symptoms was only rarely recommended. Children suffering from a physical handicap were practically never in this group. Age, gang membership, and delinquent neighborhood made no difference to the probation officer. Where parents were more cooperative with him, probation was recommended slightly more often. Economic status was not considered significant.

The child recommended to probation had both his original parents in more instances than did the child recommended for institutionalization; but marital stability was no more frequent among parents of those in the probation group than among parents of those in the other groups.

The child's school attendance, his conduct at school, and his achievements there neither qualified nor disqualified him for a recommendation to probation. Even church attendance, although it was more frequent in this group than among the institution group, was not a significant criterion for the probation officer. Neither the child's group affiliation nor his good or bad relationship with siblings, neighbors, relatives, and even his mother was significant. (The child's relationship with his peers went practically unrecorded, although more followers than leaders, more "group" delinquents than "lone wolf" delinquents were recommended for probation.) With regard to his mother's relationship with him, he did not differ from the children in the other groups. Interestingly, though, his father less frequently treated him with "severe rejection" than did the fathers of those in the psychiatric examination and institution groups. The parents' personalities, however, were not considered important criteria to the probation officer—and were seldom recorded.

Few children who had committed serious delinquent acts were recommended for probation; to the probation officer, commission of an act against the parents evidenced a family background and personality structure too disturbed to warrant probation. Thus, delinquents who had committed acts against life or property were more often recommended to probation.

Number of previous convictions was not an important criterion, but the group recommended to probation differed significantly from the others in that a larger number had previously committed delinquent acts that had not been prosecuted. If the child cooperated with the probation officer during the presentence investigation, he had a slight edge in his chances of being recommended to probation; this was also true of his parents' cooperation with the officer.

CHILDREN RECOMMENDED FOR INSTITUTIONALIZATION

Age was not considered significant in the officer's recommendations for institutionalization. As to religious affiliation, the child recommended for commitment was less likely to be Catholic than either Protestant or Jewish. He was slightly less cooperative than the child recommended for probation, and relatively more often handicapped than those in the other groups —but mental deficiency was not a significant criterion.

With respect to personality difficulties, he differed markedly from the other groups and usually had undiagnosed personality problems. A smaller number of those recommended for commitment had behavior difficulties or neurotic symptoms; few were rated as having no difficulties.

The child's family structure revealed factors important enough to influence the probation officer's recommendation. The child had only one original parent in more instances than did those in the other groups. (The number of children with one or both parents who were substitutes was not deemed an important criterion.) His economic status was the lowest of those in the four groups, but the others were just as frequently found in a delinquent neighborhood as he.

Most mothers, but slightly fewer fathers, of these children had severely rejected them, and their relationship with both parents was usually bad. The parents' marital relations were very unstable, although the symptoms characteristic of an unstable personality were found slightly less often among the mothers than among the fathers. The parents were not cooperative with the probation officer. Curiously, the sibling relationship of children in this group was not exceptionally bad.

In other social areas, the child recommended to commitment presented a less clear-cut picture. Although his attendance at church and school was the most sporadic of the four groups, he did not differ in his behavior or achievements at school. His group affiliations were not in any way distinctive, and his relationship with his peers, neighbors, or relatives was too infrequently recorded to show any trend in the probation officer's process of selection.

As to his delinquent acts: those against sexual taboos or against parents more frequently resulted in the child's being recommended to an institution than to any other disposition—a fact which explains the disproportionately high number of girls recommended for institutionalization, even when their social background was better than that of boys committing the same kind of delinquent act.

While the seriousness of the delinquent act was not significant, very few "mild" cases were recommended to an institution. The fact that most children in this group had committed their delinquent acts alone is consistent with the two kinds of delinquencies (i.e., against parents and against sexual taboos) most frequently found in this group. To the probation officers, previous convictions had some significance for this recommendation group, but previous *unprosecuted* delinquent acts had none. The same applied to gang membership. In spite of the high number of Negroes in this group, the kind of delinquent act, rather than a child's race, was what brought him into the institution.

CHILDREN RECOMMENDED FOR PSYCHIATRIC EXAMINATION

What makes the probation officer deem his investigation insufficient in determining a child's difficulties or the proper treatment to be used so that he decides to recommend a psychiatric examination? According to the reports the officers filled out, the answers cannot be found in the child's family background. With respect to family structure and to the economic situation and marital stability of the parents, *all* children recommended for psychiatric examination resembled those recommended for probation. A slightly greater number of families of children in this group, however, lived in a delinquent neighborhood, but no significant differences were reported in the familial relationship—mother to child, child to mother, father to child, child to father. There was a very slight tendency for the father to have an unstable personality, but nothing of note was reported about the mother's personality or the child's relationship with his siblings. Parental cooperation with the probation officer was slightly better in the probation group. Thus, those children recommended for psychiatric examination have family backgrounds very similar to that of the probation group.

With respect to this group's ability to socialize—and this refers to their church and school attendance, school conduct and performance, their relationship with neighbors, relatives, and other groups—no significant trends distinguished the child in the psychiatric examination group from the child in the probation group. Peer-group relationships were unrecorded in so many cases that no conclusion about them could be made. Neither age nor religious affiliation was deemed of any significance.

What *did* distinguish the child in this group from those in the others was his personality structure, which showed a major and marked difference. Here, he had every manner of severe personality disorder. But the probation officer, it is interesting to note, did not attempt to distinguish between various kinds of difficulties. Instead, he recommended to psychiatric examination an equally high number of children with neurotic or undiagnosed symptoms, disturbed behavior, and psychotic symptoms, and did not presume to diagnose certain kinds of disturbances himself. The fact that a disturbance existed was sufficient evidence for him to recommend a psychiatric examination.

Children in this group also differed significantly in their cooperativeness with the probation officer—a difference that was especially outstanding when compared with the probation group, which these children resembled for the most part. When no working relationship was established, the probation officer would ask for a psychiatric examination in hopes that this would make for a better relationship.

The relatively large number of girls recommended for examination (large when compared with those recommended to probation or discharge) could not be analyzed further because the number studied (only nine) was in such small proportion to the total. The fact that girls committed acts against sexual taboos or against parents was enough, apparently, to lead the probation officer to assume that psychiatric help was needed.

The eight Negro children in this group, although as thoroughly investigated, did not show as many personality difficulties as the white children, despite the striking similarities in many other areas—a feature which served to emphasize the importance of the child's relationship with the probation officer (rather than any extrapersonal or social factors) in selection for examination.

As to the importance of the delinquent act, previous conviction or previously committed, unprosecuted delinquent acts were obviously not significant criteria for psychiatric examination. Gang membership was, however, as was the fact that a serious act had been committed. Leadership in a group committing delinquent acts against property also had some significance for the probation officer making this recommendation. The large number of "lone wolf" delinquents corresponded to the high number of sex delinquencies and delinquencies against parents characteristic of this group, for whom the probation officer recorded a greater number of combined personality disorders. But there is no evidence that the *kind* of delinquent act alone determined the recommendation for psychiatric examination.

CHILDREN RECOMMENDED FOR DISCHARGE

Contrary to what might be expected, children were not recommended for discharge because of the mildness of their delinquent acts. However, this group did show fewer unprosecuted previously committed delinquent acts and slightly fewer previous convictions. In kind of delinquency committed, this group resembled the probation group in that their delinquencies were usually against life or property; very few were against parents or sexual taboos. But this group differed in its delinquency pattern—fewer children involved in group delinquency against life or property were recommended for discharge than were those involved in solo delinquent acts. Gang membership, however, was not any different in this group than in the others.

Slightly more indicative criteria for the discharge group were those pertaining to the child himself. Neither sex nor age of these children differed meaningfully from the sex and age of those recommended for other dispositions; but fewer Protestant and fewer Negro children were recommended for discharge than expected, considering their proportion to the total. In the incidence of physical handicaps, children in the discharge group resembled those of the other groups, although no child with a mental deficiency was recommended for discharge. Outstanding in all these cases was the fact that, by and large, the probation officer did not record any personality difficulties; the discharge group included a great number of children whom he rated "stable." These children were also more cooperative than the others.

The children's family background and superior social adjustment are the major areas which distinguish this recommendation group from the others. Most of the children had both their original parents, who were of good economic status and who had a good relationship with their child. Their marital relations were more stable than those of the parents in the other groups; and, although the father was more stable than those in the other groups, the mother did not differ. Both, however, were conspicuously cooperative with the probation officer. The child's relationship to his siblings was not too different from that of the children in the other groups (an observation seldom recorded for any group, however). These children lived in slightly less delinquent neighborhoods, attended church more frequently, and were comparatively outstanding in school attendance, conduct, and achievement. They did not differ in their spontaneous association with other children. Their relationships with neighbors, relatives, and peers were too rarely recorded to be interpreted.

Conclusions

Certain salient features emerge from analysis of the criteria for each recommendation. Seriousness of the delinquent act had only secondary significance to the probation officer in making his recommendation; of primary significance were the child's personality, his family background, and his general social adjustment. But the number of items omitted from the presentence investigation report indicates that the probation officer was unaware of the importance of the criteria he was actually using. Items most often recorded were objective in nature: identification of the child (by age, sex, religion, race), the delinquent act (kind, seriousness, role, previous conviction), the family composition and economic situation, and church and school attendance. Omitted were the more subjective, broader criteria: the various personal relationships in the family, the personalities of the parents and, especially, of the child. (The psychiatric examination group, with its highest number of children with personality difficulties, did not show more pathogenic relationships, so that no connection can be made between a child's disturbance and his pathogenic family.) This stress on reporting only the more objective data was extended to school adjustment as well—a child's attendance was much more completely recorded than were his conduct and actual achievement.

Obviously, these objective data can be more quickly and accurately recorded; but on analysis a number of these heavily recorded criteria proved to be quite useless to the probation officer in his choosing among the four kinds of recommendations. Modern casework practice considers the other kind of criteria—often obscured or lost in the records—more important to understanding the social and emotional pathology of the child and his family and crucial to his successful supervision and rehabilitation. Data on the child's personality and family situation, no matter how meagerly recorded, proved their own worth when they were actually used by the officer in distinguishing among the four groups.

More detailed records on the child's social adjustment outside the family would also be helpful. His relationship with his peers is especially important for our cases, since most of these children are in their adolescence —a period of life when peer groups have an important function in the youngster's maturation. The dynamic relationships between parent and child, child and sibling, carry over into the child-peer relationships as well. Therefore, information about the specific character of this relationship is important not only as a diagnostic tool but also as a means by which the probation officer can help effect the youngster's social rehabilitation.

The results of this study show not only a lack of application of these important criteria, but also the use of certain rather inconsequential criteria (sex, age, race, etc.) rather than consideration of the individual child. The high number of Negro children who committed delinquent acts against parents and sexual taboos and were recommended to institutions and the low number of girls who committed the same types of acts and were recommended to probation exemplify this trend.

As to the specific recommendation groups, the following can be said:

Probation. Recommendation to probation, as shown in our research sample of 200, was based on rather nebulous and limited criteria. The overwhelming majority of the cases recommended to probation did not have the personality difficulties which would require the personal and social rehabilitation that probation offers. A shift in criteria—reducing the number of cases with no personality difficulties who are recommended to probation and increasing the number of children with behavior disturbances and undiagnosed or neurotic symptoms—would bring more disturbed, but still curable, children to probation and would change the kind of delinquency "needed" to become a member of this group. Children committing sexual delinquencies or delinquencies against their parents could then receive the benefits of casework treatment. Membership in an unstable family would not necessarily mean a child's removal from home and community to an institution, but would allow instead for his inclusion in the probation caseload. This latter disposition would be especially appropriate since probation is an individual treatment situation, built on the relationship between the probation officer, the child, and the child's family. Many of those cases now recommended for probation showed adjustment difficulties that a well-conducted group program would help solve if the child were prepared by the probation officer to participate in it.

Institution. Institutional treatment is a group experience within a relatively controlled setting, but a child's need for such a group experience should be evaluated before he is sent to an institution.

Psychiatric Examination. If the family and the broader social background of the child were investigated in more detail, the group recommended for psychiatric examination would be more carefully selected by type and severity of personality difficulty and would include more children with severe pathology, with neurosis, and with undiagnosed symptoms. There would be no change in the use of the delinquent act as a criterion for recommending an examination.

Discharge. The criteria used in deciding on this recommendation are fully justified; disregard of the delinquent act is, it should be stressed, a constructive approach. The probation officer should concentrate on the juvenile delinquent's general social maladjustment rather than on its particular expression.

The proposed change in selecting children for probation would mean that a number of cases now recommended for probation would become candidates for discharge. But this shift of cases would not affect the criteria now used for this recommendation.

11. A Study of Probation Effectiveness

FRANK R. SCARPITTI and RICHARD M. STEPHENSON

OF THE twenty-two recommendations made by the President's Commission on Law Enforcement and Administration of Justice in the area of corrections, eight call for the expansion of community based treatment programs.[1] Prominent among the Commission's recommendations is a call for the expanded use of probation services for both juvenile and adult offenders. Citing the detrimental effects of institutionalization, especially on the young, the Commission's report concludes that placing an offender on probation allays these effects as well as increases his chances for a successful adjustment.[2] The negative consequences of institutionalization

Reprinted from *The Journal of Criminal Law, Criminology, and Police Science*, September 1968, pp. 361–369, by special permission of *The Journal of Criminal Law, Criminology, and Police Science* and the authors. Copyright © 1968, Northwestern University School of Law volume 59, number 3.

1. *The Challenge of Crime in a Free Society*, Report by The President's Commission on Law Enforcement and Administration of Justice (Washington, D.C.: U. S. Government Printing Office, 1967), chap. 6.
   2. *Ibid.*, pp. 165–171.

are well documented,[3] and obviously, keeping one out of the reformatory or prison will prevent his experiencing their debilitating effects. However, the effectiveness of probation as a rehabilitating program is not as well documented, and its crime or delinquency reducing impact upon offenders continues to be subject to many skeptical questions.

Conclusions regarding the effectiveness of probation are generally based upon the number of probationers who complete their supervision without revocation or the amount of post-release recidivism occurring among those who complete supervision. It can be seen that these are actually two different measures of success. In the former instance, many unknown and uncontrollable variables may influence the outcome of the probation experience: the philosophy of the probation department in revocation, the intensity of the officer's contacts with the probationer, the unknown offenses committed by the probationer while on probation, and the philosophy of the court in continuing or extending probation for known offenses. Nevertheless, England's review of eleven probation studies indicates that from 60 to 90 per cent succeed on probation.[4] A 1944 study of juvenile probationers showed that 35 per cent failed,[5] and a later study of 11,638 adult probationers revealed that only 29 per cent had their probation revoked.[6]

These success-failure rates are based upon official probation records and of course suffer from the deficiencies listed above. As such, they present a most favorable picture of probation success. Using more stringent, but perhaps unfair and unrealistic criteria of failure, the Gluecks have reported probation failure rates of 57.9 per cent for youthful offenders and 92.4 per cent for adult male offenders.[7]

Perhaps the second method of determining probation effectiveness, re-

3. Of the many studies that have attested to the anti-rehabilitation effects of total institutions such as prisons and reformatories, see, for example, Sykes, *The Society of Captives* (1958); Clemmer, *The Prison Community* (1948); Cloward, "Social Control in Prison," chap. 2 of Cloward *et al.*, *Theoretical Studies in Social Organization of the Prison* (1960); Garrity, "The Prison as a Rehabilitation Agency," chap. 9 of Cressey, ed., *The Prison: Studies in Institutional Organization and Change* (1961); Glaser and Stratton, "Measuring Inmate Change in Prison," chap. 10 of *ibid.*; Goffman, *Asylums* (1961); Ward and Kassebaum, *Women's Prison* (1965); Street, "The Inmate Group in Custodial and Treatment Settings," *American Sociological Review*, XXX (1965), 40–45; Berk, "Organizational Goals and Inmate Organization, *American Journal of Sociology*, LXXI (1966), 522–534; and Giallombardo, *Society of Women: A Study of a Women's Prison* (1966).

4. England, Jr., "What is Responsible for Satisfactory Probation and Post-Probation Outcome?" *Journal of Criminal Law and Criminology*, XLVII (1957), 674.

5. Reiss, Jr., "Delinquency as the Failure of Personal and Social Control," *American Sociological Review*, XVI (1951), 196–207.

6. *The Challenge of Crime in a Free Society*, p. 166.

7. S. and E. Glueck, *Juvenile Delinquents Grown Up* (1940), p. 153; and *Criminal Careers in Retrospect* (1943), p. 151.

cidivism, is a better indicator of the true success or failure of probation as a rehabilitation mechanism. Again, England reports that of the eleven studies reviewed, eight fall within the 70 to 90 per cent range in terms of post-probation success. These include Diana's study of juvenile probationers (84 per cent success), and England's study of adult Federal probationers (82.3 per cent success).[8] In addition, other studies of post-release recidivism among both adult and juvenile offenders show success or nonrecidivism rates of 72, 79, 88 and 83 per cent.[9] These rates compare favorably with those reported for in-program success and appear to substantiate the call for increased probation usage.

Nevertheless, the high rates of probation and post-probation success are puzzling to those who are aware of the difficulties of resocialization and rehabilitation. Probation supervision and guidance has traditionally been only superficial, generally involving infrequent and ritualistic contacts between officer and offender.[10] At the same time, few if any special programs of more intensive treatment and worker-client contacts can approximate the probation success rates.[11] Such contradictory evidence causes one to ask questions that have not yet been or have only partially been answered. Are probationers the least likely of the offender population to become recidivists? Are probationers different from other adjudicated offenders? What differentiates the in-program successes from the failures? How does recidivism among ex-probationers compare with that of other offenders who have experienced alternative methods of treatment? This paper will attempt to answer these and other questions pertaining to the effectiveness of probation as a treatment method.

The Present Study

Data presented in this paper were collected as part of a larger comparative study of delinquency treatment facilities. From January, 1962 to January, 1965 some 1210 adjudicated male delinquents between the ages of 16 and 18 from Essex County (Newark), New Jersey were admitted into

8. England, op. cit., pp. 667, 674.
9. Reported in Sutherland and Cressey, Principles of Criminology, 7th ed. (1966), p. 497.
10. England, op. cit.; Diana, "Is Casework in Probation Necessary?" Focus, XXXIV (1955), 1–8.
11. See, for example, any or all of the following: Weeks, Youthful Offenders at Highfields (1958); "The Community Treatment Project After 5 Years" (California Youth Authority, n.d.); Empey and Erickson, "The Provo Experiment in Delinquency Rehabilitation, Annual Progress Report for 1964," unpublished, report to the Ford Foundation, 1965; Stephenson and Scarpitti, "The Rehabilitation of Delinquent Boys," report to the Ford Foundation, 1967, mimeo.

the study.[12] Of these, 943 were committed to county probationary supervision, 100 to a non-residential guided group interaction center in the county, 67 to residential guided group interaction centers in the state, and 100 were sent to the State Reformatory at Annandale. All boys were followed up for recidivism until June, 1966.

The special admission criteria used by the court in committing boys to the group centers were also used to select participants in this study. Hence, all delinquents in this sample were male, 16 or 17 years of age, had no evidence of psychosis, severe neurosis or serious mental retardation, and had no prior commitment to a correctional institution. Assurance of reasonable comparability among cases, with respect to such differentiating factors as social background, psychological profiles, and delinquency history, presents a major problem in any comparative study. Ideally, it would be desirable to have boys assigned by the court to treatment facilities on a basis that would assure such comparability or, at least, on a random basis. In this study, as in others, this was not possible. However, it was felt that it would be possible to match boys across facilities on pertinent variables so as to control to some extent differences that might be found among the groups.

In order to obtain data upon which to match boys by treatment programs and to see how such data are related to progress in treatment and recidivism after release, the following information was obtained for each boy: first, social background data consisting of the usual demographic items relating to the boy and his family; second, delinquency history data consisting of the boy's entire court record (this information was up-dated during the post-treatment follow-up period); and third, a psychological profile determined by responses to questions on the Minnesota Multiphasic Personality Inventory.[13] The personality inventory was given whenever possible to each boy after his court appearance and before entrance into one of the treatment programs. Because of the large number of probationers relative to the other treatment groups, the MMPI was not administered to members of this group after January, 1964. In order to test for

12. During this period nearly 15,000 children appeared before the Essex County Juvenile Court. Some 4,761 of these youths were boys sixteen or seventeen years of age.
13. Of the several psychological instruments available, the MMPI appeared to be most feasible for this purpose. Resources would not permit an exploration in depth, nor was it possible to design, test, validate and complete an instrument more suitable for this particular study. On the other hand, the MMPI has been widely used, is readily administered, and gives a reasonably broad psychological profile. Moreover, a number of studies have used the MMPI on both delinquent and non-delinquent populations. See Hathaway and Monachesi, *Analyzing and Predicting Juvenile Delinquency with the MMPI* (1952); *Adolescent Personality and Behavior* (1963); Dahlstrom and Welsh, *An MMPI Handbook* (1960); Welsh, *Basic Readings on the MMPI in Psychology and Education* (1956).

change during treatment, the study subjects were again given the inventory at the time of their release.[14]

Hence, it was not only possible to test the impact of the probation experience as measured by program completion, psychological change, and recidivism, but also to compare the results of probation with those of other programs available to the committing judge. The programs used for such comparison can be thought of as more "intense" and confining than probation. The non-residential group center (Essexfields) program included a regimen of work and group interaction for approximately four months while the boys continued to live at home. The Group Centers program entailed the same elements for the same length of time, but boys resided in the Centers. At Annandale, the state reformatory, the program was restricted and irregular, and commitments averaged about nine months.

Characteristics of the Groups

As Table 11.1 indicates, the social background characteristics of each group are roughly associated with assignment to their treatment facility. Although the association is not always marked or consistent, Annandale tends to have a greater proportion of boys who are Negro, in the lower range of the socio-economic continuum, and more likely to terminate their education before high school graduation. Probationers, on the other hand, are equally divided racially and generally tend to be more positive on the socio-economic, family organization, and education variables. Between the extremes of Annandale and Probation are the other two treatment groups.

In addition, 37 per cent of the Probation group had completed the tenth grade or more compared with 24 per cent in the Group Centers, 18 per cent in Essexfields, and 14 per cent in Annandale. More of the Probation group also had some employment experience prior to their treatment assignment.

A fairly clear pattern of progression with respect to the association between delinquency history and treatment program is also evident. This pattern indicates that the extent of delinquency tends to increase from Probation through Essexfields and Group Centers to Annandale. This progression is most clearly indicated by the number of past court appear-

14. Since some of the boys were non-readers or failed to cooperate, it was impossible to test all in both pre- and post-treatment situations. Further attrition of cases was occasioned by changes in institutional personnel administering the tests, in-program failures, and a variety of administrative circumstances. When the inventories were scored and examined for validity, further losses were experienced. In all, there were 491 valid pre-treatment and 325 valid post-treatment MMPI inventories available.

Table 11.1. Percentage distribution of social background factors by treatment programs

Background Factor	Probation	Essexfields	Group Centers	Annandale
Race:	(N = 943)	(N = 100)	(N = 67)	(N = 100)
White	50	41	55	29
Negro	50	59	45	71
Family Income:	(N = 938)	(N = 100)	(N = 67)	(N = 95)
Welfare	15	18	12	26
Less than $2,000	2	6	3	1
$2,000–4,000	20	19	25	25
$4,001–6,000	28	33	28	24
$6,001–8,000	19	15	21	12
$8,001–10,000	9	4	8	8
$10,001 or more	8	5	3	3
Occupation of				
Breadwinner:	(N = 737)	(N = 76)	(N = 52)	(N = 67)
Unskilled	21	35	25	33
Semi-skilled	44	41	27	39
Skilled	14	12	19	8
Clerical	12	7	14	8
Owner-Manager	5	3	8	13
Professional &				
Semi-Professional	4	3	8	—
Education of				
Breadwinner:	(N = 891)	(N = 99)	(N = 61)	(N = 56)
Grammar school				
grad. or less	16	15	5	27
Some high school	59	65	66	54
High school grad.	19	17	21	11
Some college	3	3	5	7
College graduate	3	—	3	2
Parents' Marital Status:	(N = 943)	(N = 100)	(N = 67)	(N = 100)
Unknown	1	—	—	2
Never married	2	2	2	5
Married	49	47	46	40
Separated	20	22	13	27
Divorced	10	12	13	6
One or both dead	18	17	25	20
Boy Lives With:	(N = 943)	(N = 100)	(N = 67)	(N = 100)
Both parents	49	45	45	39
Parent and step-parent	11	13	15	10
Mother only	30	33	28	31
Father only	4	4	6	3
Relatives, foster				
home, or institution	6	5	6	17
Boys' School Status:	(N = 943)	(N = 100)	(N = 67)	(N = 100)
In school	48	68	48	28
Expelled	4	2	—	14
Quit	39	20	39	51
Excluded	7	9	13	7
Graduated	2	1	—	—

ances. Nearly half of the Probationers had no prior court appearance, while only seven per cent or less of the other boys fall into this category. Twenty per cent of the boys at Annandale, 15 per cent at Group Centers, 6 per cent at Essexfields, and 3 per cent on Probation had five or more appearances. Only 40 per cent of the Probationers, but over 90 per cent of the boys in the other groups had one or more prior petitions sustained by the court. ,Forty-one per cent of the Annandale boys had three or more petitions sustained, but only 5 per cent of the Probationers. Eighty per cent of the Probationers but only 19 per cent of the Annandale boys had never been on probation before. As a group, Probationers were older and Annandale boys younger at the time of the first court appearance. Almost two-thirds of the Probationers were 16 or 17 years of age at their first court appearance; less than a third of the boys in any other group were that old. Insofar as previous court history and age of first court appearance are associated with continued delinquency, the Probationers appear to be the best risks and Annandale boys the worst.

When the psychological characteristics of the four groups are examined, rather distinct differences can also be seen.[15] As with many of the social background and delinquency history characteristics, the Probation and Annandale groups are the most different, with the Essexfields and Group Centers groups falling between these two extremes. These results suggest that the Probation boys as a group are somewhat less anti-social, less delinquent (although exhibiting a distinctively delinquent personality pattern), and better emotionally adjusted than the boys in the other groups. They are also less anxious and less hostile, exhibit a slightly better attitude toward themselves, have a better work attitude, and score higher on the social responsibility dimension of the inventory.

From all indications, it would appear that Probation received the less delinquent and better socially and psychologically adjusted juvenile offender. In this sense, it becomes responsible for what might be termed "easier" cases, or boys for whom the probability of success is greater. The relationship between pre-treatment probability of success and actual success can be seen in terms of (1) program completion, (2) change during the program, and (3) post-treatment recidivism.

In-Program Success and Failure

"In-program failure" is used to refer to any boy who was sent back to the court during the course of the treatment program and who was not returned

15. In addition to the regular fourteen basic clinical and validity scales, fifteen other measures selected from Dahlstrom and Welsh, *op. cit.*, and other sources were used in the analysis of the MMPI's. For a detailed discussion, see Stephenson and Scarpitti, *op. cit.* The authors gratefully acknowledge the contribution of Dr. Richard Lanyon, Department of Psychology, Rutgers, the State University, in the analysis of these data.

by the court to the same program. It refers to those boys returned to the court for committing a new delinquent offense, being incorrigible or unmanageable while in the program, or, in the case of Essexfields and Group Centers, being socially or emotionally unsuitable for the program. In essence, the in-program failures were those boys upon whom the various rehabilitation programs had the least immediate effect, not even providing them with an opportunity to experience the entire treatment process.

Aside from Annandale, a custodial institution where program completion is not a question, the in-program success and failure rates for the other facilities were strikingly similar. Although the failure rate for Probation, 28 per cent of the committed boys, is higher than that for Essexfields, 23 per cent, and the Group Centers, 27 per cent, these differences are not statistically significant. These rates do indicate, however, that the overwhelming majority of the boys in non-custodial programs complete their treatment experiences without becoming involved in further difficulty. Using only this criterion of success, probation fares no better than some others, and theoretically more meaningful, programs of treatment. In addition, some 219 Probationers appeared in court for a new offense during their probationary period, but were given dispositions of "Probation Extended" or "Probation Continued." Hence, they were not counted as in-program failures.

Examination of pertinent background, delinquency and personality variables shows interesting differences between Probation successes and failures. In Probation, whites have a lower failure rate and a higher success rate than Negroes. Failure is also more likely to occur for those boys who were out of school at the time of their admission. The same is true for those boys with a negative educational status score, a composite index which includes present school status, number of grades completed, and number of years retarded in school. The delinquency history score, another composite index consisting of age first known to court, number of delinquent offenses, and types of delinquent offenses, presents further evidence that the less delinquent and less delinquency-prone do better on probation than the more seriously delinquent. All of these differences are statistically significant at the .05 level or better. The same relationship, however, is not necessarily found between failures and successes in the other groups. Generally speaking, failures in the other groups are similar to Probation failures, but do not differ as markedly from the successes in their groups.

The MMPI data corroborate these findings. Again, the greatest differences are found between the Probation successes and failures. Nineteen of the 29 scales used in this study differentiate these two groups at the .05 level of significance or better. Among those tests which distinguish between the groups are the psychopathic deviancy, hypomania, schizophrenia, and

F (indicating an attempt by the respondent to show himself in a bad light), as well as the delinquency, escapism, and social responsibility scales. As with the other tests which differentiate, the Probation successes score more positively than do the failures. The failures clearly have a more delinquent personality pattern, conforming closely to the classic pattern for delinquents.

All of the scores for the Probation successes indicate that they are not very disturbed and are fairly well adjusted. Probation failures, as indicated, are less so, but are similar to both the failures and successes in Essexfields and Group Centers. In these groups, there are practically no significant differences between program successes and failures as determined by the MMPI tests. Failures in both programs, however, generally score more negatively than do successes on most scales. Although many of the success-failure differences in the Essexfields and Group Centers programs are in the same direction as those found in Probation, they are milder and less able to distinguish between the criterion groups.

These data seem to indicate that the Probation successes are less delinquent and better adjusted than all other boys in this study, successes or failures. In Essexfields and Group Centers the successes and failures are more similar to each other, as well as to the Probation failure group.

Changes During Treatment

The pre- to post-treatment MMPI changes made by boys while on Probation were relatively minimal. Of the basic MMPI scales, the significant changes were an increase on the depression and defensiveness scales, and a decrease on the paranoia and social introversion scales. While this pattern of change is not readily meaningful, it becomes clearer upon examination of the remaining scales. Decreases occurred on the anxiety and neuroticism scales, although these changes tend to be inconsistent with the increase in depression. Other changes were an improvement in attitude toward others, in attitude toward self, in work attitude, in intelligence and in dominance.

These scores suggest that a definite though slight change did take place in the boys during their probationary term. However, the changes were not in the scores characteristic of delinquency (psychopathic deviancy, hypomania, and schizophrenia), but in a variety of other areas. Overall, the boys became a little less anxious, and more outgoing, secure, and intellectually efficient. Also, there was improvement in attitudes toward themselves, others, and work. The slight decrease in paranoia seems to have little meaning, since larger decreases were shown by all other groups.

Changes shown by the Essexfields and Group Centers boys were somewhat more marked than those shown in the Probation sample. Although the changes were not necessarily the type associated with delinquency reduction, they reflected general improvement in attitudes and ego-strength and a reduction of anxiety. Annandale boys, however, did not exhibit any of these positive changes and showed a greater tendency for change in a negative direction. Most noteworthy, perhaps, was an increase in the hostility score over the period of institutional confinement.

These findings indicate that the greatest positive changes, as measured by the MMPI, occurred in the group programs. Changes for the Probation group were slight, but in a positive direction. To account for Probation's more favorable initial group profile, groups within the four programs were matched on clinical scales regarded as predictive of delinquency. The changes for these matched groups were very similar to those of the unmatched groups. We might conclude then that Probation's effect in this respect is slight but positive. It is not as effective as either the non-residential or residential group programs, but much more beneficial than the reformatory experience.

Recidivism

Perhaps the most crucial indicator of probation effectiveness is whether or not boys who complete the program continue to experience difficulty with the law. Objections to the use of recidivism as a criterion of "successful" treatment may be raised on several grounds. Recidivism indicates only one aspect of the effectiveness of a program of rehabilitation. Improvement in work habits, educational orientation, family adjustment, or personality characteristics are not necessarily indicated by the fact that a new offense is or is not committed. In addition, a person may commit numerous infractions of the law without arrest or conviction and still be regarded as a "success." Nevertheless, an avowed goal of corrections is to inhibit a return to crime and delinquency. Short of daily surveillance of individual cases or reliable community sources of informal information concerning them, the available evidence for estimating effectiveness in reaching this goal is the official record of court appearances and dispositions. This evaluation therefore seeks to answer one major question: to what extent do those released from a program of treatment become involved in delinquency or crime as indicated by court action?

Boys who completed treatment and had no court appearances from their date of release to June of 1966 are clearly non-recidivists. Those who had one or more court appearances after release are not so readily disposed of since a court appearance is not sufficient to regard a case as a recidivist. A wide range of alternative dispositions are available to the court that may indicate a minor offense or even none at all. Therefore, the following court dispositions were used as the basis for determining recidivism: fine, jail, probation, Essexfields, Group Centers, reformatory, and prison. A court appearance resulting in any other disposition [16] was regarded as non-recidivism, since the court obviously did not view the case as demanding intensive correctional treatment or punitive action.

Setting aside for the moment the fact that boys in different programs differ in social background and delinquency history, it can be seen from Table 11.2 that Annandale boys have the highest recidivism rate (55 per

Table 11.2. Number of recidivists, cumulative recidivists and cumulative per cent of releasees who are recidivists by six month periods

Months	Probation (N = 671)			Essexfields (N = 77)			Group Centers (N = 49)			Annandale (N = 97)		
	#R	CR	C%	#R	CR	C%	#R	CR	C%	#R	CR	C%
6	50	50	7	12	12	16	8	8	16	20	20	21
12	37	87	13	9	21	27	5	13	27	16	36	38
18	9	96	14	8	29	38	5	18	37	9	45	46
24	5	101	15	6	35	45	2	20	41	6	51	53
30	1	102	15	1	36	47	—	—	—	1	52	54
36	—	—	—	1	37	48	—	—	—	1	53	55

N—Number of releasees (completed treatment).
#R—Number of recidivists.
CR—Cumulative recidivists.
C%—Cumulative percentage of releasees.

cent) and Probationers the lowest (15 per cent). Essexfields and Group Centers fall between these extremes, although recidivism is somewhat lower for Group Centers boys (41 per cent) than for Essexfields boys (48 per cent) and terminates earlier than that of any other program. It also is apparent that this general pattern is repeated when recidivism is calculated for each six month post-release period. The differences in rates of recidivism between Probation and each of the other three programs are statistically significant at a level greater than .001.

Among all recidivists, the highest percentage of recidivism was within the first six months, and nearly 75 per cent of the recidivism took place within a year after release. Probation recidivists appear to have the highest rate of recidivism within the first year and decrease strikingly thereafter. Noting the early termination of recidivism among Group Centers boys, the other three programs appear to spread out recidivism over a longer time span.

16. Court dispositions not regarded as recidivism included dismissal, petition withdrawn, private placement, hospital placement, restitution ordered, counseled, adjustment to be reviewed, referred to parole (no further action taken), probation extended or continued (for Essexfields and Group Centers releases), probation vacated, bench warrant issued and case pending.

Since boys in the four programs of treatment were found to differ with respect to social background and delinquency history, an attempt was made to match cases across programs. With the exception of Probation, the total number of boys in each program was relatively small. This meant that to match on more than two or three variables was not feasible. At the same time it was desirable to include as many of the relevant factors as possible. One way to handle this problem was to combine several related variables into one index. Three factors were selected for matching purposes: socio-economic status (index comprised of family income, education and occupation of family breadwinner), delinquency history (index described earlier), and race.

It was possible to match only 44 boys across all four programs on the three matching factors. After elimination of in-program failures, the following rates of recidivism were observed: Probation (N = 34), 21 per cent; Essexfields (N = 35), 49 per cent; Group Centers (N = 31), 45 per cent; and Annandale (N = 41), 56 per cent. The differences in rates between Probation and each of the other three programs are statistically significant at a level greater than .01. Probationers were then matched separately with Essexfields boys since these two programs were most similar. Ninety-nine boys were matched in each group and, after eliminating the in-program failures, recidivism rates of 19 per cent for Probation (N = 69) and 48 per cent for Essexfields (N = 76) were found. As these results from matched groups indicate, the relative proportion of recidivists for each program does not change greatly even when seemingly significant variables are controlled.

It appears that Probation is highly successful as a treatment device when compared with alternative methods of dealing with delinquent boys. Probationers who complete their treatment have lower rates of recidivism than those who complete other types of programs, even when matched on background and delinquency factors. A great difference can be observed, however, between the recidivism rates of Probationers who complete and those who fail to complete the program. This is a significant consideration because recidivism rates of in-program failures may bear upon the finding concerning recidivism among boys who successfully completed treatment.

The data suggest that boys who fail during treatment and are reassigned to another program are poor risks for rehabilitation. Although this is true for all programs in which in-program failure was possible, it is especially truc for Probation. Not only do Probation failures have a much higher rate of recidivism than failures in other programs, but they also have a significantly higher (p > .001) rate than those who complete treatment. When program successes and failures are combined, that is, all boys originally assigned to Probation by the court, the recidivism rate for Probation more than doubles, although it still remains lower than that of the other programs.

Discussion

This paper has presented data on the effectiveness of probation as a treatment program for 16 and 17 year old delinquent boys. Boys assigned to probationary supervision were compared with delinquents committed to group treatment programs and to the state reformatory. Pertinent data were collected for each group at the time of program assignment, during the programs, and after release from treatment.

As a group, boys assigned to Probation appear to be "better" or "easier" cases than those assigned to other treatment facilities. They appear to come from more stable family backgrounds, are less deprived, and have a more positive educational history. Their delinquency careers are shorter and involve fewer past offenses and official court actions. The MMPI scores suggest that Probation boys are less delinquent, less antisocial and better adjusted than boys in the other groups. Of the more than 1200 delinquent boys selected for this study, it is clearly evident that the best "risks" were assigned to Probation. As others have indicated,[17] the bulk of Probationers are not seriously delinquent and probably not in need of intensive rehabilitative efforts.

Once assigned to Probation, some 72 per cent of the group completes the program and are successfully discharged. This is comparable to the percentage completing the group programs. More significantly, however, are the differences observed between the Probation successes and failures. On practically every count, the in-program failures are worse off than the successes. These differences are not seen between successes and failures in the other programs. Probation failures conform more to the profiles of all boys in the other groups than they do to the successes in Probation. Hence, it would appear that Probation rids itself during the course of treatment of those boys who are most delinquent and hardest to resocialize.

For those who complete probation, little change is reflected on the psychological and attitudinal dimensions of the MMPI. This is not surprising since the pre-tests did not indicate gross abnormalities among these youths and since the most disturbed, who had the greatest margin for improvement, were eliminated as in-program failures. It seems significant then that even modest positive changes were found in attitude, ego-strength and anxiety. Although not as great as the changes made by boys in the group-oriented programs, they are certainly more favorable than those of the reformatory group.

17. Diana, *op. cit.*; England, *op. cit.*

In the last analysis, the crucial test of program effectiveness is recidivism, despite its many shortcomings. Again, boys assigned to Probation do much better in staying out of legal difficulty after release than their counterparts in other treatment programs. The Probation recidivism rate of 15 per cent is substantially below that of other programs. Although this low rate may result from Probationers' having the most favorable social backgrounds and delinquency histories, when boys were matched across programs, the relative rates of recidivism remained substantially unchanged.

The low rate of recidivism of the Probationers who complete treatment may partially be accounted for by the high rate of recidivism of in-program failures, on the grounds that Probation rids itself of high recidivism risks. By returning high risk boys to the court for further disposition, Probation may increase its chances of non-recidivism among boys who complete treatment. This is possible to a much lesser extent at Essexfields and Group Centers, and practically impossible at Annandale. This possibility must be considered as a strong conditioning factor in assessing the very low 15 per cent recidivism among Probationers who completed treatment.

On the basis of the criteria used in this study, Probation does appear to be an effective treatment agent, at least for certain types of boys. Those who are less delinquent and come from fairly stable backgrounds complete their treatment program and remain free of delinquency involvement. More severe cases, similar to those assigned to intensive or punitive programs, do not do as well on Probation.

These findings lead us to a note of caution. It would appear that the good performance of probation is often misunderstood and thought to mean that all offenders can benefit from being placed under probationary supervision. This is clearly not the case. If probation is extended greatly, failure and recidivism rates will grow markedly, unless, of course, there is some monumental change in treatment techniques. Barring such change, a backlash effect is possible, with the public's reacting against probation, which they will assume to be ineffectual, and demanding more incarceration. The use of probation should be expanded, but its direction must be carefully guided and those assigned to it must be chosen with rigor.

PART SIX

Training Schools and Delinquents

We have now followed the juvenile offender from the point at which he engaged in delinquency through the juvenile court and on to probation. We have seen that the state training school constitutes the "end of the line," where those lawbreakers who have failed in other correctional programs are allocated. Whatever else it is, the training school is a warehouse in which some of society's rejects are temporarily stored.

However, in the eyes of at least some of those who manage training schools and in the view of many members of the general public, the juvenile custodial institution is supposed to be more than a storage vault for social wreckage. The training school is intended to be the locale for a therapeutic endeavor which converts juvenile "bad guys" (or "bad girls") into law-abiding citizens. Moreover, the rehabilitative focus has received a good deal of implementation in California, Washington, Minnesota, New Jersey, and a number of other states, in which marked efforts have been made to organize the juvenile institution into a rehabilitative milieu.

Another perspective on the training school is often entertained by students of deviant behavior, who suggest that it operates as a "crime school"

222

which provides juvenile offenders with hardened attitudes, criminalistic self-images, and enhanced crime skills.

These three opinions contain different assertions about the effects of juvenile institutions upon wards who are incarcerated in them. The therapeutic orientation supposes that these places have positive effects, the deviance position contends that they have a negative impact upon offenders, and the warehouse view suggests that the training-school experience is a benign one which has no great impact one way or another on offenders. This third stance argues that most offenders are so enmeshed in lawbreaking by the time they get to the institution that it contributes little to their subsequent delinquent careers.

The first aspect of the training school with which we are concerned in this section is the nature of social organization in the juvenile institution. What are training schools like? How harmonious are relationships among different employee groups in these places? What are the main lines of behavior which can be observed in them? What kinds of social patterns grow up among inmates? What kinds of views about the training school do wards exhibit?

There is a growing literature on juvenile institutions, and a considerable stock of evidence now exists on a variety of training schools.[1] The picture that emerges from this material is a complex one, much too detailed to be discussed at length here. But some of the major elements of the evidence point to the following generalizations. First, punitive-custodial institutions are still in the majority. Here the major focus of the program centers about the restriction of freedom of the wards. The staff members of these schools are poorly trained, and few of them are conversant with treatment themes. The focus on control of wards, regimentation, and prevention of escapes often leads to physical punishment as a routine disciplinary tool. Second, treatment-oriented institutions have grown up in some number, in which staff members view themselves as professional

1. A sample of this material would include Gordon H. Barker and W. Thomas Adams, "The Social Structure of a Correctional Institution," *Journal of Criminal Law, Criminology, and Police Science*, XLIX (January-February 1959), 417–422; Sethard Fisher, "Social Organization in a Correctional Residence," *Pacific Sociological Review*, IV (Fall 1961), 87–93; R. L. Jenkins, "Treatment in an Institution," *American Journal of Orthopsychiatry*, XI (January 1941), 85–91; Lloyd E. Ohlin and William C. Lawrence, "Social Interaction Among Clients as a Treatment Problem," *Social Work*, IV (April 1959), 3–13; Howard W. Polsky, *Cottage Six* (New York: Russell Sage Foundation, 1962); David Street, Robert D. Vinter, and Charles Perrow, *Organization for Treatment* (New York: Free Press, 1966); George H. Weber, "Conflicts Between Professional and Non-Professional Personnel in Institutional Delinquency Treatment," *Journal of Criminal Law, Criminology, and Police Science*, XLVII (May-June 1957), 26–43; Weber, "Emotional and Defensive Reactions of Cottage Parents," in Donald R. Cressey, ed., *The Prison* (New York: Holt, Rinehart and Winston, 1961), pp. 189–228, much of this material is summarized in Don C. Gibbons, *Society, Crime, and Criminal Careers* (Englewood Cliffs, N.J.: Prentice-Hall, 1968), pp. 478–485.

rehabilitation agents. At the same time, the focus on control of inmates persists, so that a marked degree of tension develops between cottage workers, who have the responsibility for orderly behavior, and the case-workers, teachers, and other members of the treatment staff. Third, a well-developed inmate social-status system is found in both custodially oriented and treatment-oriented schools. Under this system, more sophisticated wards are involved in victimization of younger, less mature, low-status inmates.[2]

The first essay in this section was drawn from a larger report of an experimental program at Fricot Ranch for Boys, a California Youth Authority training school. This selection was chosen because it provides the most vivid and detailed characterization of life in the juvenile institution which can be obtained short of actually serving time in such a place. The flavor of training-school life is captured in this excerpt from the Fricot Ranch report.

It ought to be noted that Fricot Ranch is an institution that is on the far end of a treatment-custodial continuum, an institution in which a major effort at rehabilitation has been mounted. But, as the essay makes clear, discipline and control still remain overpowering concerns in this place. Whatever the long-range effects that incarceration in this school may have upon the boy who experiences it, it can hardly be argued that Fricot Ranch is a warm, friendly, therapeutic institution. One remarkable thing about this paper is the candor with which this negative portrayal of the training school is made, in view of the fact that the selection is taken from a report produced by the state agency which controls Fricot Ranch.

The second facet of the training school with which this selection is concerned is that of impact. Most of the evidence on parole violations or subsequent criminality on the part of wards released from juvenile institutions indicates that these places turn out mostly "failures."[3] Unlike probation, in which three-fourths or more of the probationers refrain from further delinquency (or at least are not observed in misconduct), training schools discharge inmates into the community who frequently become reinvolved in lawbreaking. The main exception to this dismal report on the training school is the institution for girls, for female parolees commonly succeed on release from the facility.

However, the meaning of these figures is not clear. Do parolees become caught up in misconduct due to negative social-psychological changes which occurred on their part? Although this is one possibility, it is equally plausible that the training school is only a neutral experience. Perhaps

2. One study dealing with a number of juvenile institutions, in which these features are reported, is Street, Vinter, and Perrow, *op. cit.*
3. Evidence on training school results can be found in Don C. Gibbons, *Delinquent Behavior* (Englewood Cliffs, N.J.: Prentice-Hall, 1970), pp. 247–254.

high failure rates are the consequence of antisocial attitudes which wards bring with them into the institution and which are not modified by the experiences there.

One recent investigation conducted by Adamek and Dager, of a Catholic training school for girls suggests that that school has at least a benign effect on many of the girls who proceed through it.[4] These researchers found a number of wards in that school who showed a positive identification with the institution. These same girls showed improved self-esteem and other signs of positive change during their stay in the school. Adamek and Dager also discussed the authoritarian but benevolent social structure of this girls' school, which they claim produced much of the success of the place. However, they were quick to point out that such a highly structured regime might not produce the same results if it were imposed upon a boys' institution. At any rate, this study provides one exception to the contention that training schools are inevitably harmful in impact.

The study by Eynon and Simpson bears on this theme. Their investigation is a comparative one, dealing with a large training school in Ohio and several camps in that state. Although the combined findings of that research do not point in exactly the same direction, one major conclusion is that boys in this state training school showed some improvement in attitudes. The Eynon and Simpson study provides little encouragement for those claims about the deleterious effects of the juvenile institution.

4. Raymond J. Adamek and Edward Z. Dager, "Social Structure, Identification and Change in a Treatment-Oriented Institution," *American Sociological Review,* XXXIII (December 1968), 931–944.

12. The Fricot Ranch Study

CARL F. JESNESS

The Fricot Ranch School for Boys

The formal Fricot organization, headed by the superintendent, includes a staff of approximately 110 persons who care for and treat an average population of slightly over 220 boys, in five living units. Under the superintendent and his assistant, on the organization chart, are four major division heads—Business Manager, Supervisor of Special Treatment (social work staff), Supervisor of Academic Instruction, and Head Group Supervisor. The Home Life division, under the Head Group Supervisor, is the direct descendant of the traditional custodial department of penal institutions. It is this staff, by far the largest division at the institution, which has responsibility for the daily care and treatment of the boys.

The relationship between the social work staff headed by the Supervisor of Special Treatment and the staff of the Home Life section is imprecisely defined and has been in a state of evolution for several years. Fricot has been a leader in integrating the services of social work and psychological staff into the entire program rather than having them func-

Reprinted from Carl F. Jesness, *The Fricot Ranch Study* (Sacramento: State of California, Department of the Youth Authority, 1965), pp. 8–14, 28–34.

tion in isolated settings in individual therapy. During most of the last two years of this study, after the small staff had been increased, one social worker was assigned to each of the five lodges, where he worked closely with the supervisors on all aspects of the program. As individual therapy is not an important aspect of the program, the social worker has had to develop new approaches to treatment. Such a change of role necessarily takes time, and there is still conflict to be resolved in defining areas of responsibility.

The role of the academic school teacher is akin to the traditional one, and seemed to present fewer difficulties in definition. One major problem noted appeared to hinge on the reluctance of teachers, who have often had considerable formal training in the treatment of children, to give over the main responsibility for treatment to the Home Life staff. Their role as "treaters" remains ambiguous. Another problem faced by the teachers was the sustaining of enthusiasm and high productivity goals in the face of the lack of feedback from community and parents, the limited time invested in each boy's development, and the indifferent, sometimes hostile attitudes of many of the wards.

It is the group supervisor around whom the daily program revolves; with him a boy deals most often outside school hours. The supervisor's job embodies an enormous variety of skills and responsibilities. His role combines the tasks of friend, counselor, group manager and lodge administrator. Each boy entering Fricot is assigned a "Fricot Dad" from among the supervisors in his lodge. This special counselor will follow the boy's case closely, recommend referral to parole when he judges the boy ready for release, and will give him individual attention and advice wherever possible. Thus, the supervisor is a most important person, not only in determining the milieu of the living unit, but also in deciding the fate of the ward. Almost any Fricot staff member, asked to define the Fricot treatment program and how it differs from that of other institutions, is likely to mention the assignment of "Fricot Dads" as a key concept, and it is on the supervisor that our attention will be focused.

The daily program at Fricot is a busy one, with planned activity filling almost every hour of the day. The routine for a boy in any one of the lodges would run much as follows:

> Lights are turned on at 6:05 A.M. The group is on silence during dressing and washing up, then the boys line up in the hallway, where quiet talking is allowed until they leave for the dining room at 6:35. On the dining hall ramp the boys stand silent at attention until the "At ease, quiet talking" order is given. In the dining room low talking is allowed, but no horseplay or trading of food. After breakfast the group is moved to the lodge yard, where the supervisor takes a count and runs a bathroom call. He selects crews to sweep and mop the lodge washroom,

locker room, day room, dormitory, honor room hall and office, and supervises the work. At 8:25 the boys are ordered into formation, the supervisor takes another count and then accompanies the group to the academic school building. When classes are let out at 11:30 A.M., boys go directly to the dining hall ramp, met by their supervisor, who takes a count before the group enters. After lunch the boys go to the lodge, usually for a quiet period in the day room or on their beds, sometimes going on a short hike or playing outdoors. At 1:05 P.M. they are ordered into formation for a count, then move again to the school building, followed by the supervisor. School is dismissed for the day at 4:15, and the boys go directly to their lodge yard, met by their supervisor, who takes a count, then usually allows free play. By 4:30 P.M. the boys are moved into the lodge to wash up before dinner, and they leave the lodge about 5:05 P.M. to march to the dining hall. After the meal the group moves back to the lodge for a count, a bathroom call, and a brief period of free play outdoors or in the lodge. At 6:15 P.M. the group is split, following the preferences of the boys, for the evening activities, which may include a hike, organized games, or supervised crafts. Activities end at 8:00 P.M., when the boys are returned to the lodge. They brush their teeth, undress, put their shorts, socks and tee shirts into laundry bags, and take showers by groups. As soon as they have showered, the boys go to their beds, and there is "package call"— which means that those who have received from home packages of cookies, candy, and toys, may enjoy these treats until 9:30, when all boys must be in their beds. No boy is allowed out of bed after 10:30 unless it is to go to the bathroom, and during the night the supervisor quietly moves through the lodge to take a count of the boys three times every hour.

While the routine activities, or "program," provides the vehicle for the interpersonal relationships which are the basis of treatment, the nature of these interactions are shaped as much by the assumptions and preoccupations of staff as by the officially stated goals. Officially, the program is meant to provide a basis for warm, meaningful relationships through which the children can mature. Unofficially, the problems of managing large groups often seem to interfere. At Fricot, as at other institutions, control is a major concern of administration and staff. The supervisor who achieves quick, certain response from a group, with a minimum of disorderliness, often is designated by staff as a "strong" supervisor; whereas one who has difficulty in obtaining obedience is considered a "weak" supervisor. Group supervisors are more often known by their control techniques and effectiveness than their counseling abilities.

The achievement of control leads to a conspicuous smoothness of operation; on the surface the school seems to be run with great efficiency. However, there is a cost in the methods by which firm control is achieved.

It is when discussing the use of punishment and the other effects of the emphasis on control that the researcher must rely on direct observation for generalizations rather than depend upon the consensus of the custody staff, for many of the influences which impinge upon the wards are unverbalized, unrecognized and unlabeled, and to some extent denied by staff. The staff's need for self-deception begins mildly at this point but often reaches to where staff members lose sight of control as a necessary concomitant of orderly management, and see it as an end in itself.

The emphasis on control is not difficult to understand. In addition to the ancient precept that punishment must follow transgression, there is the penology tradition which assumes that without punishment, misbehavior will recur. There is also the community pressure which shows itself in the preoccupation with prevention of escape, even though at Fricot the possibility of dangerous behavior by an escaped ward is not great due to age of youth and geographic isolation. Once these concerns gain priority, a "tone" is established which tends to place emphasis on control. At Fricot, for instance, "sight supervision" is required at all times; a boy must always be in the direct line of vision of the person supervising him.

Even without historical precedents and tradition, a very realistic reason for emphasis on control is the fact that when one man supervises 50 impulsive, aggressive, emotionally disturbed children, the simplest routines such as getting to meals, going to and from school, washing hands, and making beds, become major problems in logistics and technique.

Staff status pressures add another reason for firmness. There can be painful embarrassment of a supervisor when boys in his charge are disorderly or out of control. The wards themselves seem to understand this, and it may be by more than chance that such incidents happen more often when the supervisor is not well liked by the boys, and occur, moreover, in public places such as the dining room or the playfield.

Obtaining obedience so dominates the thinking of staff that a new supervisor coming on duty is instructed primarily in control techniques, with his role as counselor and friend to the wards relegated to a minor position. Because it is assumed that a new supervisor must gain control solely by inspiring fear, the door is open for such extremes as the advice given to new supervisors by some superiors that they should not smile at the boys for at least the first six weeks.

The need to enforce conformity leads to the second major unverbalized treatment variable, common to both experimental and control lodges, and that is the ever-present threat of punishment. In a research interview, an experienced supervisor bluntly stated, "You have to be mean as hell to get control." Because of the official policy against the use of corporal punishment, techniques are valued which enable punishment to be executed as inconspicuously as possible. Nevertheless, punishment is a constantly observable part of the daily scene. In the Gremlin control lodge, over the periods observed, group punishment was commonplace, occurring almost every day. It took the form of standing at attention for long periods, or strenuous group calisthenics, or sitting in silence, or "suffer hikes" over difficult terrain, or retiring early to bed. Physical violence, never condoned, occurs fairly routinely, although supervisors learn to make rather mild physical punishment inspire fear and seem much worse than it is by their accompanying gestures, threats, and noise.

There are other attitudes, largely unverbalized, which seem to characterize the Fricot approach. Among them are the following:

1. There is a feeling that a boy should be tough and self-sufficient, and should not show dependency on an adult. Such independence is encouraged in part because of the apparent necessity for self-sufficient behavior in a 50-boy unit where staff attention cannot be given to every minor demand. The dilemma is that, with many of these boys, part of their problem may be precisely that they have been neglected and have never been involved in any close or dependent relationship with an admired adult.

2. There is a belief by many that the ideal boy is one who does not hesitate to be aggressive. Physical aggression is felt necessary for a boy to take care of himself among peers, and therefore a good fighter is admired so long as he "fights fair." (It should be noted that this is a totally masculine environment except for the addition of one female training intern to each lodge during the summers. Staff resistance to and resentment toward these women interns is sometimes clear enough to be felt by the interns, as the research staff learned through interviews.)

3. An assumption is made that a boy learns primarily by being told. The learning-through-lecture theme pervades the "counseling" relationships as well as other verbal exchanges. More often than not, a "counseling" session might be better described as a "chewing-out."

4. The question of whether or not a boy has respect for authority, and whether or not he is "sincere," are major points on which his rehabilitation is rated. Staff feel they can judge earnestness of intent, and one of the highest compliments they pay a boy is to say he is "really trying."

5. An important element often unverbalized or even denied is the need to form alliances with those boys who have the most peer influence. These are not consciously made "deals" but the arrangements that all persons running large groups apparently need to make to work in cooperation with existing group leadership. The research team, after many hours of observation, became convinced that it would be almost impossible for a supervisor to maintain control solely through coercive, punitive methods. Often, however, the arrangement results in partiality towards wards whose influence is sought. Boys are extremely sensitive to this and often men-

tioned to the research staff the lack of fairness of certain supervisors. On the other hand, boys understood that almost all supervisors tended to favor their own "Fricot Sons" and were less perturbed by this favoritism. Although some supervisors tried to be scrupulously fair, they often had trouble because of it, since punishment of a member of the leadership clique could lead to disruption of group functioning—at times even reprisals.

Associated with the strict control required by authoritarian leadership is the rigid "structuring." A boy at Fricot has little need for thought, initiative, or decision-making during his entire day—a lack of responsibility clearly enjoyed by many. When, as at Fricot, the staff assumes the entire burden and responsibility for operations, it leads to cumbersome and laborious details such as in the following excerpt from procedure instructions to supervisors for leaving the Fricot gymnasium after the showing of movies:

> Boys put on shoes when the movie is over. The Gremlins leave last, following the movie, and it usually is done as follows: first group stand and move out to the door, each row making a right face, until the entire group is there and formed in a column of twos. Take a count. The boys are then moved to the top of the stairs and from there to the lodge door and on into the lodge, single file to the washroom doorway. Take a count. Move the honor room boys into the washroom for brushing of teeth and getting drink, and then move them into the hall where they will sit down. Move in half of the dormitory boys for the same procedure, and finally the remainder of the group.

To the observer, the Fricot atmosphere is rather rigidly formalized and punitive, with one day much the same as another and the activities repetitious, routinized and predictable. The external pressures which impinge on our subjects are, on the surface extremely uniform. It is well to remember, however, that what a boy himself may see in the emphasis on control and the frequent punishment depends upon his previous experience. For many of these boys, who have lived with chaos, rejection and neglect, leading to painful anxieties, conflicts and insecurities, Fricot is by contrast secure and serene. A boy may arrive at Fricot after a succession of turbulent experiences—arrest, juvenile hall and a court hearing, testing at the Reception Center and Clinic. At Fricot the rural setting and absence of locked doors are usually an agreeable surprise, and, furthermore, here is a place he knows he will settle down in, to remain for a considerable time. To many of these boys, the routine implies security and certainty, the apparent emotional distance from staff is like warmth after complete rejection in the home; and the punishment fades to nothing when compared to previous brutality known. At the same time, another boy may see Fricot as much more stringent and punitive than it is.

The Peer Subculture

For the inmates, life at Fricot is clearly peer-centered. Aside from the boys' interactions with their own teacher and with less frequency, their Fricot Dad, contacts with staff on an individual basis are limited. However, the boys are constantly interacting with one another, and as is the case with young people generally, there is developed a set of values and understandings—a subculture with distinct characteristics.

The functional value of testing reality through peer interaction and play must not be underestimated; at Fricot the general maturing or socializing process is speeded for many boys who have not had friends prior to their stay at the school. Sociometrics taken by the research team demonstrate that with few exceptions the boys are able to improve their ability to develop friendships and get along with peers by the time they leave.

It would be unwise, however, to assume that all peer influences are helpful and healthy. Without objective measures, which the research staff had neither the time nor ingenuity to devise, evaluation of the impact of the peer culture is difficult, for interpretation is particularly susceptible to coloration by the subjective views of the observer. One of the research staff placed great emphasis on the negative impact of the group.

An early observation made by this member of the research team was as follows:

> Two of the more salient behavioral practices among inmates are victimization and patronage. Several varieties of these practices are observable among inmates. Victimization is a predatory practice whereby inmates of superior strength and knowledge of inmate lore prey on weaker and less knowledgeable inmates. The ends sought by aggressors range from "getting even" for some capricious grudge to acquisition of commodities such as toys and candy. Three of the common forms of victimization on Lodge G are physical attack, agitation and exploitation. (Fisher, 1961.)

An observer can, indeed, make such an interpretation of what occurred. But over time and hundreds of hours of observation the research staff learned to evaluate its observations using a wider frame of reference. For example, the staff had noticed that the game of Foursquare offered an unusually clear picture of the functioning of the power clique. The strong boys could maintain themselves in squares as long as they wished, and there was tacit understanding that lower-status boys were not to put them out. Clique boys could establish their own rules, which appeared on the surface to be cheating, especially to boys very new to the institution. The blatant exploitation of the weak by the strong at first seemed clearly a function of the institutional setting and a manifestation of the delinquent subculture. However, the following quotation will illustrate why this was soon seen in a different perspective:

> In Foursquare there are things called Friendsies, when you don't try to get any of your friends out. And then there's Homesteading where nobody else can play except the people you want. If there's two, that's all there is, and if there's four, then there's four. . . . Sometimes the kids standing in line quit and go to another square. Sometimes if you accidentally put out one of your friends the other kids might come running back and say, "That was my place, so I'm in D now," and then sort of get into a fight. . . . The ones you don't like are put out by giving them fast balls, and also they never get "overs," and the popular kids keep getting "overs."

The quotation above did not come from one of our subjects, but from the eight-year-old daughter of one of the research team members, describing the game as played in the local public school. The similarity of structuring by the power clique suggested we go slow in attributing their behavior to the existence of a special "deviant subculture." Whether they are deviant or "normal," of course, the peer values are influential and must be understood before any judgment can be made as to whether the subculture of the adolescent tends to facilitate or to subvert treatment. It is clear that many of the practices were not sanctioned by official policy or viewed as desirable.

The most conspicuous fact of the boys' world is the existence of a power structure. Despite periodic staff efforts to eliminate his role, the duke is the one person in every lodge who is well known and easily identified. Surrounding the duke is a clique of "strong boys" who form the most influential social body within the unit. The strong clique, ordinarily aggressive and domineering, sets the informal rules and establishes precedent. With boys of this age, the structure may be unverbalized and understood at only a subconscious level, but nevertheless its presence is understood by all.

For example, at a time when a particularly "strong" clique was functioning in one unit, it became apparent that a certain part of the recreation area was the clique's "territory." Boys who did not understand this, or who were indifferent to it, were punished by the clique for infringing on its ground. But actually most of the weaker boys not in the group or on a friendly basis with it, appeared to find this convenient, since at least during the time when the clique boys were playing within their own territory, they could play uninterrupted elsewhere.

How influential is a duke on the lodge? How conscious of his power is the duke himself, and the other boys, and the supervisors? We can allow them to answer in their own words from recorded interviews selected to illustrate the point.

Speaking of his relationship with a duke who had just been paroled, a boy recalls, "Sometimes I was afraid that we'd have an argument or something, and he would get me. . . . Sometimes in the afternoon when we'd fall in, he wouldn't want those guys to mess up, so he wouldn't have to suffer for it. So he would tell them to quit messing around, and they would do it."

A lodge duke, speaking of a supervisor who once gave him trouble, concludes, "But he doesn't mess with me no more. I got mad one day and told some boys I was going to kill him, and we was up at summer camp, and we stole some knives off the kitchen. We was waiting for him to come back to the tent. Then after a little boy had told on us we threw the knives away, but he ain't messed with me no more since then."

When asked how the strong boys keep their names off the demerit lists at times, a duke explains, "We talk. We say to the supervisor, 'Oh, you just take my name for nothing!" We start talking real loud, and a lot of guys say this together with you. We get with each other and keep saying it, and then he would erase your name."

A boy describes how group punishment increases when a duke is paroled and the hierarchy is upset, and compares the present duke with his predecessors: "When Mike leaves for home, it will be just the same as after Harry and Cliff left. Everybody will be suffering, all the time. A lot of boys act like they are afraid of Mike, but Mike does not really fight very often."

A low-status boy reports: "I tell you, sometimes a supervisor is afraid to get on the big dukes of the lodge. Cause they're afraid that they're going to get them. That's when I get scared, sometimes."

Another boy describes what happens when he gets a package from home and the duke sees it. "Sometimes he would press you for candy, but sometimes he wouldn't, and you were afraid if you didn't give it to him he would beat you up."

The supervisors are not unaware of the duke's influence. In emphasizing the power of a particular duke, a supervisor states, "Then if he turns around and says, 'Okay, make noise on Mr. S.' and these other kids don't—watch out! Because they know that all his friends will get them. Then you've got hell on your hands."

A second supervisor relates, of another duke, "This duke is leading this bunch, and oh boy—what he says goes. If I say 'Shut up,' and he says 'Talk,' they talk. It makes no difference whether I'm standing taking names or not. If the duke says 'Talk,' they'd better talk, or the duke will kick the —— out of them."

A duke explains how he protects his friends: "If somebody mess with them, they run over and tell me, and I just say, 'Stop hitting on him,' and they stop."

The power hierarchy in the lodge extends from the duke and the strong clique at the top through the middle boys to the "messups" at the very bottom of the heap. The few lowest-status boys tend to cause friction and problems for themselves and, as we shall point out, for everyone else in the lodge as well.

In addition to the dukes and messups are other types which tend to be characteristic. Among the most conspicuous at Fricot are the following:

1. "Finks," or tale-bearers, are unpopular and scorned. Because they are not to be trusted, they are left out of intimate groups. There is considerable accuracy in the group in being able to pick out the finks, except for the finks themselves, who are so closely identified with the official program that they do not apply the label to themselves. Boys with high peer status, particularly those in the strong clique learn who not to trust and can describe and identify the lodge finks with accuracy and consensus. Other boys trusted none of their peers when they came, and none when they left.

2. The "kissy" who may sometimes also be a fink, ingratiates himself with supervisors and despised here as elsewhere. This may be partly because he seems too close to the adults, to whom all the boys would probably like to relate if they were not prevented by their reluctance to show emotion and their repression of dependency feelings. The kissies rarely achieve high standing as measured by sociometrics.

3. A "messup" is scorned because his inappropriate behavior brings group punishment upon all members of his lodge, corresponding to the "outlaw" described by Sykes (1958). The messup can also cause concern because he arouses in the group feelings which must be repressed or denied. In addition, a messup is often socially unaware, insensitive, and may embarrass others and cause arguments or problems among his peers even when the ultimate results is not group punishment. Some of these boys were extremely slow in learning the fundamentals of group membership despite enormous peer and staff pressure.

4. A "chicken" is a boy unwilling to fight or accept challenges. Because part of lodge social prestige comes from daring and aggressive behavior, a chicken is not respected. One of the first steps toward gaining status is to show willingness to stand up and fight, and this is particularly approved if the opponent is an established scapegoat. While an occasional fight was condoned by staff, they were usually stopped as quickly as possible.

5. In this subculture, as in most nondelinquent societies, a person who cheats—except under certain sanctified situations—or who fails to pay off obligations, or who lies—particularly at the wrong time—is not respected. There is a time and a place for cheating, and for lying; and it is particularly against protocol to lie so as to get another boy in trouble if the other boy has some social status.

As numerous examples would indicate, the staff to some extent adopts, or brings into the setting, many of these values, using the same terms to describe boys as the boys themselves. Many practices maintain themselves because they function to introduce some organization of the group and facilitate management. As has been amply shown by several investigators, staff here as elsewhere tends to enable the peer power structure to function. Equally important in the establishment of norms, however, is the resourcefulness and aggressiveness of the peer leadership.

As in settings with nondelinquents, social power among the delinquent boys is associated with a variety of talents (Rosen, 1959). The lodge leaders at Fricot seem to exemplify the skills and daring which most boys of this age idealize. Dukes have qualities of leadership, of social sensitivity, and of being likeable. Race did not seem important, although on occasion was obviously a factor in the formation of certain cliques. Physical strength was necessary but not sufficient. A boy who attempted to duke his way on the basis of physical power alone was never known to establish stable leadership status. The strong clique which developed sometimes excluded him altogether, although more often he was taken in later as a lieutenant under the clique control. The true duke who sets the standard often shows positive qualities—or at least qualities the other boys would like to see in themselves.

However, at least a part of the power of the duke and his strong clique comes about through their use of physical aggression. The threat to "get" somebody is commonplace as a strong-arm method of gaining control over peers, who are in further jeopardy if they fink. This puts lower-status boys in an uncomfortable position, wanting revenge but at the same time wishing to avoid further trouble from their stronger peers. As boys become socially tuned-in they learn to conform and "take low," refusing to fink to staff about the punishment meted out by the strong clique.

The use of agitation, in exerting pressure on boys to conform to peer standards, is a rather clever means by which official punishment can be brought onto those who do not fall in line. As examples, "sex talk," "mother talk," and "race talk" are common methods of causing a boy to become angry enough to blow up. The victim "fires at"—hits—someone, and a member of the clique will report his behavior or it will be noticed by the supervisor, who then punishes the boy for his apparent aggression. Successful use of agitation requires a social sensitivity and adeptness not possessed by many of the low-status boys.

Perhaps the most powerful means of getting boys into line is through excluding them from high-status social groups. In the ultimate—the "stone-out" situation seen in older boys' institutions—no one will speak to the boy at all, and anyone who might speak to him is also stoned out. At Fricot the exclusion is less refined; the boy who breaks taboos and does not learn his position in the hierarchy is merely told to get out of a group, and is not allowed to join in desirable activities. It is the very lowest boys in the hierarchy who seem to have the most difficulty in learning protocol, and the group has the poorest control over them. Many of these boys are mentally disturbed and are not aware of protocol, are socially immature, and have little control over their own feelings or actions which they express immediately and directly as they experience them.

As implied above, the simplest way for a boy to deal with the strong clique is to conform to its requirements. Taking low, and playing the part of the obedient follower, is a convenient way to gain some acceptance. In learning his place, the new boy perceives that this group is powerful, that he cannot successfully fight them, and had better join them. This means he must follow the rules they set down—not putting them out in Warball games, not finking on them, not getting ahead of them in chow line, giving them help where they require it, and so on.

Not only obedience, but material possessions also, may be demanded by the duke and his lieutenants or by more aggressive individuals. The low-status boy must learn to share his packages from home without too much protest, and must not fink when he is pressured for candy and other treats. These tributes do not buy him permanent status, however; even a boy with a steady supply of boxes from home does not improve his position unless he can gain prestige through other means as well and loses whatever status he has when his supply is cut off.

It is clear that the institutional experiences of a high status boy, and one of low status who is one of the ruled rather than the rulers, are very different, and the effects in terms of developing confidence, obtaining rewards from satisfactory peer relationships, the establishment of values and so on, may often be the opposite of those desired.

13. The Boy's Perception of Himself in a State Training School for Delinquents

THOMAS G. EYNON and JON E. SIMPSON

THERE have been three approaches to the study of the impact of correctional institutions on inmates. The prediction-of-outcome method, used by Burgess and the Gluecks, is based mainly on preinstitutional factors. The prison-community approach of Clemmer and others views impact as socialization into an inmate subculture. The Reckless self-reporting approach used in the study reported here sees institutional impact through inmate responses to structured questionnaires.[1] The self-reporting method

Reprinted from *Social Service Review*, March 1965, pp. 31–37, by permission of *Social Service Review* and the authors. Copyright 1965 by The University of Chicago Press.

1. Since 1948, a series of impact studies, under the direction of W. C. Reckless, used the inmate's perceptions of his own view of his institutional experience. These studies include the following: E. J. Galway, "A Measurement of the Effectiveness of a Reformatory Program" (Ph.D. dissertation, Ohio State University, 1948); M. S. Sabnis, "A Measurement of Impact of Institutional Experience on Inmates of a Training School" (Ph.D. dissertation, Ohio State University, 1951); D. E. Bright, "A Study of Institutional Impact upon Adult Male Prisoners" (Ph.D. dissertation, Ohio State University, 1951); M. R. Moran, "Inmate Concept of Self in a Reformatory Society" (Ph.D. dissertation, Ohio State University, 1954); H. Zibners, "The Influence

assumes that the non-disturbed and non-retarded inmate perceives what happens to him during his institutional stay and is able to tell whether he has been helped or worsened. It is assumed that the inmate's perceptions of his experience in the correctional institution can be used as data for studying the impact of the institutional environment upon him. Studying the impact of the institution through perceived changes in the inmate is akin to studying marital happiness or marital roles through the perceptions of marriage partners and/or persons who have known them well. This method is systematic and objective. It can be checked for reliability, and it has predictive value. The carefully constructed questionnaire can discount conventional and evasive answers. It provides an operational and meaningful picture for correctional administrators.

In this paper comparisons are made between some of the findings from a study of inmate perceptions at the Boys' Industrial School at Lancaster, Ohio, and inmate perceptions at the two open camps operated by the parent institution.[2] The data for the paper, collected in 1960 and 1961, are a small part of the total data collected in a three-phase study of consecutive first admissions to the school during a six-month period.

A previous study had indicated that boys were better integrated into the large residential bureaucracy than anticipated and that they improved as a result of their stay. These findings were in disagreement with commonly held opinions that incarceration in a large state-operated juvenile institution is criminogenic and that inmates become "prisonized" as a result of their exposure to the inmate subculture. These findings, of course, applied not to hard-core criminals but only to delinquent boys who remain in the institution for an average of six months.

Since the boys in the school either did not change or changed for the better, it was expected that boys in open permissive camps would show even more favorable impact. The small camps, which provide more individual attention, have come into great favor among correctional administrators. However, very few studies have been reported indicating the rehabilitative impact of camps for delinquent boys.

The school is one of the oldest and largest state-operated training schools in the United States for boys committed by juvenile courts. The average

of Short-Term Institutionalization upon Emotionally Disturbed and Delinquent Children" (Master's thesis, Ohio State University, 1954). These studies are summarized in Walter C. Reckless, "The Impact of Correctional Programmes on Inmates," *British Journal of Delinquency*, VI (September, 1955), 138–147.

2. The Boys' Industrial School, which opened in 1857, has been one of the most "surveyed" schools for delinquents in the United States. Albert Deutsch, in *Our Rejected Children* (Boston: Little, Brown, 1950), characterized it as an institutional slum. Ashley Weeks, in *Survey of Facilities for Delinquent Children in Ohio* (Columbus: Bureau of Educational Research, Ohio State University, 1955) saw it as a giant deepfreeze.

daily population in 1960–61 was 887 boys. The two open camps, located at Zaleski and Mohican State Forests, begun in 1956, have an average daily population of 65 boys selected by the camp directors a few weeks after their admission to the school.

The Sample and the Data

Four hundred and eighty-five boys were originally studied at the point of admission and also at the point of release. These cases represented a consecutive sample of boys admitted for the first time during the period roughly from February 1 to July 1, 1960. (Boys who had previously been at the school were eliminated.) The findings presented herein are based on 446 of these boys whose admission and release schedules were both completely filled in. Of this group only 37 were transferred to camps, while 409 remained in the parent institution.

Most of the boys came from lower-class areas of the large cities of Ohio. Seventy-one per cent were white, and 29 per cent were Negro. The average age at commitment was sixteen. According to age-grade placement the boys were, on the average, two years retarded in school. They had about four contacts with the juvenile court before commitment. Their average onset age for official delinquency was 13.5 years, but their onset age for first professed (unofficial) delinquency was 11.8 years. About 66 per cent were committed for property offenses. Half came from broken homes. The boys were below average in intelligence, as measured by the Henmon-Nelson Intelligence Test. The camp boys were, on the average, older, started their delinquency later, had fewer contacts with authority, and scored higher on the Stanford Grade Placement Test but lower on the intelligence test. They had older fathers. The difference between the school boys and the camp boys on degree of delinquency orientation, as measured by the DE scale of the California Personality Inventory, was non-significant. (Each group had a mean score of 27, the same as other institutionalized delinquent boys.)

Background data were collected from the case record of each boy, but the study data came from questionnaires administered by the authors. The number of boys completing a questionnaire during a given session varied from 1 to 35, depending upon the number of commitments or placements for a week. If a boy had difficulty reading the questions, he was interviewed, while others were instructed to raise their hands when they needed assistance from the investigators. Extensive efforts were made to establish rapport and to control the testing situation so that there would be a minimum of communication between the boys.

The intake and release questionnaires contained the same questions. but in different sequence and format. Thus, one segment of both questionnaires contained twenty-five value-orientation items designed to measure the respondent's views concerning the merits of ambition, responsibility, self-reliance, violence, aggression, rationality, forethought, and respect for property. Another section contained the Agreeableness Scale of the Guilford-Martin Personnel Inventory. A high score on the Agreeableness Scale indicates a lack of quarrelsomeness and domineering qualities; a low score reflects a belligerent, domineering attitude and an overreadiness to fight about issues of slight importance. A third section of the questionnaire contained 36 questions which sought to elicit the boys' feelings about themselves. Finally, two additional sections were composed of approximately 125 impact questions designed to obtain the boys' perceptions of various facets of their institutional experience. To facilitate analysis of the data, questions were clustered according to their content.

The internal consistency of each inventory (section) developed in this manner was tested and demonstrated by item analysis. First, the total sample was dichotomized in terms of the median score for all the items in an inventory. The responses of the "high" and "low" subcategories for each question were compared.[3]

Mean scores for the specific inventories, based upon individual scores for the boys, were derived in the following manner: The unfavorable response alternative for each question was given a score of 1, while the favorable alternative was given a score of 0. A constant of 10 was added to facilitate the data analysis. Thus, a score of 10 on a particular inventory indicated that the respondent answered all the questions in a favorable direction, a score of 11 reflected an unfavorable response to one question, a score of 12 indicated two unfavorable responses, and so forth. The Value Orientation and the Agreeableness Scale scores do not include a constant, and the scoring is reversed, so that the higher scores are indicative of socially approved value orientations and a willingness to participate with others in an agreeable manner.

The Findings

Integration of the boys into the school and the camps was measured by three inventories—"helplessness," "rules of the game," and "impersonality." In their perceptions of helplessness and/or futility, frustration, and powerlessness in coping with the institution, the school boys did not differ from the camp boys at intake and did not change from intake to release. However, as shown in Table 13.1, the camp boys' responses were significantly more favorable at release than those of the school boys.

3. The chi-square test was used, and the .01 level of significance was accepted.

Both groups by the time of release perceived that it was less necessary to "play it cool," keep one's mouth shut, and keep out of the way of adults—items covered under perceptions of the "rules of the game." This is change in the favorable direction. The camp boys subscribed less to these rules of the institutional game than the school boys.

Table 13.1. Comparison of mean scores for school and camp boys at admission and release

Inventory and Group	Score[a]		Inventory and Group	Score[a]	
	Admission[b]	Release[c]		Admission[b]	Release[c]
1. Helplessness			6. Self-labeling		
School	12.49	12.31	School	12.45	12.37
Camp	12.43	**11.42**	Camp	12.69	12.39
2. Rules of the Game			7. General		
School	13.11	**12.59**	Improvement		
Camp	12.78	**11.92**	School	12.93	**13.20**
3. Impersonality			Camp	12.67	**11.75**
School	Not given	11.89	8. Self-Improvement		
Camp	Not given	11.28	School	Not given	12.46
4. Outlook			Camp	Not given	11.67
School	13.70	**11.91**	9. Value Orientation		
Camp	13.81	**11.94**	School	15.69	**17.62**
5. Self-Feelings			Camp	17.78	**19.03**
School	11.58	**11.23**	10. Agreeableness		
Camp	11.19	10.92	School	29.66	**31.50**
			Camp	31.30	31.28

[a]Release scores significantly different from admission scores appear in boldface type. The *t*-test was used, and the .01 level of significance was accepted.

[b]At admission the camp boys, compared to the school boys, had less agreement with "rules of the game," had "better self-feelings," "more middle-class value orientation," but were not significantly "more agreeable" than the school boys.

[c]At release the camp boys, compared to the school boys, were less "helpless," had less agreement with "rules of the game," "less impersonality," had less "general improvement," less "self-improvement," but more "middle-class value orientation" than the school boys.

The "impersonality" inventory was not included at intake; however, the camp boys felt slightly less impersonality in staff-boy relations at release than the school boys. They rated their relations to the staff as somewhat more intimate and personal, probably due to the small size of the camp, compared to the school.

Changes in "self-concept" (perceptions of self or self-image) were measured by three inventories. The "outlook" inventory pertained to the boys' feelings of bitterness, tension, anxiousness, hopelessness, and isolation. Although there was no difference between camp boys and school boys at either intake or release, each group had a better outlook at release than at intake. Apparently, the camp had no more favorable impact on these perceptions than the school experience. At intake the camp boys felt a little better about themselves on the "self-feeling" inventory (items such as "having a lot of problems" and "getting a raw deal") than the school boys, but did not differ from the school boys at release. The school boys improved somewhat by the time of release. It appears that the camp receives boys who start with better self-feelings but does not change them, while the parent institution retains the large residue of boys with poorer self-feelings and their perceptions improve.

On the "self-labeling" inventory, the boys indicated whether they viewed themselves as delinquents, boarding-school pupils, military school privates, institutional inmates, or criminals. There was no difference between the school boys and camp boys at intake or release, and neither group changed during the stay. The boys viewed themselves primarily as delinquents at the beginning and at the end of the institutional experience.

Whether or not the boys perceived that they had profited by their stay was measured by the two improvement inventories. The "general improvement" inventory brought some interesting findings. At intake, both school and camp boys had the same expectations about what they would get out of their stay, but at release the camp boys indicated that they got more out of their stay than they had expected at intake. The school boys said that they got somewhat less than they had expected. In short, the camp boys perceived a small profit, while the school boys perceived a small loss during their stay.

The "self-improvement" inventory, not included at intake, requested the boys to indicate whether they perceived improvement in themselves as a result of their stay. The camp boys reported more improvement than the school boys.

The "value-orientation" inventory indicated significant improvement for both school and camp boys. The camp boys, however, had a more middle-class value orientation than the school boys at intake and release. The values in the inventory concerned "getting ahead," "responsibility," "planning for the future," "respect for property," "saving money," and "working for a living." [4]

A high score on the "agreeableness" inventory indicates good social adjustment. Both school and camp boys scored lower than the norms for the general population, and there were no significant differences between them at either intake or release. Although the camp boys scored higher at intake, the school boys caught up with them, thus indicating

4. A considerable body of literature has been developed concerning the components of the delinquent subculture and focal concerns of the lower class, which have been presumed causal for delinquency. If these speculations are valid, then the findings reported in this article have implications for treatment, since they indicate that both the school and the camp experience changed the boys to a more favorable value orientation or moved them from values which caused them to become delinquent. Analysis of postinstitutional adjustment will bear on this point.

significant improvement. An unanticipated finding was that the school boys were more "agreeable" at release than at intake, while the camp boys remained the same.

In the release schedule the boys were asked about the pressures put on them during their institutional stay. The percentage comparisons on four key questions are shown in Table 13.2. On three of these items the

Table 13.2. Comparison of responses for school and camp boys on perceptions of inmate pressures

Questions	Percentage Giving Affirmative Answer [a]	
	School Boys	Camp Boys
1. Did any of the other boys pick on you while you were here?	40	22
2. Did you have trouble getting along with the other boys here?	27	8
3. Do the boys make it hard on the boys who take religion seriously?	30	16
4. Has any group of boys "put the nut" on you [b] while you were here?	61	81

[a]There is a significant difference between school and camp boys on all four questions.
[b]Made a fool of you.

school boys perceived a greater amount of negative pressure from fellow inmates than the camp boys. On Question 4, the camp boys seemed to be much more alerted to inmate pressure than the school boys. (The small size of the camp probably enhanced the ability of the boys to make fools out of each other.)

In the release schedule the boys were also asked a series of questions designed to get at impact of staff members, as the boys perceived it. Each boy was asked to check a list of institutional adult figures from cook to psychologist and to choose the staff member who knew him best, the one with whom he would share good news, the one with whom he could best talk about personal problems, and the one who helped him the most. The staff member most frequently chosen on all four of the above characteristics by the school boys was the cottage supervisor. The next was the work supervisor. Trade instructors, teachers, and counselors were much less frequently chosen, while social workers were infrequently chosen and psychologists hardly ever chosen. In the simple staff structure of the camps, the counselor was the most frequently chosen. The cottage supervisor was the second most chosen; the cook, third; the work supervisor, fourth. (There were no teachers, social workers, or psychologists in the camps.)

Still other items were used in the release schedule to gauge the perceived impact of staff on the boys. Twenty-five per cent of the school boys and 84 per cent of the camp boys professed that "all or most" of the staff members knew them; 52 per cent in the school and 84 per cent in the camps said "all or most" of the staff members did all they could to help. Forty-two per cent of the school boys, versus 70 per cent of the camp boys, believed that none of the staff tried to make them think they were criminals.

One final item was used in the release schedule to measure acceptance or rejection of the institution: "If a friend of yours got into trouble, would you want him sent here?" Thirty-one per cent of the school boys and 87 per cent of the camp boys gave the affirmative answer.

Conclusions

1. The camp boys perceived their integration into the camp structure more favorably than the school boys perceived their integration into the large training school; this perception tends to be more favorable at release than at intake.

2. Confinement at either the school or the camps appears to have a favorable impact on outlook, general improvement, and value orientations.

3. The school experience also appears to have had a favorable impact on self-feelings and agreeableness, but the camp boys did not improve along these lines.

4. At release, the school boys perceived a greater amount of negative pressure from their fellow inmates than did the camp boys.

5. The school boys believed that the cottage supervisor and the work supervisor had the greatest impact on them, while the camp boys considered the counselor, the cottage supervisor, and the cook, in this order, the most significant staff members for them.

6. Camp boys perceived a much more favorable staff influence upon them than did the school boys.

7. Camp boys were overwhelmingly accepting of the camps, while a majority of the school boys rejected the institution as a place to which they would want a friend to come if he got into trouble.

Discussion

An impact study using inmate perceptions is not easy to interpret. The inventories used so far are still in a primitive state. But impact studies must continue. It is not enough to observe inmate structure, as several sociologists have done.[5] The part of the inmate structure which is internalized is the most important aspect. Eventually, impact must be measured by reliable assessments of inmate perceptions.[6]

The findings indicate, at least from the boys' point of view, that a large state institution for delinquent boys is not a "crime school" processing boys into an inmate subculture. Open camps, because of their relaxed atmosphere, may become highly effective treatment centers, if their programs are accelerated. As open camps may be getting the more promising boys, perhaps their staff and program must function at a different level.

Very important is the finding that the boys in the institution apparently develop a closer relationship with cottage parents, work supervisors, and counselors than with social workers, psychologists, doctors, and chaplains. This finding certainly has implications for the staff of an institution for delinquent boys, but translating research findings into treatment principles is beyond the intent of this discussion.

5. Donald Clemmer, *The Prison Community* (Boston: Christopher Publishing House, 1940); Hans Reimer, "Socialization in the Prison Community," in *Proceedings of the American Prison Association* (1937), pp. 151–155; Norman S. Hayner and Ellis Ash, "The Prison as a Community," *American Sociological Review*, V (April 1940), 577–583; Kirson Weinberg, "Aspects of the Prison's Social Structure," *American Journal of Sociology*, XLIV (March 1942), 717–726; Clarence Schrag, "Leadership among Prison Inmates," *American Sociological Review*, XIX (February 1954), 37–42; and Stanton Wheeler, "Socialization in Correctional Communities," *American Sociological Review*, XXVI (October 1961), 697–712.

6. The recent study by Rose and Weber recognizes the need to study changes in the attitudes of youthful inmates as a result of institutional stay. See Arnold M. Rose and George H. Weber, "Changes in Attitudes among Delinquent Boys Committed to Open and Closed Institutions," *Journal of Criminal Law, Criminology, and Police Science*, LII (July-August 1961), 166–177.

PART SEVEN

Conflicting Perspectives on Correctional Decisions

OUR OPENING remarks in this book indicated that one important aspect of correctional organization analysis centers around the views or perspectives of those who are influenced by these structures. Three groups can be identified whose attitudes and opinions are of interest to us: the public in whose name correctional processes operate, the workers who manage these agencies, and the offender raw material serviced by them.

Part VII presents some evidence on the organizational perspectives of these persons. However, earlier contributions in this volume have already identified some of the main outlines of this evidence. Thus we saw in the opening selection by Werthman that the views of delinquents about the schools, police, and other community institutions diverge markedly from those of the persons who manage these systems. Then too, the Piliavin and Briar essay on police encounters with juveniles contained some information on the orientations of juvenile offenders toward policemen. Finally, the papers by Jesness and by Eynon and Simpson involved a good deal of information on the attitudes of training school wards toward these institutions and the workers who operate them.

248

The attitudes and organizational views of various employee groups within the law enforcement–correctional system also were touched upon in a number of places in preceding parts of this book. Piliavin and Briar, along with Wilson, provided us with a good deal of insight into the views of police officers toward their work, juvenile offenders, and the juvenile court. The essay by Walther and McCune contained some information about the orientations of juvenile court judges toward their role, suggesting that they view their responsibilities differently than do other judges. Finally, the studies by Cohn and Gross dealt in part with the perspectives of probation officers as they go about processing youthful offenders.

One matter about which little has been said so far in this book is the issue of public orientations to correctional agencies. While citizen views have not received much attention by sociologists, the scanty evidence available points to several conclusions. An "out-of-sight, out-of-mind" attitude prevails among the citizenry, such that most laymen are grossly ignorant of the workings of the justice and correctional system. The attention of the citizen is caught by dramatic or bizarre instances of crime, but he quickly loses interest in them once the offender has been apprehended. Punitive and repressive sentiments about offenders and tactics for dealing with them are voiced by large numbers of citizens. They believe that society should deal harshly with deviants, and they judge that lawbreakers are being dealt with in a lenient or "mollycoddling" fashion.

In one recent inquiry, a statewide survey in California showed that most citizens are quite unaware of penalties currently being dealt to adult offenders.[1] When respondents were asked to indicate the penalty for eleven different offenses, the mean number of correct answers was 2.6. Most of the citizens *underestimated* the severity of sentences currently being imposed, thinking that the courts deal more leniently with criminals than they do in fact. Regarding their perceptions of the nature of the crime problem, all the laymen claimed that crime rates are excessively high. The younger, better educated persons generally opted for ameliorative approaches to the crime problem, while older respondents favored strict penalties and repressive approaches to offenders.

Another indication of general ignorance of correctional processes can be found in a study by Gibbons, in which a sample of laymen in San Francisco were presented with a questionnaire testing their knowledge about a wide range of correctional practices in the state of California.[2] Although most of the respondents had lived in the area for a long time, virtually none of them knew the identity of the juvenile court judge, the chief probation

1. Assembly Committee on Criminal Procedure, *Deterrent Effects of Criminal Sanctions* (Sacramento: Assembly of the State of California, 1968), pp. 10–18.
2. Don C. Gibbons, "Who Knows What About Correction?" *Crime and Delinquency,* Vol. IX (April 1963), pp. 137–144.

officer of the county, or the directors of the adult and juvenile state correctional systems. Most of them know that the California Youth Authority was the agency dealing with incarcerated delinquents but few knew the location of any training school. Only about one-third of the citizens viewed California's juvenile correctional system as better than that of other states, even though that program has been widely hailed in correctional circles as the most well developed and progressive in the nation.

Several examples are available evidencing citizen preferences for harsh penalties, particularly when directed at adult criminals. In an investigation by Rose and Prell, in which citizens (college students) were asked about the penal sentences appropriate to a range of criminal activities, the respondents tended to select punishments which bore little resemblance to the penalties actually imposed upon offenders.[3] In another study, Rooney and Gibbons elicited citizen views of appropriate punishments for persons involved in "crimes without victims" (abortion, homosexuality, and drug addiction).[4] Many of the laymen advocated severe penalties for homosexuality and drug addiction. In much the same way, Gibbons conducted another investigation in which citizens were asked to elect punishments they felt appropriate for twenty different criminal offenses.[5] In many cases the choices of laymen exceeded in severity the penalties currently imposed in the state.

Parallel evidence on the national level can be found in 1968 Gallup poll results, in which adults across the nation were asked: "In general, do you think the courts in this area deal too harshly, or not harshly enough with criminals?"[6] For the total sample, 63 per cent of the respondents answered that the courts do not deal harshly enough with lawbreakers. The Joint Commission on Correctional Manpower and Training has reported similar results from a 1968 national citizen survey.[7] In that study, most of the subjects averred that crime rates are rising and that law enforcement agencies do not discourage people from crime. About one-half expressed the opinion that the courts are too lenient in their handling of offenders, while about half said that the prison system fails to rehabilitate offenders. The laymen offered different judgments about appropriate penalties for varied kinds of

3. Arnold M. Rose and Arthur E. Prell, "Does the Punishment Fit the Crime? A Study in Social Valuation", *American Journal of Sociology*, Vol. LXI (November 1955), pp. 247–259.
4. Elizabeth A. Rooney and Don C. Gibbons, "Social Reactions to 'Crimes Without Victims'", *Social Problems*, Vol. XIII (Spring 1966), pp. 400–410.
5. Don C. Gibbons, "Crime and Punishment: A Study in Social Attitudes", *Social Forces*, Vol. 47 (June 1969), pp. 391–387.
6. *Gallup Opinion Index*, Report No. 33 (March 1968), p. 15.
7. Joint Commission on Correctional Manpower and Training, *The Public Looks at Crime and Corrections* (Washington, D.C.: Joint Commission on Correctional Manpower and Training, 1968), pp. 4–11.

offenders; nearly all would impose long sentences on armed robbers, murderers, and persons caught selling drugs to minors, and most of them would deal more leniently with burglars, prostitutes, or embezzlers. Three-fourths of the citizens indicated that they would place juveniles involved in petty thefts on probation, but most of them would deal more harshly with juvenile muggers or car thieves. To a considerable extent, the differential sentencing choices of citizens seem to parallel the actual policies of courts, even though laymen may not be aware of the congruence between their choices and actual dispositions made of youthful offenders. Indeed, this is a point treated in the first essay in this section by Parker.

The three following papers deal with perspectives on correctional organizations. All three of the essays are original ones, prepared specifically for this book. The first contribution by Parker deals with citizen attitudes toward the juvenile court in four Washington State communities. Parker reports that laymen in these cities voiced a general desire for punitive courts, but perceived them to be overly lenient in operation. When the citizens were asked about dispositions they thought appropriate for specific cases, they volunteered choices close to the actions which had actually been taken against the offenders. Yet at the same time these community residents believed that the juvenile court was considerably more lenient toward delinquents than it was in fact.

The second essay by McMillin and Garabedian deals with the opinions expressed by different groups of employees within a large probation department on the issue of due process for juvenile lawbreakers. Their data suggest that attitude toward due process is in part a function of the job experiences of the control agents. Work experiences for line personnel, the deputy probation officers, appear to be related in a curvilinear fashion to legalistic orientations. Both novice probation officers and those with a good deal of experience tend to endorse the idea of providing procedural safeguards for juvenile offenders. In addition, the occupational experiences of the supervisors apparently promote even more favorable legalistic attitudes.

Garabedian's paper deals with the attitudes of probation officers and policemen toward a variety of job responsibilities and policy questions frequently raised when these groups process delinquents. His data shows that there is little agreement over "who should do what and how," adding further evidence to the picture of role confusion and fuzzy occupational boundaries currently found in the correctional machinery. These articles should caution us against any assumption that the "people-processing, people-changing" system is a finely-tuned mechanism in which all the parts mesh in quiet harmony.

14. Juvenile Court Actions and Public Response

HOWARD A. PARKER

Introduction

The development of formal agencies of social control has been one major aspect of the growth of modern, urban, complex societies. The small New England town of the 19th century could rely heavily on informal mechanisms of social control such as public ridicule, shunning, ostracism, and so on, supplemented with a limited set of formal mechanisms, such as laws or other forms of rule. Similarly, organizations designed to implement the formal rules were few in number and small in size until relatively recently. For example, many small towns operated with only a constable and justice of the peace as the agents of order. The actions of these persons were quite visible to most members of the community and generally evoked little criticism. However, with the growth of large-scale communities, informal mechanisms have become less effective, formal

The author would like to express his appreciation to William J. Chambliss and Herbert Costner for their advice during the planning stages of the research. Acknowledgment is also due to Don C. Gibbons for commenting on an earlier version of the manuscript.

252

rules have proliferated, and organizations designed to implement and enforce these formal rules have increased.

The development of formal organizations designed to exercise social control has been accomplished in the name of the citizenry. These agencies are said to be needed in order to "protect the community" or to "protect society." However, the workings of these structures are complex, and therefore these actions may not be visible to most citizens. It may well be that many laymen are only dimly aware of the activities which go on in these systems of control. Then too, there may be a number of citizens who hold negative views of various social control agencies, believing them to be involved in practices and tactics which the laymen oppose. As a result, it may be quite misleading to speak of social control structures as though they are agencies that are directly carrying out the wishes of the citizenry. Perhaps the attitudes and beliefs of many citizens are out of sorts with the practices and policies of control systems.

Although this line of argument is plausible enough, the plain fact is that we know relatively little about the opinions and preferences of citizens as they have to do with control agencies.[1] The study reported here is an inquiry into these matters, for it deals with the perceptions of citizens concerning the juvenile court and its operation.

Consider the case of the juvenile court and public sentiments about it. It can be argued that citizens probably are particularly ill-informed about the juvenile court, given the facts that this court operates informally, that persons not having specific business there are not allowed to witness hearings, and that, in other ways, the operation of the court is less visible than are the workings of criminal courts.[2] Consequently, the citizen must get his information regarding the court primarily through speculation, the mass media, vocal opinion leaders, or through other indirect communication channels. The mass media tend to provide information concerning rising juvenile crime rates and the more sensational juvenile offenses, but usually offers little information of a positive nature with respect to the court. Likewise, opinion leaders usually are vocal regarding the court only when they are concerned about particular instances of lawbreaking, and rarely do they speak out in defense of the court. In addition, messages received through the less formal communication structure are dis-

1. A major exception is the national survey of public attitudes and opinions toward corrections recently conducted. See Joint Commission on Correctional Manpower and Training, *The Public Looks at Crime and Corrections* (Washington, D.C.: Joint Commission on Correctional Manpower and Training, 1968).

2. Recent trends suggest that juvenile court proceedings will become more visible. See, for example, the decision recently rendered by the Supreme Court of the United States, *in re Gault*, reported in The President's Commission on Law Enforcement and Administration of Justice, *Task Force Report: Juvenile Delinquency and Youth Crime*, (Washington, D.C.: U. S. Government Printing Office, 1967), pp. 57–76.

torted by the time they reach the average community member. Consequently, it might be expected that an individual's perception of the court would be somewhat negative. More specifically, for those persons who believe that strict reactions to deviance operate as a deterrent, it might be anticipated that they would perceive the court to be relatively lenient in its dealings with juvenile offenders, at the same time that they would prefer stricter action. This would be especially true where community concern was high.

However, juvenile court judges and other court workers are influenced by their perceptions of public opinion. The judge and his aides do take periodic soundings of community opinion, so that the judge presumably orients his on-the-bench activity to these citizen attitudes. It follows that the judge who is sensitive to public opinion may render decisions which are not overly lenient, that is, which are not markedly less punitive than preferred by citizens. Public views of the court, therefore, may not be too accurate. Citizens may see the court as more lenient than it is in fact. Similarly, the level of preferred strictness voiced by laymen may be closer to the actual level of court strictness than the average community member might expect.

Information and opinions about the court are not likely to be uniform throughout the community, nor are all citizens equally knowledgeable about juvenile problems in general. Instead, community leaders and influential citizens should be better informed about court actions and procedures than ordinary residents. Community leaders quite probably experience more interaction with court officials, they probably are in contact with more mass-media sources of information about juvenile policies, and in other ways, they are more informed than other citizens.[3] In particular, those influential community figures who are involved in children and youth activities in the community ought to be particularly well-informed about court operations.

The following general hypotheses can be drawn from this brief introductory conceptualization of public sentiments about the juvenile court:

1. Members of the general public voice preferences for punitive court actions that exceed the degree of punitiveness they perceive to be involved in court dispositions.
2. Community leaders prefer less punitive responses to juvenile offenders than do other members of the general public.
3. Community leaders are more accurate in their assessment of actual court punitiveness than are other members of the general public.
4. Community leaders who have the most contact with the court will show the greatest accuracy of perception of court actions.

3. Robert K. Merton, "Patterns of Influence: Local and Cosmopolitan Influentials," *Social Theory and Social Structure* (Glencoe, Ill.: Free Press, 1957), pp. 387–420.

5. In general, the level of punitiveness of actual court actions will be closer to the punitive preferences of citizens than to their perceptions of court punitiveness.

These hypotheses were investigated in the research reported below.

Design of the Research

SAMPLE SELECTION

In order to test the preceding hypotheses, data were collected from four small cities in the state of Washington during 1964. Each of the four cities was the county seat in which the juvenile court resided. The communities had populations ranging from 12,000 to 32,000, and each had approximately the same delinquency rate.

Multi-stage area probability samples of 115 persons over 21 years of age were selected in each city, making a total sample size of 460 respondents. In addition, 17 community leaders active in the general area of children and youth were identified by the Chamber of Commerce in each community, so that a total sample of 68 community leaders was selected.[4]

THE QUESTIONNAIRE

A questionnaire was constructed which, in addition to questions of a general demographic nature, asked the respondents to respond to four delinquency cases abstracted from the juvenile courts in question.[5] The citizens were asked to indicate (1) what action they felt the court actually took, (2) what action they felt the court ought to have taken, and (3) what action most members of the community would have preferred. The respondents were confined to answering in terms of several general alternatives open to the court. These seven actions were as follows: (1) remand to the adult court, (2) special institutional placement (menal institution, etc.), (3) commitment to the Department of Institutions (placement in a correctional institution), (4) foster care, (5) formal probation, (6) informal probation, (7) warning. In addition to the case histories, each person was asked to respond to two general questions concerning court punitiveness. One question was: "How strict do you feel

4. The technique used to identify influentials was similar to that employed by Hunter in "Regional City" and in various modified forms by subsequent researchers. See Floyd Hunter, *Community Power Structure,* (Chapel Hill: University of North Carolina Press, 1953).

5. The case histories were taken from each of the four juvenile courts. These four cases were then abstracted and submitted to all four judges for their opinions: (a) Was a decision possible on the basis of the information given? and (b) If so, what would they have done? The judges all agreed that a decision could be made and all agreed substantially with the original decision in the case.

the juvenile court actually is with juvenile offenders?" The other was: "How strict do you feel the juvenile court ought to be with juvenile offenders?" Questions also were included which assessed the degree of contact of all persons with the court and the amount of exposure of leaders to local *vs.* extra-community literature, etc., regarding children and youth.

The four delinquency cases are presented below, in the same form as included in the questionnaire:

Case 1. Robert A. is a white male, 17 years of age. Robert has two older brothers, 21 and 20 years of age, and one older sister who is 18. Robert's mother and father were married as teen-agers and were divorced when Robert was 7 years old. Robert remained with his mother who remarried when he was 10. Robert was referred to the juvenile court for the first time during that year for breaking windows. He was referred twice more in the same year for vandalism (destroying property) and for "breaking and entering" (burglary). His mother was divorced when Robert was 11 and Robert did not get into trouble for several months afterward. She remarried when Robert was 12. Her third husband is an older man in his late fifties, with a good job that pays him about $8,000 a year, and the marriage has been relatively stable. Since Robert was 12, he has had thirteen referrals to the juvenile court, the offenses ranging from vandalism to burglary. Previous actions taken by the court have included commitment to the State Department of Institutions for diagnosis and treatment. He is presently before the court because of his involvement in the theft of an automobile.

Case 2. John H. is a white male, 17 years of age. He is a junior in high school with a generally poor academic record. John has two older brothers, 18 and 20 years of age, who are currently in the Army. John's father and mother are both employed. John's father is a bus driver, earning $5,500 a year, and his mother is a clerk in a department store earning $4,000 a year. John has been referred to the juvenile court by the police on two occasions, both times for public intoxication. On both occasions the intoxication resulted from a teen-age drinking party. No malicious acts were committed on either occasion by any of the participants. His most recent referral came as the result of his being stopped by the police for operating an automobile with a defective stop light, at which time he was found to be intoxicated and arrested for public intoxication.

Case 3. William B. is a white male, 16 years of age. William currently attends high school where he has established a poor record, being considered by his teachers to be a troublemaker. William is the younger of two children, having an older sister aged 18. His parents were divorced when William was 12 years of age, his mother obtaining custody of both children. His mother has since remarried. Her present husband is a truck driver who earns approximately $6,000 a year. She is not employed outside of the home. William has been referred to the court on four separate occasions. At age 15 he stole $6.00 from a grocery store cash register and was placed on informal probation. Two months later he was referred as an accessory to an auto theft resulting in his being placed on formal probation. Four months later he ran away from home, wanting to go to live with his natural father. William's most recent referral to the court resulted from his participation in the burglarizing of two stores.

Case 4. Albert K. is a white male, 16 years of age. He is presently attending high school where his performance has been generally poor. Albert has an older brother and sister and a younger brother and two younger sisters. His father is employed by an airfield at a salary of $5,500 a year. His mother does not work outside of the home. Albert and another boy were referred to the juvenile court by the police for car theft. In the course of one evening they stole three cars, abandoning one of them when it ran out of gas, and returning the other two to the spot from which they had taken them. None of the cars had been damaged in any way. This was the first time that either Albert or his companion had been referred to the juvenile court.

COLLECTION OF DATA

The questionnaires were hand-carried to each respondent by an interviewer who returned after two days and collected the completed questionnaire. The overall response rate was 81 per cent. Subsequent comparison of available age and sex data for nonrespondents with that of respondents indicated only slight differences. What differences occurred seemed to indicate an underrepresentation of males and of older and younger respondents in the sample. Subsequent comparisons of respondent characteristics with the 1960 census confirms the underrepresentation of males; however, no systematic biases were revealed with respect to age, education, income, or occupation.

Findings

CITIZEN PREFERENCES FOR COURT DISPOSITIONS

Let us begin with the general responses of citizens to questions about court actions. As noted above, respondents were asked to indicate how strict they perceived the court to be, and also how strict they thought the court ought to be with juvenile offenders. The responses of average citizens and community leaders in the four communities are shown in Tables 14.1 and

Table 14.1. Distribution of responses to the question "How strict do you feel the juvenile court actually is with juvenile offenders?" (percentages)

| | Very lenient | | | | Very strict | No | | Leik's |
	1	2	3	4	5	Response	N	D
General public	21.7	17.3	34.5	6.7	8.4	11.4	359	.48
Community leaders	11.9	27.1	49.2	10.2	1.6	0.0	68	.32

14.2. Clearly, most citizens view the court as quite lenient, in that 73.5 per cent of the members of the general public and 88.2 per cent of the community leaders said the court was only moderately strict. On the other hand, most citizens hold that the court ought to be more strict in its operations, for the responses of 70.2 per cent of the general public and 73.3 per cent of the leaders fell into categories 4 and 5 of the punitive choices. In short, when citizens are quizzed about their general reaction to the court, Hypothesis 1 in confirmed. Most citizens see the court as lenient or "soft" on offenders, while most of them would have the court be more severe in its dealings with juvenile lawbreakers.

Table 14.2. Distribution of responses to the question "How strict do you feel the juvenile court ought to be with juvenile offenders?" (percentages)

| | Very lenient | | | | Very strict | No | | Leik's |
	1	2	3	4	5	Response	N	D
General public	1.9	0.8	16.2	26.7	43.5	10.9	359	.38
Community leaders	1.7	1.7	23.3	55.0	18.3	0.0	68	.25

A second observation from Tables 14.1 and 14.2 bears upon Hypothesis 2, which held that community leaders prefer less punitive responses than do general citizens. Among the general public, 70.2 per cent of the respondents said that the court should be quite strict (response categories 4 and 5), while 73.3 per cent of the leaders offered this view. As far as general perspectives on court operations are concerned, community leaders appear to be as punitive as other citizens, so that Hypothesis 2 is not supported by these data.[6]

But, how strict is "strict"? What do citizens have in mind when they assert that the court is not strict enough? What kinds of penalties do they they have in mind when they opt for strictness in the court? Conceivably,

6. Leik's D, a measure of dissensus, is reported in most of the tables that follow. This statistic measures the degree of rank dissensus for a distribution. Perfect dissensus exists when the cases are equally distributed into the two extreme ranks. Perfect consensus is the condition where all cases fall in one rank. The statistic varies from zero (perfect consensus) to 1.00 (perfect dissensus). See Robert W. Leik, "A Measure of Ordinal Consensus," *Pacific Sociological Review,* IX (Fall 1966), 85–90.

many members of the general public may mean, by strict penalties, punitive actions which are markedly more severe than those handed out by the courts in their actual operations. Yet it might also be the case that laymen mean, by strictness, punitive policies which are less severe than those actually handed out in juvenile courts. In short, we ought to examine the preferred dispositions which citizens might offer for specific cases of delinquency, in addition to asking them about their general feelings about court actions.

The questionnaire used in this study did inquire about laymen's preferences for court action in terms of four actual delinquency cases. The actual disposition made in Case 1 was remanding to adult court; in Case 2 the offender was placed on informal probation; in Case 3 he was committed to a juvenile institution; and in Case 4 he was placed on formal probation. The judges of the four juvenile courts in question all agreed with the actual disposition made of these four offenders. Now, the question is: Do citizens think that more severe actions should have been taken against these delinquents?

Table 14.3. Distribution of degree of preference for court punitiveness (percentages)

	Low Punitiveness			High Punitiveness		No Response	N	Leik's D
	1	2	3	4	5			
General public	3.9	36.8	49.6	6.4	1.4	1.9	359	.27
Community leaders	1.5	39.1	51.6	6.3	1.5	0.0	68	.26

Table 14.3 presents the summary responses of citizens concerning preferred dispositions of the four cases. The punitiveness index for the case histories was derived by arbitrarily weighting the seven possible alternative actions from 1 to 7; 1 for warning, 7 for remand to adult court. The weights were then summed across the four case histories, yielding a range of scores from 4 to 28. These scores were then broken down into five categories (4–8, 9–13, 14–18, 19–23, and 24–28). The lowest scores reflect low punitiveness, while high scores reflect the highest punitiveness. The actual dispositions made of the four cases resulted in a total score of 17, or an intermediate score of 3 on the punitiveness scale.

It can be seen from Table 14.3 that 90.3 per cent of the general citizens made moderate or low punitive choices (score of 1 to 3), while 92.2 per cent of the community leaders opted for relatively low degrees of punitive handling of the offenders. Hypothesis 2 regarding the less punitive posture of community leaders must again be rejected, on the basis of these findings.

However, there is something more startling about the results in Table

Table 14.4 Distribution of types of court actions preferred by the public for the four cases (percentages)

Course of Action	Case 1	Case 2	Case 3	Case 4
Remand to Adult Court	18.9	4.5	6.2	1.9
Special Institutional Placement	21.5	1.4	8.0	0.3
Commitment	18.7	2.8	44.6	1.9
Foster Care	14.5	3.0	24.6	0.6
Formal Probation	15.4	34.3	10.6	23.4.
Informal Probation	6.9	37.7	1.9	35.7
Warning	1.4	13.0	1.1	32.6
No Response	2.7	3.3	3.0	3.6
Total Percentage	100.0	100.0	100.0	100.0
N	359	359	359	359
Leik's D	.45	.41	.26	.26

14.3. It is at this point that we begin to see that the matter of public sentiments about court punitiveness is a complex phenomenon. In brief, the results to this point picture citizens as "hard-liners," who say in general terms that they would "crack down" on youthful offenders and who see themselves as sterner than court officials. Yet these same citizens elect relatively lenient penalties for specific cases of juvenile delinquency when their responses are measured against the actual dispositions made by the court.

Let us look more closely at this matter of citizen preferences and actual court actions. Tables 14.4 and 14.5 show the distribution of types of actions preferred by citizens and community leaders for each of the four delinquency cases. Take the first case of delinquency which resulted in remanding to the adult court as the actual disposition. One-quarter or less of the citizens and leaders gave this disposition as the one they would

Table 14.5. Distribution of types of court actions preferred by leaders for the four cases (percentages)

Course of Action	Case 1	Case 2	Case 3	Case 4
Remand to Adult Court	26.5	2.9	5.9	0.0
Special Institutional Placement	13.2	0.0	0.0	0.0
Commitment	17.6	2.9	67.6	0.0
Foster Care	14.7	0.0	8.8	2.9
Formal Probation	20.6	38.2	8.8	22.1
Informal Probation	1.5	39.8	1.5	50.0
Warning	0.0	8.8	0.0	17.6
No Response	5.9	7.4	7.4	7.4
Total Percentage	100.0	100.0	100.0	100.0
N	68	68	68	68
Leik's D	.45	.26	.15	.16

prefer, so that their preferences were for punitive actions that are less severe than those actually dispensed by the court! In Case 2, which actually resulted in informal probation, 72 per cent of the general public chose either this disposition or formal probation, while 78 per cent of the leaders also elected one of these two actions. Citizen preferences for action in Case 2 are relatively close to the disposition actually handed out by the court. In much the same way, 69.2 per cent of the laymen and 76.4 per cent of the leaders chose foster-home placement or institutional commitment for Case 3, which actually had been dealt with by institutionalization. For Case 4, 68.3 per cent of the citizens and 67.6 per cent of the leaders chose informal probation or a warning, while the delinquent was actually placed on informal probation. On the whole, the penalties preferred by citizens and community leaders for the four cases of delinquency were close to the actual dispositions made, while in a number of instances citizens chose penalties which were less severe than those handed out by the court.

A second observation from Tables 14.4 and 14.5 is that Hypothesis 2 again failed to receive support by the data. Community leaders were not more lenient in their penalty choices for the four delinquent cases than were general citizens.

PERCEIVED COURT ACTIONS

It is already apparent from material considered to this point that citizens' perceptions of the juvenile court are inaccurate, for laymen respond in general that the court is too lenient at the same time that they choose penalties for offenders which are less strict than those handed out by the court. However, Table 14.6 throws further light on this issue. Recall that

Table 14.6. Distribution of perceived court punitiveness (percentages)

	Low Punitiveness			High Punitiveness		No Response	N	Leik's D
	1	2	3	4	5			
General public	10.9	40.1	38.2	3.9	1.1	5.8	359	.33
Community leaders	6.3	60.4	33.3	0.0	0.0	0.0	68	.20

the level of punitiveness of actual court dispositions was 3 on the 5-point punitiveness scale. But when citizens and leaders were asked to estimate the punitiveness of court actions, 51 per cent of the general citizens and 66.7 per cent of the leaders judged the court to be less harsh with youthful offenders.

Further details are added to this picture of citizens underperceiving the severity of court actions by the data in Tables 14.7 and 14.8. These tables

Table 14.7. Distribution of types of court actions perceived by the public for the four cases (percentages)

Course of Action	Case 1	Case 2	Case 3	Case 4
Remand to the Adult Court	9.7	3.1	5.8	0.3
Special Institutional Placement	11.4	0.8	4.2	0.6
Commitment	30.6	2.2	45.7	3.6
Foster Care	7.5	1.4	11.4	0.6
Formal Probation	18.7	25.6	16.2	17.3
Informal Probation	9.5	33.1	4.7	32.0
Warning	4.2	25.9	2.5	37.0
No Response	8.4	7.8	9.5	8.6
Total Percentage	100.0	100.0	100.0	100.0
N	359	359	359	359
Leik's D	.44	.29	.31	.26

show the responses of citizens and community leaders to the query concerning the actions the local court would have taken in the four delinquency cases. In the first delinquency case, the youth was remanded to the adult court, but only 9.7 per cent of the general citizens and 7.4 per cent of the community leaders supposed that he would have received this disposition from the court. The second delinquent offender was actually placed on informal probation, but 25.9 per cent of the general public and 25 per cent of the leaders estimated that he would have received a lesser penalty in the court. The third offender was sent to a training school, but 34.8 per cent of the citizens and 33.8 per cent of the leaders thought that he would receive a lesser sentence. Finally, the fourth offender was placed on informal probation, but 69 per cent of the general citizens and 70.6 per cent of the leaders supposed that he would have been given a lesser penalty.

Table 14.8. Distribution of types of court actions perceived by leaders for the four cases (percentages)

Course of Action	Case 1	Case 2	Case 3	Case 4
Remand to Adult Court	7.4	0.0	2.9	0.0
Special Institutional Placement	7.4	0.0	0.0	0.0
Commitment	30.9	1.5	55.9	0.0
Foster Care	8.8	0.0	8.8	1.5
Formal Probation	25.0	26.5	23.5	20.6
Informal Probation	8.8	39.7	0.0	38.2
Warning	1.5	25.0	1.5	32.4
No Response	10.3	7.4	7.4	7.4
Total Percentage	100.0	100.0	100.0	100.0
N	68	68	68	68
Leik's D	.42	.20	.24	.20

The findings above support Hypothesis 5, which held that the actual court actions will be closer to the punitive preferences of citizens than to their perceptions of court punitiveness. This relationship can be seen more clearly in a comparison between Tables 14.4 and 14.5 and Tables 14.7 and 14.8. Thus 18.9 per cent of the citizens would remand Case 1 to adult court, but only 9.7 per cent of them supposed that the juvenile court would take this action. Similarly, only 13 per cent of the citizens believed that a warning was an adequate response to Case 2, but 25.9 per cent of them suspected that the court would make this disposition. Regarding Case 4, 59.1 per cent of the citizens felt that the offender should be placed on formal or informal probation, but only 49.3 per cent of them thought the court would handle the case in this way. Inspection of Tables 14.5 and 14.8 show that the preferred levels of punitiveness of community leaders also exceed their anticipation of court action.

The preceding data do not lend much support to the hypothesis that community leaders are more accurate in their perceptions of court actions than are citizens generally. But what of Hypothesis 4 which argues that community leaders who have frequent contacts with court officials will be more accurate than others in their perceptions of court responses?

To begin with, let us examine the interaction of citizens and leaders with juvenile authorities. Findings on this matter are shown in Tables 14.9

Table 14.9. Distribution of frequency of contact of the general public with certain juvenile authorities (percentages)

	Frequent [a]	Occasional [b]	Infrequent [c]	None	No Response	N
Judge	0.8	0.8	5.6	81.3	11.4	359
Probation Officer	0.8	1.9	7.0	78.6	11.7	359
Other Court Employees	1.7	1.1	6.4	78.8	12.0	359
Police	5.0	7.5	16.2	62.7	8.6	359

[a]Once a week or more
[b]Less than once a week but at least once a month
[c]Less than once a month

and 14.10. Table 14.9 indicates that over three-quarters of the general citizens report no contact at all with juvenile court judges, probation officers, or court employees, while nearly two-thirds of them indicate that they have no interaction with police officers. However, the community leaders report considerably more interaction with judges, probation officers, court officials, and policemen. This is not surprising, in view of the fact that the leaders were selected in the first place as persons with involvement in children and youth problems. Even so, Table 14.10 indicates that many of these community leaders are only infrequently in contact with juvenile authorities of one kind or another.

Table 14.10. Distribution of frequency of contact of leaders with certain juvenile authorities (percentages)

	Frequent *a*	Occasional *b*	Infrequent *c*	None	No Response	N
Judge	4.8	19.0	50.8	23.8	1.6	68
Probation Officer	4.8	20.6	44.4	27.0	3.2	68
Other Court Employees	4.8	15.9	38.1	36.5	4.8	68
Police	38.1	28.6	25.4	6.3	1.6	68

aOnce a week or more
bLess than once a week but at least once a month
cLess than once a month

Contact with juvenile authorities does seem to have the effect of providing community leaders with relatively accurate perceptions of court actions. Findings on this point are to be found in Table 14.11, so that it can be seen that more of the high-contact leaders perceived the court as moderately lenient in its operations than did the low-contact influentials. More of the latter were found exhibiting views that the court is very lenient in its actions.

Table 14.11. Distribution of perceptions of court punitiveness for leaders having varying degrees of contact with the judge and probation officers (percentages)

	Very lenient 1	2	3	4	Very strict 5	No Response	N	Leik's D
High-Contact Leaders	0.0	54.5	45.5	0.0	0.0	0.0	22	.23
Low-Contact Leaders	12.5	65.0	22.5	0.0	0.0	0.0	40	.18

Conclusions

The findings reported in this paper were generally consistent with the five hypotheses outlined at the beginning of the report. Members of the general public voice harsher sentiments about dispositions of juvenile offenders than they believe are implemented in the court, although community leaders did not appear to be less punitive than citizens generally. Also, the hypothesis holding that community leaders are more accurate in their assessment of actual court punitiveness than other citizens was not supported by the data reported here. However, those community leaders who have relatively frequent contacts with court were more accurate in their perceptions of court actions than were other citizens. Finally, and most importantly, the actual levels of court punitiveness are not much different from the preferred levels voiced by citizens, although citizens generally suppose that the court is quite lenient and "soft" in its dealings with law-breakers. Indeed, the actual dispositions handed out by the court are more severe than the preferred levels identified by many citizens.

The reader should recall that the results reported here were obtained in relatively small communities. Even greater disparity between public knowledge and court action might be expected to exist in larger, more anonymous urban communities. Certainly, there appears to be a major problem of communication and public relations facing juvenile courts. It appears that court officials receive ambiguous, general messages from the community in the form of inarticulate demands for greater punitiveness. Apparently judges reflect this public attitude by making somewhat stricter decisions than they might ordinarily prefer to make. In short, the process may work like this: juvenile crime increases (or people believe that it is increasing), the public becomes concerned, the court is viewed as lax by the public, these views are disseminated through the communication channels to the court, the court then responds by becoming somewhat more strict. However, accurate information flowing back to the public from the court gets no further than those who are in closest contact with the court. Thus public anxiety is not allayed and the pressure on the court remains, even though its actions vary little from what the public would do if given the opportunity. If judges are concerned with reducing public pressure upon them, better communications between the court and public will have to be developed.

15. Attitudes of Probation Officers Toward Due Process for Juvenile Offenders

JAMES D. McMILLIN and PETER G. GARABEDIAN

IN RECENT years there has been growing awareness of the role of social policies in delinquency and crime causation. Attention has been shifting from the study of the individual delinquent and criminal to the study of social policies that either "criminalize" human actions or underlie the existence of social injustices in the society. In large measure, this trend, which has been called the age of reconstruction and reintegration,[1] assumes that crime can be effectively controlled by modifying such policies rather than focusing entirely on the business of changing the delinquent's attitudes.

The research reported in this paper was made possible by grants from the President's Committee on Juvenile Delinquency and Youth Crime, Department of Health, Education and Welfare (No. 6220), and the College Committee on Research, Washington State University (No. 711). The authors wish to thank James F. Short, Jr., for his generous support of the study, Mr. Harold Muntz, Los Angeles County Probation Department, for his assistance during the survey, and Don C. Gibbons, for his helpful comments on an earlier draft of the manuscript.

1. The President's Commission on Law Enforcement and the Administration of Justice, *Task Force Report: Corrections* (Washington, D.C.: U. S. Government Printing Office, 1967), pp. 6–13.

An important category of policies and practices that has increasingly been the target of criticism is that concerned with the procedural aspects of the criminal law. Though stemming back to the *Adamson* case in 1947, the concern with articulating procedures and safeguarding the constitutional rights of accused persons has become especially evident with the *Gideon* case in 1963, followed in relatively rapid succession with the *Escobedo* and *Miranda* decisions in 1964 and 1966, respectively.[2] More recently, in 1967 the Supreme Court rendered its decision *In re Gault*.[3] In this case, which is surely to become a landmark decision, the Court held that juveniles should be given formal notice of charges against them and should be informed of the right to counsel, the right to confront and cross-examine witnesses, the privilege of not testifying against oneself, the right to a transcription of the hearing, and the right of appeal. To date, the Gault decision represents one of the clearest expressions of the due process trend, especially in the adjudicatory stage, and as Cohen has recently noted, the due process trend is almost certain to move into the post-adjudication phases of corrections.[4]

Behind the *Gault* decision lies an extensive history of controversy centered on the issue of constitutional guarantees of due process both prior to, during, and after the juvenile court hearing. Apologists for the system have argued that the court is responsible for protecting children who need help and that it should follow through with this help. Those who disagree assert that the juvenile court should have the same philosophy and approach as any other equity court.[5] Critics of the court have maintained that it operates behind a glib ideological facade, reinforced by legal slogans such as *parens patriae* and *in loco parentis,* that deprives juveniles of their basic constitutional rights.[6]

As noted by Lemert, many of the critics of juvenile courts, and those most responsible for generating the pressures that ultimately led to *Gault,*

2. The trend toward scrutinizing and articulating procedural aspects of the justice system has been called by Packer the Due Process Model. See Herbert L. Packer, *The Limits of the Criminal Sanction* (Stanford: Stanford University Press, 1968), pp. 149–246. See also his "The Courts, the Police, and the Rest of Us," *Journal of Criminal Law, Criminology, and Police Science,* LVII (September 1966), 238–243.

3. 387 U. S. 1 (1967).

4. Fred Cohen, *The Legal Challenge to Corrections* (Washington, D.C.: Joint Commission on Correctional Manpower and Training, 1969). See also his "Sentencing, Probation, and the Rehabilitative Ideal: The View from *Mempa v. Rhay*," *Texas Law Review* (December 1968), pp. 1–59; and "Legal Norms in Corrections," in The President's Commission on Law Enforcement and the Administration of Justice, *Task Force Report: Corrections,* pp. 82–92.

5. Gustav L. Schramm, "Philosophy of the Juvenile Court," in Sheldon Glueck, ed., *The Problem of Delinquency* (Boston: Houghton Mifflin, 1959), pp. 271–272.

6. Gilbert Geis, "Publicity and Juvenile Court Proceedings," *NPPA Journal,* IV (1958), 333.

were persons not directly connected with the operation of juvenile courts.[7] Sociologist Paul Tappan, for example, who was an outspoken critic of juvenile courts, argued that various methods of applying court treatment without a full and fair judicial trial of the issue of guilt for a given offense are hazardous and unnecessary.[8] He argued for the same sorts of procedural safeguards that have recently been articulated by the Supreme Court in *In re Gault*. Indeed, Tappan is one of the major thinkers from whom the justices drew in their arguments in the *Gault* decision.

Variations on this theme have also been expressed by other critics. Dunham has maintained that when the juvenile court attempts to "help" a child by "treating" his disorder, it is, in effect, using the child to collect data to substantiate certain theories of child behavior while at the same time "chipping away at the concept of legal responsibility."[9] Similarly, Diana has stated that reactions against the extremes of the legal codes has led, in many instances, to the removal of virtually all procedural safeguards and the formation of a concept which makes the juvenile court a child-guidance agency supported by the power of the state.[10]

Though *In re Gault* is a formal expression of disapproval by the highest tribunal in the country of the use of informal procedures, the decision by no means guarantees that due process will in fact be accorded to youth referred to juvenile courts. For example, in 1961 in the state of California, the law was revised so as to make a mandatory separation of the adjudication hearing from the disposition hearing. Yet in a 1965 survey, Lemert found that two-thirds of the California juvenile court judges were still reading the social investigation prior to (rather than after) the adjudication hearing.[11] Moreover, whereas there was a statutory provision for legal counsel in delinquency proceedings, the practice of using attorneys in juvenile court hearings varied widely, as did practices of admitting various types of hearsay information as evidence.[12] Lemert's survey clearly shows that the 1961 revisions in the California law governing juvenile proceedings had relatively little effect on juvenile court practices. There

7. Edwin Lemert, "The Juvenile Court—Quest and Realities," in the present volume, pp. 135–167.

8. See the following works by Paul Tappan: *Juvenile Delinquency* (New York: McGraw-Hill, 1949), pp. 167–286; *Crime, Justice, and Correction* (New York: McGraw-Hill, 1960), pp. 387–395; and *Comparative Survey of Juvenile Delinquency, Part I: North America* (New York: United Nations, Department of Economic and Social Affairs, 1958).

9. H. Warren Dunham, "Juvenile Court: Contradictory Orientations in Processing Offenders," *Law and Contemporary Problems*, XXIII (1958), 221.

10. Lewis Diana, "The Rights of Juvenile Delinquents: An Appraisal of Juvenile Court Procedures," *Journal of Criminal Law, Criminology, and Police Science*, XLVII (January-February 1957), 561.

11. Edwin Lemert, in the present volume, p. 157.

12. *Ibid.*, pp. 158–162.

is little reason to believe that the picture for the country as a whole would be significantly different since *In re Gault* in 1967.

This paper is a report of the attitudes of probation officers in the state of California toward providing procedural safeguards for juveniles as they are processed through the justice system. The data were collected in 1963 after California had revised its laws regarding procedures in delinquency hearings, but prior to the *Gault* decision. This paper first examines the social and occupational correlates of "legalistic" thinking among probation officers and, second, assesses the role of legalistic orientations in the decision-making process. In general the data show that education, position in the formal organizational structure, and experience on the job tend to differentiate those probation officers who support the idea of having procedural safeguards from those who do not. Additionally, the data suggest that decision-making is influenced by legalistic orientations in the case of serious offenses but not in the case of minor offenses.

Research Procedures

The data reported in this paper are based on the responses to self-administered questionnaires by 292 probation officers employed in the Los Angeles Country Probation Department. The department is organized into four operating divisions: Administrative Services, Field Services, Juvenile Facilities, and Medical Services. Probation services are decentralized throughout the county in twelve area offices. Six of the twelve offices were randomly selected, and questionnaires were administered to all of the probation officers who were present on the day of the data collection. The schedule was also administered to a group of probation officer trainees and their training supervisors. These two groups were located in the central office, since training is a part of the Administrative Services division.

The Los Angeles Country Probation Department services not only youth who have been adjudicated as delinquent but also adults who have been found guilty of a felony by the criminal courts. Thus the department has the dual function of processing juvenile and adult offenders. Consequently, the sample consists of probation officers and their supervisors having responsibility over adult probationers, juvenile probationers, or both. Of the 292 respondents, 97 were supervising adult offenders, 106 were supervising juvenile offenders, 6 were supervising both juveniles and adults, 48 were connected with the training program (trainees and instructors), 5 were directors of the area offices, and 30 did not identify their formal position in the organization.

Four Likert-type items were used as the basis for the construction of a "due process index": (1) a juvenile should not be required to testify against himself in a juvenile court hearing; (2) in a juvenile court hearing, the juvenile should have the right to be represented by a lawyer; (3) a juvenile should have the right to appeal a juvenile court decision to a higher court; and (4) juveniles who are suspected of breaking the law should not be questioned by the police without being told of their right to have a lawyer. Factor analysis was used for selecting the above four items from a larger set of thirty statements.[13]

Each of the four items contained five response categories—strongly agree, agree, undecided, disagree, and strongly disagree—to which arbitrary weights of 1, 2, 3, 4, and 5 were assigned, respectively. The individual's score was summed to yield a composite score. The resulting distribution of composite scores was then trichotomized, with cutting points being determined by the mean and standard deviation of the distribution.[14] By employing this method, 100 probation officers, with scores ranging between 4 and 7, were defined as *legalistic*, that is, favorable toward the idea of providing due process for juvenile offenders. Those with scores of 8 through 10 ($N = 110$) were defined as *somewhat legalistic,* and those with scores ranging from 11 through 20 ($N = 82$) were designated as *not legalistic.*

Social and Occupational Correlates of the Due Process Index

In this section, a number of social and occupational characteristics of officers are examined in order to assess their relationships to scores on the due process index. Such variables as amount and type of education, involvement in professional activities, age, length of time employed, and extent of contact with delinquent youth, will be discussed with the aim of uncovering patterns of relationships. It appears reasonable to assume that the different amounts and types of experiences encountered by probation officers will influence the way they view the question of providing procedural safeguards in juvenile proceedings.

AMOUNT AND TYPE OF EDUCATION

In the literature dealing with probation, as well as within probation agencies, much debate has centered around the question of how much and

13. A correlation matrix containing 30 Likert-type items was factor-analyzed using the principal axis method and entering unity for communality estimation in the main diagonal. The above four items, along with a fifth, emerged as a single factor. While the loading of the fifth item was relatively high ($-.44$), it also loaded relatively high with two other factors. Since the other four items had loadings ranging from .61 to .72, and did not show high loadings on other factors, it was decided not to use the fifth item in the construction of the due process index. For a detailed description of the interrelations and factor analysis, see James D. McMillin, *Attitudes of Probation Officers Concerning Issues in the Handling of Juvenile Offenders* (unpublished master's thesis, Washington State University, Pullman, Wash., 1965), chap. 2.

14. The mean of the distribution of composite scores was 8.90 and the standard deviation 3.21.

what type of education should be required for juvenile and adult probation officers. As the debate has continued over the years, the educational requirements have increased. Formerly a bachelor's degree was deemed sufficient, but in recent years expectations have been raised. Many large, professionally oriented juvenile probation departments have increasingly encouraged the pursuit of a graduate education, so that it is not uncommon to find sizeable numbers of probation officers possessing advanced degrees. Indeed, of the 292 probation officers completing the questionnaire, 51 (almost 20 per cent) had earned advanced degrees at the time of the study.[15]

Even more debate has centered on the question of the type of education most suitable for the field of juvenile probation. The literature generally has recommended training in the field of social work, with less emphasis on related fields. Basically, the debate has concerned training in social work *vs.* training in the behavioral sciences. At the time of the study, two-thirds of the probation officers had received some graduate training beyond the bachelor's degree. Of these, 20 per cent had majored in social work, 34 per cent in one of the behavioral sciences, and 45 per cent in "other" disciplines.[16]

From the above discussion, it might reasonably be inferred that both *amount* and *type* of education may be related to the legalistic orientations of probation officers. Table 15.1 shows the relationship between the due

Table 15.1. Level of education and attitude toward due process

		Percentage with Legalistic Scores
Completed College or Some Graduate Work	32	(238)[a]
Completed Graduate Work	45	(51)

[a]In this and the following tables figures in parentheses represent the total N on which the percentage is based.

process index and level of education for the 292 probation officers. The trend suggested by the data is evident; probation officers who have completed their graduate training tend to more strongly favor due process than either those possessing only a bachelor's degree or those having had

15. This, of course, may be an extreme case. Level of education varies with size of the department. In general, probation departments located in urban areas will have higher educational requirements than those located in less urbanized areas.
16. The "other" category includes the physical and biological sciences, engineering, and art.

some graduate education.[17] One of the apparent consequences of an advanced degree is greater awareness of the political and legal implications involved in processing juvenile offenders. Increased education may sensitize the probation officer not only to basic constitutional guarantees in general but also to the many points in the process of delinquency proceedings where these rights might be denied or overlooked.

Social work curricula generally stress the philosophy of "protection" and "treatment" when dealing with clients in general and with juvenile offenders in particular. Behavioral sciences, on the other hand, are more concerned with the scientific study of human behavior. This suggests, then, that probation officers with training in social work might be less concerned with procedural safeguards (because they are more interested in "helping" their clients) than those who have majored in behavioral sciences.

However, this expectation is not entirely confirmed by the data presented in Table 15.2. This table shows the relationships between level of

Table 15.2. *Level of education, major field of study, and attitude toward due process*

| | Percentage with Legalistic Scores | | | |
	Some Graduate Work		Completed Graduate Work	
Social Work	18	(27)	46	(13)
Behavioral Science	28	(53)	29	(14)

education, type of major, and attitudes toward due process.[18] It can be seen that for each educational level the relationships are in different directions. Among probation officers who have less than a graduate degree, those who majored in social work tend to be *less* legalistic than those who majored in one of the behavioral sciences. The reverse is true for those who have completed their graduate training. The social work majors in this group are *more* concerned with procedural safeguards than the behavioral science majors. In addition, the data indicate that there is little

17. There is no difference in due process index scores between those with only a bachelor's degree and those with some graduate work. These two groups have therefore been combined in the analysis.

18. Those probation officers who did not major in either social work or one of the behavioral sciences are excluded from this analysis. One of the major points of debate has revolved around the question of the effectiveness of social work in the training of correctional personnel. Generally, the debate has centered around a comparision of the merits of social work vs. psychology, sociology, or some other behavioral science. It is, therefore, for this reason that non-social work and non-behavioral-science majors have been excluded. This latter group tends to be more legalistic than either the social work majors or behavioral science majors. See James D. McMillin, op. cit., pp. 45–48.

difference between behavorial science majors with different levels of education, suggesting that the content of the behavioral science curriculum does not change sufficiently from the lower to the advanced levels to alter the attitudes of probation officers. But at the same time the data suggest that the content of the social work curriculum does change from the lower to the advanced levels. No doubt there is greater stress placed on notions of "helping" and "humanitarianism" on the beginning level. In the more advanced levels, leading directly to the master's degree, the professional and technical aspects of social work become increasingly important.

PROFESSIONAL INVOLVEMENT

In the literature dealing with standards in juvenile probation, it is not uncommon to find statements asserting that involvement in the profession-at-large is necessary for continued professional growth. These statements assume that professional involvement will have an impact (in a desirable direction) on attitudes and performance. Lack of professional involvement implies that the worker will exhibit undesirable attitudes and substandard performance. Though these assertions appear with a good deal of frequency in the literature, there is little in the way of systematic evidence to shed light on the matter one way or the other.

Table 15.3. Professional involvement and attitudes toward due process

	Percent with Legalistic Scores	
Number of Articles Read		
None or one	40	(55)
Two or more	33	(239)
Conferences Attended		
None	40	(82)
One or more	32	(210)
Offices Held		
Yes	45	(44)
No	33	(247)

Three items in the questionnaire were designed to provide some indication of the respondent's professional involvement. These were: the number of magazine or journal articles read during the past month; the number of local, state, or national professional conferences attended during the past three years; and whether or not the respondent ever held office in a local, state, or national organization related to his profession. The results of these queries, related to the due process index, are presented in Table 15.3

Two trends appear to be evident in the data. Professional involvement, either in terms of reading magazine or journal articles or in terms of attending professional meetings, is inversely related to attitude toward due process in delinquency proceedings. Those probation officers who have attended at least one conference or have read two or more articles (during the past month) are less likely to endorse the idea of legalism in the processing of juvenile offenders.

However, another measure of professional involvement reveals a second trend. Those probation officers who have held an elective office in a professional organization tend to have more favorable legalistic orientations that those who have never been elected to some position. The data in Table 15.3 suggest that different types of professional involvement have different consequences for legalistic attitudes. Greater exposure to the literature and frequent participation at professional meetings are associated with unfavorable attitudes toward due process. Apparently the humanitarian and treatment traditions, which traditionally have opposed legalistically-oriented delinquency proceedings, continue to occupy a large part of the content of the literature and topics for discussion at meetings which probation officers attend. But professional involvement on the level of being elected to office is related to a more legalistic position regarding delinquency proceedings.

POSITION IN THE FORMAL ORGANIZATION

Previous research has shown that systematic variations exist between position occupied in the formal organizational hierarchy and attitudes, perceptions, and behavior. For example, in a recent survey of a national sample of correctional workers (juvenile and adult corrections, as well as those employed in the field and in institutions) by the Joint Commission on Correctional Manpower and Training, systematic differences were found to exist between those occupying different positions.[19] The administrators, first-line supervisors, functional specialists (professional personnel), and line workers varied systematically according to their perceptions of the criminal justice system and their attitudes toward their particular agency and job.

As stated in an earlier section, the Los Angeles County Probation Department has the dual function of supervising adult and juvenile probationers. Thus the supervisory staff and deputy probation officers are divided according to juvenile and adult divisions. Also, a training program exists at the central office designed to acquaint newly hired probation officers (trainees) with policies and programs of the department. This program is conducted by a number of training supervisors. Finally,

19. Joint Commission on Correctional Manpower and Training, *Correctional Personnel Look at Corrections* (Washington, D.C.: Joint Commission on Correctional Manpower and Training, 1968).

the department is decentralized into twelve area offices each having a director. Table 15.4 presents the distribution of due process scores according to both formal position and major function (juvenile *vs.* adult probation).[20]

Table 15.4. Formal position, major function, and attitude toward due process

	Percent with	Legalistic Scores
Directors	40	(5)
Training Program		
Supervisors	57	(7)
Trainees	31	(41)
Juvenile Probation		
Supervisors	36	(11)
Deputy P. O.'s	26	(95)
Adult Probation		
Supervisors	44	(9)
Deputy P. O.'s	37	(88)

The first trend to note in Table 15.4 is that the supervisory staff in each of the three major divisions (juvenile, adult, and training) is more legalistic than the lower echelon in each of the respective segments. Training program supervisors are most likely to hold favorable attitudes toward due process, while supervisors in the juvenile division are least likely to. Adult division supervisors occupy an intermediate position. No doubt those occupying supervisory positions, especially in large urban probation departments, are more attuned to the legal problems that arise as juvenile offenders are processed. Indeed, from their vantage point, procedural and other administrative considerations become paramount for the maintenance of a smooth-running organization.

However, the reverse is true for the deputy probation officers so that the data exhibit a second trend. Rather than being concerned with procedural problems, this group is more likely to consider delinquents as sick and in need of treatment rather than protection of constitutional rights. Among members of this group, probation officers in the juvenile division are least likely to endorse the idea of providing procedural safeguards for juvenile offenders, while adult division officers are most likely to endorse legalistic procedures. Trainees occupy an intermediate position. Deputy probation officers in general, and juvenile probation officers in particular,

20. As mentioned in an earlier section of this report, 30 deputy probation officers did not specify whether they were supervising primarily juvenile or adult probationers. These individuals are not included in the analysis. In addition, on the day of the study, one of the area office directors was ill, and therefore not able to complete the questionnaire. Thus, of the six area offices contacted, five of the directors completed questionnaires.

are more likely than other categories of correctional personnel to be committed to the rehabilitative ideal. They are also likely to be the most experienced and knowledgeable in juvenile treatment resources, programs, and techniques. Attempts to formalize delinquency proceedings are likely to be viewed as undue restraints, having little to do with treatment and rehabilitation. Formalization of delinquency proceedings amounts to increased "red tape" and paper work in the daily routine of the probation officer. Any move in this direction is therefore likely to be viewed with some skepticism and disfavor by the deputies.

AGE, LENGTH OF TIME EMPLOYED AND CONTACT WITH DELINQUENTS

If there is any merit to the above argument, then it is reasonable to expect that the experienced probation officers would be less favorably disposed to the idea of procedural safeguards for juvenile offenders than less experienced deputies, because they are most likely to be knowledgeable about treatment strategies, resources and programs.

Table 15.5. Length of time employed, contact with delinquents and attitude toward due process

	Percent with Legalistic Scores	
Time Employed		
Less than two years	31	(76)
Two years or more	35	(216)
Contact with Delinquents		
Less than three	41	(100)
Three to eleven	30	(94)
Eleven or more	31	(93)

It can be seen that one of the measures of "experience" (contact with delinquents) is consistent with the above view. However, the second measure (length of time employed) is not. Probation officers reporting contact with fewer than three delinquents per week are more favorably disposed to the idea of due process than are those agents who are more heavily involved with juvenile offenders. But the scores of those employed for two or more years tend to be the same as those probation officers who have been employed fewer than two years.

"Length of time employed" measures experience in terms of tenure on the job, and "contact with delinquents" represents an indirect measure of involvement with "clients." It is therefore entirely possible for the two measures to vary independently. The probation officer with little tenure on the job might have a high degree of contact with many probationers, and the probation officer with greater job tenure may be relatively isolated from such contacts. With these considerations in mind, the joint relationship between time employed, contact with delinquents, and attitudes toward due process is presented in Table 15.6 and shown separately for juvenile and adult probation officers.[21]

Table 15.6. Time employed, contact with delinquents, major function, and attitude toward due process

	Percent with Legalistic Scores			
	Employed less than two years		Employed two years or more	
Juvenile Probation				
Contact				
Less than 3	40	(15)	—	(2)
3-11	29	(28)	22	(31)
11 or more	20	(15)	31	(45)
Adult Probation				
Contact				
Less than 3	44	(9)	40	(40)
3-11	40	(5)	39	(28)
11 or more	50	(2)	33	(30)

The data suggest that when the two measures of "experience" are considered jointly, relatively clear trends are observed for the juvenile probation officers, but not for those from the adult division. For the latter group, attitudes toward due process are not strongly associated with length of time employed or contact with delinquents. However, among the juvenile probation officers, those with little time in the job become less legalistic as they have more contact with delinquents, while the reverse is true for those employed for two years or more. As these persons have more contact with delinquents, they become more favorably disposed toward the idea of due process. These data suggest that as probation officers spend more time on the job, they become not only more knowledgeable about treatment strategies, programs, and community resources, but they also tend to become somewhat more skeptical than their less tenured colleagues about the accomplishments of treatment efforts. More than any other of the deputies, juvenile probation officers with a fair amount of time on the job are likely to perceive the discrepancy between the rhetoric and reality of treatment efforts. As they become more skeptical (and perhaps more disillusioned) about treatment, they are more willing to at least provide juveniles with the same rights as are accorded adults.

21. Only two of the deputy probation officers working in the juvenile division reported having contact with fewer than three delinquents per week. The trainees, who also supervise juvenile probationers, are therefore included in the analysis, and this increases the number of juvenile probation officers who have contact with less than three delinquents per week.

However, the data in Table 15.6 suggest that this might be part of the later stages of a larger process that is operating. There is the suggestion that legalistic orientations do not develop in a simple linear fashion, so that not all persons become either progressively more or less legalistic with the accumulation of experience. Rather, the trend suggested is curvilinear or U-shaped. It will be seen that probation officers who are the least experienced (in terms of tenure and contact), as well as those who are most experienced, are also the most legalistically-oriented. Probation officers with intermediate degrees of experience (either in number of years employed or number of delinquents contacted) tend not to be in favor of due process. It appears that at the outset novice probation officers are not sure of themselves nor well-acquainted with treatment strategies and techniques. Lacking such knowledge, they fall back on the law and "go by the book" in processing delinquents. It is interesting to note that of this group (less than two years on the job and less than three delinquents contacted per week) 63 percent are trainees. But as a degree of experience is gained, either in terms of tenure on the job or contact with delinquents, concerns with legal safeguards become secondary to the emerging rehabilitation concerns of the probation officer. He begins to develop a sense of omniscience regarding the welfare of the delinquent and becomes aware of the "tools" of his trade, and moreover, is anxious to have the opportunity to apply them. This concern with therapy is likely to promote an unfavorable view of legal procedures and safeguards. But as the probation officer becomes highly experienced and knowledgeable of therapeutic efforts in delinquency control, he begins to draw conclusions regarding their effectiveness, and he finds little basis for optimism. Thus legalistic concerns reappear among those who are very experienced, but now out of a sense of disillusionment with the treatment ideal. It is, of course, possible, that among this very experienced group of deputies, many anticipate eventual movement upward in the organizational hierarchy, and thus they become more legalistic.[21]

Attitudes toward Due Process and Decision-Making

As suggested above, there has been increasing attention paid to the decision-making processes of correctional agents in recent years. Much of this concern has been reflected in research dealing with the decisions of police. Gibbons has noted that the main concern of research in this area has been with the role of offense behavior in dispositions and summarized the studies as follows:

> The main thread throughout all of these investigations has to do with the role of offense behavior in dispositions. Youths who have been involved in offenses which arouse members of the community, who com-

mit law violations which result in sizable financial suffering to the victims, and those who are repeaters, are the ones who most often get placed on the transmission belt to the training school. Ethnic characteristics, sex, age, and other demographic variables seem to be related to dispositions through their interconnection with offense variations. Thus many girls get taken off to institutions when they offend members of the community with their displays of sexual promiscuity and other "wild" behavior.[22]

Thus it appears that offense behavior is a very important consideration underlying the decisions of correctional agents. The role of organizational variables is less well understood, which is also true of the personal orientations of probation officers in the decision-making process.

In an attempt to enlighten the relationship between legalistic orientations and decision-making, the sample was presented with a list of acts representing a fairly wide range of offense behaviors. The probation officers were asked "What do you think should be done with a boy who commits . . . (the act)?" [23] The response categories ranged from informal sanctions, such as "counsel the boy" or "detain him temporarily at the police station," to more formal disposition alternatives, such as "court referral followed by probation" and "court referral followed by commitment." [24]

To derive some indication of how seriously each of the behaviors is viewed by the sample, the distribution of responses for the three major disposition alternatives is presented in Table 15.7. In general, the acts that are defined by the group as being most serious are those with the modal percent in the "commitment" category, followed by those acts with the modal percent in the "probation" category. Using this scheme as a measure of seriousness, Table 15.7 shows the following acts are defined as most serious: using heroin, rape, armed robbery, negligent homicide, and assaulting a small child. The less serious offenses appear to be getting drunk, being in a gang fight, breaking street lights, running away from home, and skipping school.

Table 15.8 presents the disposition alternatives that were selected by persons with different due process index scores. Two trends are suggested by the data. First, in the case of the serious offenses, score on the due process index is related to the type of disposition alternative selected by probation officers. The legalistically-oriented probation officers are clearly less prone to select "commitment" as the appropriate disposition. Those

22. Don C. Gibbons, *Delinquent Behavior* (Englewood Cliffs, N.J.: Prentice-Hall, 1970), p.58.
23. The only other information provided was that the "boy is fifteen years old, commits the act alone, and has never been in difficulty before, unless otherwise specified."
24. The less severe disposition alternatives are: "ignore the act," "boy should be chewed out," "should be detained at the police station, and have his parents pick him up." These three alternatives have been combined and called "informal sanctions."

who are committed to the idea of due process for juvenile offenders are no doubt more cautious in selecting disposition alternatives, especially since the facts surrounding each of the offenses are not known. Thus, the data suggest that they base their decisions on more information than those who are not in favor of procedural safeguards. This interpretation is given added support when the offense of armed robbery is considered. Knowledge that a weapon was involved in the offense diminishes the difference between probation officers having high and low due process scores.

Table 15.7. Choice of disposition alternatives for selected offenses (percentages)

Offense	Unofficial Action	Probation	Commitment	Total	
Uses heroin and other "hard" narcotics	3	32	65	100	(287)
Rapes a fifteen-year-old girl	5	33	62	100	(287)
Engages in armed robbery of a gasoline station	8	41	51	100	(285)
Kills a pedestrian because of reckless driving	7	68	25	100	(285)
Beats up a young child	13	67	21	101	(288)
Gets drunk	13	87	—	100	(280)
Engages in a gang fight	24	67	8	99	(289)
Deliberately breaks street lights	49	49	2	100	(289)
Runs away from home	56	44	—	100	(300)
Skips school	75	25	—	100	(299)

The second trend runs in the opposite direction. For the lesser offenses, due process index scores are not as highly associated with the selection of disposition alternatives as is the case for the serious offenses. In fact, for two offenses ("breaks street lights" and "runs away from home") probation officers having high scores are just about as likely to choose a given disposition as those officers having low due process scores. Apparently, if an offense is minor, then procedural safeguards become secondary for those who would otherwise be concerned with them. Thus concern with due process is not an important consideration in the disposition of minor cases. Of course, the "upper limits" of the disposition of minor offenses are quite frequently less severe than those associated with serious offenses. Consequently, decisions can readily be made almost independently of due process considerations.

Table 15.8. Choice of disposition alternative for selected offenses and attitude toward due process

Offense and Attitude Toward Due Process	Unofficial Action	Probation	Commitment	Total	
Uses heroin and other "hard" narcotics					
Legalistic	4	41	55	100	(101)
Somewhat-Legalistic	2	30	68	100	(106)
Not-Legalistic	5	24	71	100	(78)
Rapes a fifteen year old girl					
Legalistic	5	40	55	100	(101)
Somewhat-Legalistic	4	34	62	100	(105)
Not-Legalistic	3	24	73	100	(79)
Engages in armed robbery of a gasoline station					
Legalistic	9	45	46	100	(100)
Somewhat-Legalistic	10	36	54	100	(104)
Not-Legalistic	6	40	53	99	(79)
Kills a pedestrian because of reckless driving					
Legalistic	11	70	18	99	(98)
Somewhat-Legalistic	6	74	20	100	(106)
Not-Legalistic	4	57	39	100	(79)
Beats up a young child					
Legalistic	12	74	14	100	(101)
Somewhat-Legalistic	12	67	22	101	(105)
Not-Legalistic	16	58	27	101	(80)
Gets drunk					
Legalistic	16	82	2	100	(77)
Somewhat-Legalistic	8	85	7	100	(105)
Not-Legalistic	13	73	14	100	(101)
Engages in a gang fight					
Legalistic	23	62	15	100	(101)
Somewhat-Legalistic	26	66	8	100	(106)
Not-Legalistic	25	72	3	100	(80)
Deliberately breaks street lights					
Legalistic	51	48	2	101	(101)
Somewhat-Legalistic	49	51	0	100	(106)
Not-Legalistic	45	48	6	99	(79)
Runs away from home					
Legalistic	56	44	—	100	(81)
Somewhat-Legalistic	60	40	—	100	(106)
Not-Legalistic	53	47	—	100	(102)
Skips school					
Legalistic	28	72	—	100	(78)
Somewhat-Legalistic	24	76	—	100	(105)
Not-Legalistic	18	77	5	100	(101)

Conclusions

This paper has attempted to account for differences in attitude among probation officers concerning due process in juvenile proceedings. In addition, the relationship of legalistic orientations to decision-making has been examined.

Several conclusions emerge from the analysis. First, it appears that both education and professional involvement are related to favorable attitudes toward due process. However, the qualitative aspects of each appear to be more relevant than sheer quantitative considerations in generating favorable legalistic attitudes. For those probation officers with less education, a behavioral science major is more often associated with favorable attitudes toward due process. For those with a higher level of education, a social work major appears to be more related to favorable legalistic attitudes. In addition, holding elective office, rather than attending conferences or journal reading, is related to concern with procedural safeguards.

The second major conclusion pertains to the impact of job experiences on attitudes toward due process. The data show quite clearly (although at times the number of cases is small) that occupying a supervisory position in the organization is related to favorable attitudes toward procedural safeguards. It should be borne in mind, however, that supervisors are by no means overwhelmingly in favor of the legalistic point of view. Indeed, only two of the five district directors were definitely in favor of due process. The general posture of the supervisory staff (and also of the deputy probation officers), at least in this study, is one that is clearly not in accord with recent trends as reflected in *Kent* and *In re Gault*. But notwithstanding this general a-legalistic position, the supervisors cannot ignore the administrative and procedural problems faced by their organizations. It is evident that providing due process for juvenile offenders is part of that administrative task. A total neglect of legal procedures would lead to too many problems that would tend to create serious organizational strains and disrupt the existing social structure.

The situation is different for deputy probation officers. The deputies are "line" personnel in the sense that they have the greatest contact and involvement with their charges. The manifest goal of probation is to implement the treatment ideal. But it takes a certain amount of time and experience to assimilate the prescriptions of this model so that it can be implemented. Thus, in the early stages of his career, while the probation officer is learning these prescriptions, he adopts a more formalized approach, including legalistic procedures, in his relationships with juvenile offenders. But in later stages, as he assimilates the prescriptions of the treatment model, he changes his "style" with probationers. "Going by the book," and other more formalized procedures, are abandoned in favor of the more free-wheeling approaches called for by the model. Therapeutic, not procedural, considerations become foremost in the perspective of the probation officer. Juvenile offenders require treatment and therapy—not due process—and every resource must be mobilized to accomplish that end. However, with the passage of time and the accumulation of experience, the probation officer begins to question the effectiveness of his efforts. He comes to be acutely aware of the inadequacies of the community's treatment resources, the superficiality of his own efforts, the increasing size of his case load, the primacy assigned by the organization to maintenance rather than instrumental goals, and the increasing visibility of his failures when dealing with juvenile offenders. With this fund of experience dissonance is created and it becomes increasingly difficult to rationalize it. The probation officer is forced to acknowledge the gap that exists between the rhetoric of treatment and its reality. It is out of a sense of frustration and disillusionment with the rehabilitative ideal that the probation officer comes to support the idea of due process for juvenile offenders. It should be kept in mind, however, that only a longitudinal study of probation officers can provide the necessary data to test the validity of this interpretation.

It should also be noted that the deputy probation officers do not become as legalistic as their supervisors. Apparently, the experience of upward mobility in the organizational structure promotes added concerns with legal procedures. The differences between the deputies and their supervisors are probably great enough to generate a degree of conflict and organizational strain. At the present time many perceive an inherent contradiction between the treatment ideal and adherence to legal procedures. It is frequently said that one is accomplished to the detriment of the other. Lack of experience on the part of juvenile probation departments in accommodating their policies to the broad guidelines of *In re Gault* no doubt makes it difficult for many to agree that an optimal balance between the two can be achieved. However, it is likely that effective accommodations will be made and that the broad mandates outlined in *Gault* will not seriously impede the effectiveness of treatment.

Finally, the data suggest that the legalistic orientations of probation officers are related to their decisions, but not in all cases. Consistent with previous research in this area, type of offense is the major consideration in selecting dispositions. It tempers the way in which one's ideas about procedural safeguards are related to the decision-making process and whether due process can be invoked. When the offense behavior is serious, attitudes toward due process play an important role in the selection of an appropriate alternative, with legalistic attitudes being related to the less severe dispositions. But in the case of minor offenses, the decisions of those who would otherwise be concerned with due process are not significantly different from those who do *not* support the idea of due process for juvenile offenders.

The implications of this finding are not as yet clear, but at first glance it would suggest that policies concerned with protecting the constitutional rights of juvenile offenders have not been articulated with sufficient clarity—especially in the "gray" area where most of the minor offenses fall—to provide useful guidelines for probation officers who are making decisions about juveniles. In other words, in the case of relatively minor offenses it is difficult to specify appropriate behavior prescriptions for probation officers with any degree of specificity and confidence. Thus, the problems confronting probation officers in the area of decision-making are not too different from those found in the area of police discretion. Recently, James Wilson has ably pointed out that one of the major problems facing the police today is their inability to articulate clear-cut policies for the patrolman to use in handling "order-maintenance," rather than "law-enforcement," situations.[25] The former type of situation involves police discretion on such matters as disorderly conduct, family quarrels, and other types of public and private disputes. The latter involves making decisions on relatively clear-cut matters, such as stopping a burglary in progress or chasing a bank robber. Although the patrolman encounters order-maintenance situations much more frequently than law-enforcement situations, he does not have at his disposal a set of clear policies that will help him decide on an appropriate course of action. The patrolman is thus left to his own devices to make these types of decisions.

It is not difficult to imagine the probation officer in similar situations involving juveniles. Like the patrolman, he has been vested with broad discretionary powers to implement correctional sanctions and programs. The probation officer makes decisions that can have serious consequences for the careers of the persons they supervise. Yet such decisions are seldom based on well-articulated policies and criteria that are defensible on *a priori* grounds. Rather, as Cohen has pointed out, decision alternatives are a matter of idiosyncratic choice, and each probation department has more or less randomly developed its own policy or "discovered" it by looking back to determine what it has previously done.[26] Such *ad hoc* policies in probation are in large measure due to the existence of ill-defined delinquency statutes, especially the "omnibus" clauses found in most juvenile codes throughout the country. It is in the area of the offenses falling under these broad categories that due process is most difficult to define and translate into operating procedure. Until this dilemma is solved, juvenile courts and probation departments will continue to show symptoms of disorganization that are the result of ambiguous and inconsistent policies.

25. James Q. Wilson, *Varieties of Police Behavior* (Cambridge: Harvard University Press, 1968), pp. 1–139.
26. Cohen, *op. cit.*, pp. 3–5.

16. Policy Questions in Delinquency Control: Perspectives of Police and Probation Officers

PETER G. GARABEDIAN

OVER THE years the task of controlling delinquency has become more complicated as it has come to involve many different occupational groups. Formerly, the task was implemented in a relatively simple and uncomplicated fashion, with traditional institutions such as the family, the church, and the neighborhood cooperating in a common endeavor to control juvenile misbehavior. However, since the middle of the 19th century, this country has witnessed a number of social trends that have resulted in rising delinquency rates and increased public attention to the problem of youth

This project was supported by a curriculum development grant from the President's Committee on Juvenile Delinquency and Youth Crime, Department of Health, Education, and Welfare (No. 6220), and from the College Committee on Research, Washington State University (No. 711). The author wishes to thank James F. Short, Jr., director of the Curriculum Development Project, for his generous support of the present study, and John Lillywhite for his assistance in constructing the items which form the basis for this report. Grateful acknowledgement is also due to the chiefs of police and chief probation officers of the agencies contacted during the survey. Without the assistance of these persons, this investigation would not have been possible. The author also wishes to thank Don C. Gibbons for his helpful comments on an earlier version of the manuscript.

crime. Foremost among these has been the rapid growth of population in urban centers of the nation, accompanied by developments in transportation and communication. Municipal police departments, originally established to accomplish peace-keeping tasks (quelling public disturbances and riots; controlling violence), have been assigned the responsibility of controlling delinquency and crime.[1] County and state agencies have also been established to help curb the rising tide of youth crime. Thus, the task of delinquency control has increasingly fallen to specialized agencies, so that today most of the serious juvenile offenders are processed by the police, juvenile courts, probation departments, and institutions for juveniles.

While all of the agencies of delinquency control ultimately share the common objectives of individual and general prevention, each has been assigned more immediate and concrete objectives. The police have the responsibility of identifying youthful lawbreakers and referring the most serious cases on into the control system. Probation departments have the immediate responsibility for conducting investigations of court referrals and supervising those youth who have been officially adjudicated by the juvenile courts. Each agency has developed its own policies and programs to achieve its particular objectives. However, as Schrag and others have noted, the policies developed by a given agency to implement its immediate programs may at times be in contradiction to the policies and programs of other agencies.[2] The existence of contradictory program objectives means that success in one agency may be associated with failure in another.

This condition is exacerbated by two notable trends that have had an effect upon the delinquency control system since World War II. The first and most obvious trend has been the sharp rise in juvenile delinquency, necessitating the recruitment of large numbers of specialized personnel into the various control agencies. A second trend, brought on by the growing dominance of treatment, has been the assignment of multiple objectives to each of the control agencies, especially police and probation departments. Traditionally, the major tactic of the police has been to control delinquency and crime by enforcing the law and by keeping the community under surveillance. However, this emphasis has shifted so that currently the police are also treating and reforming juveniles who come to their attention. Thus, at the present time, police organizations

1. An exceptionally well-documented account of the fact that police agencies initially performed peace-keeping, rather than crime-control, functions is found in Roger Lane, *Policing the City: Boston 1822–1885* (Cambridge: Harvard University Press, 1967).

2. See Clarence Schrag, "The Correctional System: Problems and Prospects," *The Annals of the American Academy of Political and Social Science*, CCCLXXXI (January 1969), 11–20.

have the dual objectives of control and treatment. This is seen in the existence of juvenile or crime prevention bureaus in many urban police departments and in the emergence of new police roles such as school-resource officer and community-services officer. Although the reformation of juveniles has become an important police function, it is not likely that the police would be in complete agreement as to the propriety of this objective.

Probation departments have emerged in response to humanitarian concerns along with the growing importance of the treatment philosophy, especially as articulated in the field of psychiatry. Although the ideology of probation has traditionally been one of treatment, in actual practice its major objective has been the control and surveillance of offenders in the community. But, over the years, the treatment ideology has become more pronounced in probation departments as they have attempted to recruit more professionally trained treatment agents into the field. Currently, the objective of treatment and rehabilitation is receiving very strong *verbal* support by probation officers. But at the same time, they continue to perform important control functions. A recent study of adult probation and parole officers clearly suggests the existence of dual objectives in the field, and, while there is widespread disagreement over procedures, this study shows that many of the agents feel that it is entirely appropriate to assist the sheriff in arresting an absconding probationer, to make unexpected home visits, to contact the probationer's employer to check on work behavior, or engage in other surveillance activities.[3] Thus, on the level of rhetoric probation departments clearly see treatment as a major function, but on the behavioral level they continue to perform important control functions.

In brief, the delinquency control system has become increasingly complex and differentiated.[4] The growing prominence of the treatment philosophy is changing traditional functions and blurring traditional boundaries. Control agencies, especially police and probation, have been assigned incompatible or not entirely harmonious functions. The net result of such changes has been to produce strains between and within the various agencies.

This paper is a report of the attitudes of police and probation officers toward a variety of policy questions that commonly arise in the process of controlling delinquency. The results indicate that precious little agreement exists between these two important groups on the procedures that should be used when processing juvenile offenders through the control system. The findings suggest that the system of delinquency control may

3. Dale E. Van Laningham, Merlin Taber, and Rita Dimants, "How Adult Probation Officers View Their Job Responsibilities," *Crime and Delinquency*, XII (April 1966), 97–108.
4. Wheeler and his associates have provided an incisive commentary and have collected systematic evidence documenting this general point of view. See Stanton Wheeler, *et al.*, "Agents of Delinquency Control: A Comparative Analysis," in Stanton Wheeler, ed., *Controlling Delinquents* (New York: Wiley, 1968), pp. 31–60.

be disorganized to a point where it is operating at a considerably less-than-optimal level.

Methods and Description of Sample

The data reported here are based on a survey of 55 municipal police departments and 38 juvenile probation departments in the state of Washington. The size of the law enforcement agencies varied from one-man departments to the Seattle Police Department with over one thousand employees. Questionnaires from a total of 668 police officers, or slightly more than 80 per cent of those distributed by field workers, were completed and returned. One hundred twenty-seven juvenile probation officers completed the questionnaire, representing a return rate of over 90 per cent of the juvenile probation officers employed in the state at the time of the study. In addition to this group, 292 probation officers employed by the Los Angeles County Probation Department also completed the questionnaire. Thus, the sample included a total of 419 probation officers. The probation departments ranged in size from one-man operations in the sparsely populated counties of eastern Washington to the Los Angeles County Probation Department, which at the time of the study employed between six and seven hundred probation officers.

An examination of basic demographic characteristics shows that, compared with the probation officers, the police are older, more likely to be male, more likely to be married, and considerably less likely to have even one or two years of college training.[5] However, only 2 out of the sample of 668 police report being nonwhite. This compares with 17 per cent of the probation officers who reported being nonwhite.

In terms of community background and geographic mobility, the police are considerably more likely to have spent their childhood years in communities of less than 10,000 population, whereas the probation officers (either from Washington or from Los Angeles County) are more likely to have spent their early years in communities of over 50,000 residents. In addition, the police are more likely than the probation officers to have lived for longer periods of time in the state and in the community in which

5. For a more detailed description of the background characteristics of juvenile-probation officers, see Seymour Z. Gross, "Biographical Characteristics of Minnesota Probation Officers Who Deal with Juvenile Offenders," *Crime and Delinquency,* XII (April 1966), 109–116. For a description of the background characteristics of police, see David H. Bayley and Harold Mendelsohn, *Minorities and the Police: Confrontation in America* (New York: Free Press, 1969), pp. 1–33; John H. McNamara, "Uncertainties in Police Work: The Relevance of Police Recruits' Backgrounds and Training," in David Bordua, ed., *The Police* (New York: Wiley, 1967), pp. 191–195; and James Q. Wilson, "Generational and Ethnic Differences Among Career Police Officers," *American Journal of Sociology,* LXIX (March 1964), 522–528.

they were residing at the time of the study. Thus the data make it quite clear that, as far as members of this sample are concerned, the police are considerably less mobile, geographically, than are the probation officers.

Finally, as a group the police tend to be drawn from the lower socioeconomic brackets. Compared to the probation officers, the police are almost twice as likely to be drawn from families where the father held a job that is ranked "low" by the Census Bureau's "socioeconomic index." In addition, the data suggest that some of the probation officers had formerly held jobs in the field of law enforcement, but the reverse is not true. In no instance in the present sample is there a police officer who had formerly been a probation officer. Apparently, law enforcement leading to probation represents a route for upward mobility among control agents.[6]

This paper reports data relevant to four major policy question areas. First, findings are presented on the way in which police and probation officers define their own and each other's roles. Second, the opinions of the two groups are assessed with respect to police juvenile procedures. Third, data are presented on the opinions of the two groups regarding procedures adopted in juvenile court hearings. Finally, information is presented on the opinions of the two groups regarding procedures in the field of juvenile probation.

Role Definitions

As the process of delinquency control has broadened, official agents have taken on new tasks in addition to their more traditional ones. The police, for example, are not only concerned with law enforcement but have moved in the direction of implementing programs designed to prevent delinquency-producing situations. They have also moved in the direction of reforming or redirecting the activities of juveniles who have been identified as potential or actual delinquents. Probation departments have also moved in the past quarter-century away from a simple surveillance function and have taken over major responsibilities for the treatment and rehabilitation of offenders. Thus, as suggested earlier, these changing role definitions have resulted in problems related to the integration and coordination of delinquency control efforts.

The subjects were asked to respond to two items designed to provide some indication of how each group defines its own and the other's role. Although based on responses to only two items, the data presented in

6. It is, of course, possible that many police officers leave the field of law enforcement because they do not have the personality characteristics necessary to do effective police work. These personality characteristics are summed up in the term "cop mentality." The field of probation may be a more congenial occupational setting for some of these individuals.

Table 16.1 suggest that there is little consensus on how each group defines the other's role. Indeed, there is no overwhelming agreement within each of the groups over the definition of its own role. The data show that police officers are more inclined to see the reformation of juveniles as one of their tasks than the probation officers are willing to grant. The latter are more inclined to define the police role in more traditional terms. Four out of ten probation officers agree that the police should restrict their activities to the investigation of delinquency complaints and not attempt to reform delinquents.

Table 16.1. Role definitions of police and probation officers (percentages)

	Police	Probation
Police should investigate delinquency complaints, but not try to reform those juveniles who come to their attention		
Agree	29	40
Disagree	67	54
Undecided	4	6
	(660) [a]	(418)
When a complaint is filled for juvenile court action, the probation officer and not the police should investigate		
Agree	39	65
Disagree	50	27
Undecided	11	8
	(664)	(418)

[a]Figures in parentheses represent the total N on which the percentages are based.

At the same time, however, 54 per cent of the probation officers would support the efforts of police to reform juveniles. Perhaps this item is tapping the issue of whether or not the police should play a "screening" function in processing juvenile offenders. It is well known that large numbers of juveniles who fall into the hands of the police are not referred on to the courts but are handled informally by the police. The data suggest that about half the probation officers believe that the police should continue this screening function, so as to exert a positive influence and reform the less serious delinquents who are generally handled on an informal basis, but that the more serious offenders should be referred on for the "treatment specialists" to handle. If this interpretation has merit, then 40 per cent of the probation officers would argue that the police should not act as screening agents, and should refer the great majority of cases on for the professionals to decide on the appropriate course of action to be taken.

Thus, the question "Who should have responsibility for reforming delinquent youth?" fails to elicit a clear and unequivocal answer from these workers. Probation officers are more divided on this question than are the police. In general, those probation officers who would expand the police role to include reformation of juvenile offenders tend to be younger, better educated, have less time on the job, but have considerably more contact with delinquents than their older and more tenured colleagues.

When it comes to the question "Who should investigate delinquency complaints that are awaiting some sort of court action?" the probation officers reverse their position. As a group they are considerably more likely than the police to include investigative tasks in their own role. This, of course, is not surprising in light of the fact that case investigation has been a traditional role obligation of probation officers. However, it is surprising that 35 per cent of the probation officers *fail* to see investigation as a legitimate part of their job, and this again constitutes a significant division of opinion within the group. The police are also divided on this question, with 50 per cent of them opposed to the idea that investigation should be a part of the probation officer's role.[7]

Thus, while there is a moderate degree of consensus within each of the groups regarding the definition of its own role, at the same time a sizeable minority holds divergent views. Two-thirds of the police believe that reforming juveniles should be a legitimate part of the police role; one-third of them either do not adhere to this view or are undecided. Similarly, almost two-thirds of the probation officers agree that the investigation of cases is a legitimate part of the probation officer's role; but again one-third either do not hold this view or are undecided. At the same time, there is virtually no agreement within each of the occupations in their perceptions of the other group's role. In brief, the data in Table 16.1 are consistent with the general hypothesis set forth in the beginning of this report, that the delegation of multiple responsibilities to social control agencies has resulted in a state of affairs where the agents are not certain where their responsibilities begin and end.

Police Juvenile Procedures

In recent years a good deal of controversy has revolved around the policies and practices of law enforcement agencies in processing juvenile offenders. Disputes have occurred over such issues as whether or not juvenile of-

---

7. The lack of agreement among the police officers on this question might be partly a function of item ambiguity. It is possible that the police did not understand the context within which the term "investigate" was used. The police initially investigate delinquency complaints. But probation officers traditionally have investigated cases once they have been referred (by the police) to them.

fenders should be fingerprinted, photographed, charged with specific crimes, and otherwise handled in the same way as adult suspects. Table 16.2 presents the responses of police and probation officers regarding police juvenile procedures.

Table 16.2. Attitudes toward police juvenile procedures (percentages)

	Police	Probation
Juvenile offenders arrested for serious crimes should be fingerprinted and photographed by the police		
Agree	93	45
Disagree	5	41
Undecided	2	14
	(663)	(417)
Police records on juveniles should be available to all law enforcement		
Agree	91	68
Disagree	6	23
Undecided	3	9
	(665)	(417)
Police should not transport juvenile offenders in marked vehicles		
Agree	9	35
Disagree	86	41
Undecided	5	24
	(666)	(419)
Police should arrest and book juvenile offenders for specific crimes		
Agree	46	15
Disagree	44	77
Undecided	10	8
	(663)	(417)
Juveniles suspected of breaking the law should not be questioned by the police without being told of their right to have a lawyer		
Agree	25	54
Disagree	64	35
Undecided	11	11
	(666)	(419)

It can be seen from the table that there is almost unanimous agreement among the police regarding questions of whether or not juvenile offenders should be fingerprinted, photographed, whether or not police records should be made available to all law enforcement agencies, and whether or not juveniles should be transported in marked vehicles. The police are clearly in favor of policies that lead to the official recording and identification of juveniles as lawbreakers. However, the same level of support for such procedures does not exist among the probation officers. They are much less inclined to endorse policies that would officially identify (perhaps permanently) juveniles as offenders. Indeed, one of the traditional concerns of probation has been over the stigma that is associated with coming into contact with law enforcement and corrections agencies. Many have argued in favor of adopting informal and less visible procedures when processing juveniles. The clearest expression of this concern may be seen in the provision for confidentiality of juvenile court records that are subsequently destroyed once the youth reaches his maturity.

But while it is clear that probation officers *as a group* exhibit less enthusiasm for law enforcement procedures, it is also clear that they do not stand united in their opposition to them. With the exception of the question of confidentiality of police records (68 per cent of the probation officers believe that they should not be confidential), the data clearly suggest that there is little consensus among probation officers regarding police juvenile procedures. Some would support the policies of fingerprinting, photographing, and transporting juveniles in marked vehicles, while others would not. This lack of agreement reflects the contradictory orientations and the occupational dilemmas to be found in the field of probation. Probation officers view juvenile offenders not only as "clients" but also as recalcitrant youth who have run afoul of the law. On the one hand they must be controlled, but on the other hand they must be protected. The net result is an ambivalent attitude that has been generated from contradictory objectives and conflicting community demands.

The only police juvenile procedures on which probation officers appear to have some consensus is whether or not juveniles should be arrested and booked for specific crimes in the same way as adults. Slightly more than three-quarters of the probation officers disagree with such a policy. No doubt some of their consensus is based on the knowledge that a great many juveniles come into contact with the police for minor offenses, and in their opinion these juveniles do not require arrest and booking.[8] Thus, probation officers would support the general principle that not all youths should be handled like adults when being processed by the police.

But if such a principle unites the probation officers, it divides the police, for while as a group they support such a policy more than do the probation officers, there is virtually no agreement among themselves. Approximately the same number of police support a policy of arresting and booking juveniles for specific crimes as oppose it. Perhaps somewhat unexpectedly, the opponents of such a policy are the older police officers who

8. It should be noted, however, that this item does not specify whether *all* juveniles should be booked, and thus is somewhat unclear as to its precise meaning.

have spent a long time on the job. Level of education does not differentiate between supporters and opponents. Apparently, as police officers gain more experience on the job, they become more reluctant to treat all juveniles in the same way. Those who oppose the formal handling of juveniles might be similar to the police studied by Wilson in Eastern City.[9] In that department the officers did not trust the juvenile court, and handled delinquents selectively and on an informal basis.

Finally, the data in Table 16.2 suggest that the police tend to be opposed to the idea of informing the juvenile suspect of his right to have a lawyer before being questioned.[10] Although agreement is considerably less than unanimous, over six out of ten of the police disagree with this policy. On the other hand, while probation officers generally support it somewhat more, they again exhibit little in the way of consensus.

In summary, Table 16.2 generally suggests that probation officers not only differ sharply from the police in their advocacy of procedures that would tend to make the juvenile more visible as an offender but are also sharply divided among themselves in their ideological positions. The police, on the other hand, clearly support the establishment and maintenance of official (and permanent) records that would aid in identifying juveniles who come to their attention.

Juvenile Court Procedures

Following police referral, the intake segment of the probation department decides whether the case will be adjusted informally (dismissal, referral to another agency, or unofficial probation), or whether a petition will be filed for court action. Once the petition is filed, a number of questions become relevant, one of which is whether or not to place the juvenile in detention while awaiting his date for a hearing.

In recent years, a growing number of questions have been raised about the procedures used in the juvenile court hearing itself. These questions have come in the wake of a more general concern with procedural safeguards, especially prior to adjudication. This concern has spilled over into juvenile court proceedings where questions of fair notice of hearing, rules of evidence, the right to confront witnesses, the right to appeal, and so forth have been raised. The recent decisions of *Kent* and *Gault* would

9. James Q. Wilson, "The Police and the Delinquent in Two Cities," in the present volume, pp. 110–124
10. The legal rights of juveniles have not been articulated as yet in the intake and custody stages of the correctional process. The major Supreme Court decision setting forth procedural guidelines for juvenile offenders is *In re Gault* in 1967; however, this case was aimed primarily at the adjudicatory stage. See Fred Cohen, *The Legal Challenge to Corrections* (Washington, D.C.: Joint Commission on Correctional Manpower and Training, 1969).

appear to indicate that the "due-process model," to use Herbert Packer's phrase,[11] has indeed made headway in the field of juvenile justice.

Table 16.3 presents the opinions of police and probation officers about a number of juvenile court procedures. Several trends are evident in the

Table 16.3. Attitudes toward juvenile court procedures (percentages)

	Police	Probation
A juvenile should not be placed in detention unless court action is planned		
Agree	48	63
Disagree	48	34
Undecided	4	3
	(668)	(417)
Anyone testifying in a juvenile court should do so under oath		
Agree	95	88
Disagree	3	8
Undecided	2	4
	(667)	(419)
A juvenile should not be required to testify against himself		
Agree	36	46
Disagree	53	43
Undecided	11	11
	(665)	(417)
In a juvenile court hearing, the juvenile should be told of his right to counsel		
Agree	62	94
Disagree	27	3
Undecided	11	3
	(666)	(418)
A juvenile should have the right to appeal a juvenile court decision		
Agree	45	70
Disagree	42	19
Undecided	14	11
	(665)	(419)

data. First, on the question of detention of juveniles, probation officers are quite a bit more likely than the police to believe that detention should not be used unless court action is planned. There is no consensus among the police on this matter. About half of them support the idea of detention

11. Herbert L. Packer, *The Limits of the Criminal Sanction* (Stanford: Stanford University Press, 1968), pp. 149–173.

even when court action is not planned, and about half are opposed to the idea. In general, those police officers favoring detention are older but inexperienced (as measured by length of time employed, and extent of contact with delinquent youth). No doubt part of their endorsement is based on the idea that detention will teach the delinquent a lesson and thus play an important crime preventive role.

Second, there is no substantial difference of opinion between police and probation officers over the question of whether those testifying in court should do so under oath, and whether a juvenile should be required to testify against himself. However, on the latter item, it is again clear that a basic confusion exists among the two groups. Virtually no consensus exists either among the police or the probation officers over the question of whether juveniles should be protected against self-incrimination.

Third, there is considerable difference between the two groups over the questions of right to counsel and right to appeal. An unexpected finding is that probation officers support policies that would limit the court's power, although the extent of this support is not nearly so great when it comes to the question of appealing a juvenile court decision. The data show that almost an additional one-quarter of the probation officers support the right to counsel than support the right to appeal. No doubt they have concluded that when the juvenile court arrives at a decision it will be a good, professional one, and thus should not be questioned by appealing it. It is also of interest to note that whereas six out of ten police officers support the idea of right to counsel in juvenile court hearings (Table 16.3), six out of ten also oppose the idea of right to counsel when the police are interrogating a juvenile suspect (Table 16.2).

The final point suggested by Table 16.3 is the clear lack of consensus among the police over many juvenile court procedures. Considerably more agreement exists among the probation officers, with the single exception of whether the juvenile should testify against himself. No doubt some probation officers feel that this type of policy would severely limit their ability to get information that would otherwise be helpful in making recommendations to the juvenile court judge. In general, those probation agents who feel that the juvenile should not be required to testify against himself are younger and better educated, but at the same time they are less experienced (in terms of extent of contacts with delinquent youth). Police supporting this policy are generally older and have been employed for long periods of time.

Juvenile Probation Procedures

Since probation is by far the most common correctional alternative for juvenile offenders, it should not be surprising that policy questions will arise over the proper techniques of administering it. One of the major dimensions around which such questions have revolved is the "controller-helper," one which has already been discussed. Some officials view probation and the probationer with suspicion and thus stress control and surveillance. Others see the main function of probation more permissively, as helping the juvenile overcome some of his personal and social difficulties.

Table 16.4. Attitudes toward juvenile probation policies (percentages)

	Police	Probation
Main purpose of probation is to keep a "watchful eye" on the juvenile offender		
Agree	53	5
Disagree	43	94
Undecided	4	1
	(663)	(418)
Unexpected home visits better than making appointments in supervising juvenile probationers		
Agree	89	41
Disagree	5	45
Undecided	6	14
	(667)	(417)
Probation officers who make delinquents "toe the line" get better results than those who are lenient		
Agree	58	34
Disagree	16	41
Undecided	26	25
	(667)	(419)
Probation officers with small case loads will have greater success than those with large case loads		
Agree	82	80
Disagree	8	10
Undecided	10	10
	(666)	(418)

Table 16.4 presents the responses of police and probation officers to a number of items dealing with the "controller-helper" dimension. Not surprisingly, the overall trend suggests that the police favor the implementation of "control" policies to a greater extent than do the probation officers. As a group, the latter are more permissive and define the main objective of probation more in terms of helping the juvenile offender than of keeping him under surveillance.

However, the most impressive picture derived from the table is the almost unanimous agreement among probation officers regarding the major purpose of probation and at the same time the complete lack of agreement regarding appropriate probation procedures. Thus 94 per cent of the probation officers do not believe that keeping a "watchful eye" on the juvenile offender is the major function of probation, suggesting that they verbalize an ideology of treatment rather than one of surveillance and control. But when it comes to questions more directly related to *practice*, such as home visits and making delinquents "toe the line," there is almost complete *dissensus*. This finding is consistent with the general position outlined earlier in this report. In recent years the field of probation has increasingly verbalized the ideology of treatment, but it nevertheless continues to fulfill important control functions. The probation officer's dilemma is suggested by the divisions of opinion that appear with respect to probation practices.[12] These observations are also consistent with those of other investigators and suggest that the disagreement and confusion over procedures is not characteristic of any single probation department but is, rather, the result of the organization of the controller-treater roles in the occupational structure of probation.[13] It is also of interest to point out that there is about as much dissensus among the police over probation practices as there is among the probation officers themselves. The only procedure on which police agree is in the area of home visits, and they definitely believe that unexpected visits are better than making scheduled appearances.

The single area in which both groups exhibit a significant amount of agreement is on the issue of the size of the probation officer's case-load. Both groups firmly believe the shibboleth that probation officers with small case-loads will have greater success than those with large case-loads. It is interesting that these firm opinions are held despite the fact that research has shown that small case-loads of themselves will not assure a reduction in recidivism.[14] Among other things, the type of offender being supervised must be taken into account in any assessment of the question of case-load size.

12. For an excellent discussion of the dilemmas facing the social worker in probation and parole, see Lloyd E. Ohlin, Herman Piven, and Donnell M. Pappenfort, "Major Dilemmas of the Social Worker in Probation and Parole," *NPPA Journal,* II (July 1956), 211–225. For additional evidence on the disagreement and confusion that exists among probation and parole officers, see Van Laningham, Taber, and Dimants, *op. cit.*

13. Probation officers who support the "control" procedures tend to be older, have less education, and have more time on the job than those probation officers who oppose "control" procedures.

14. The President's Commission on Law Enforcement and the Administration of Justice, *Task Force Report: Corrections* (Washington, D.C.: U. S. Government Printing Office, 1967), p. 29.

Summary and Conclusions

The foregoing descriptive analysis leads to a number of conclusions. First, while there is a degree of consensus within each of the groups regarding the definition of its own role, it is clear that there are significant differences of opinion as well. In addition, there is little agreement on how members of each group view the other group's role. The data suggest that probation officers are especially reticent to accept the changing role of the police officer in the delinquency control process.

Second, as one might have expected, there are significant differences of opinion between the police and probation officers regarding delinquency control policies. In almost every instance, whether dealing with police juvenile procedures, juvenile court procedures, or juvenile probation policies, the two groups hold sharply divergent views. In general, the police tend to support procedures that would officially identify juveniles as offenders, to oppose procedural safeguards in juvenile court hearings, and to favor control and surveillance methods of probation supervision. The posture adopted by the probation officers tends to be in direct opposition to the above. They oppose official records and identification devices, are in favor of due process for juveniles, and tend to view probation in more permissive and "helping" terms. The two groups agreed on only a limited number of relatively superficial policy questions.

Third, not only are there differences of opinion expressed between groups but within groups as well. The police are generally in agreement when it comes to their own policies. They are divided over the various policy questions in the juvenile court hearings and juvenile probation. Probation officers tend to agree on three of the five juvenile court procedures. The dissensus arises over police juvenile procedures and, unhappily, over their own probation policies.

The above findings are clearly suggestive of the fractures that exist in the system of delinquency control. Indeed, there is no reason to believe that the situation would be different had juvenile court judges and institution personnel been included in the survey. Under these conditions it is difficult to achieve any degree of system-wide coherence in delinquency control efforts. The containment of delinquency therefore awaits a more orderly and systematic planning and coordination of control efforts. Without them, the objectives of individual and general prevention will continue to remain illusory.

Index